A Doctor In Strange Places

John Rogans M.D.

Many factors affect our paths in life. Genes play a major role. There are genes for every disease, and for every personality trait. Genes explain the wanderer, leading me all over the world. My father was Dutch, and they are famous for their itchy feet. He also had a fondness for the sweet softness of the gentle sex and passed that gene along.

My profession led me to many strange places. In Saudi Arabia lifting the veil is forbidden - examining a sore throat is impossible for a male doctor, yet searching for a pea sized tumor in a breast is readily allowed.

Medical skills are highly portable. In Canada, in the U.S., Saudi, Mexico, Laos, and the Amazon the problems faced are very different, but the human physiology is very similar and equally fascinating.

How a gene for good luck works I have no idea, but my path through life has been drastically altered many times by a little bit of luck.

Love, luck, and an urge to wander.

These threads meander through the following story. It starts slowly. After all, I was a shy young boy with no ambition, growing up in wartime London. My father was a disabled chef, my mother's only skill was cleaning houses.

Instead of colorful tales of potty training I will start with a little adventure that came after I retired. It contains two of the threads. I will get back on track afterwards.

For Bradley and Jewel, Brandon, Ashley, and Juliana.
And James, Jack, Jett, and Jolie.
Who knows, you might learn from the mistakes of an ancestor.
Also for Jack and Carole Berryman, whose energy, enthusiasm, and
eagle eyes prodded this into production.

"A Doctor In Strange Places"
Library of Congress Registration Number
Txu 1-854-372
Originally appeared as "The Wandering Medico"
Library of Congress Registration Number
TXu 1-799-474
Copyright © 2012 by John Rogans
ISBN -13:978-1482338911
ISBN- 10:1482338912
Canasted Literary
PO Box 3920, Brownsville
Texas, 78521

A Doctor in Strange Places

Chapter	Pages
1. The water buffalo. Unwanted. Sparrow's Gang.	5
2. Historic Accident. Evacuated and educated.	20
3. The Balcony. Engineer Officer. The Merchant Navy.	28
4. University of London. Getting into Movies.	46
5. Spain. Love.	61
6. Graduation. Labrador. Code of The North.	67
7. The Canary Isles. Vancouver. 3276 W 11th Avenue.	81
8. She. Large ocean, small boat. Guardian Angels.	92
9. Transmogrification. The House of Lords.	104
10. Yellowpoint. The MD gets a wife. Bradley.	110
11. No pulse. Matheson.	116
12. Routine Delivery. Julia. Exotic Spain Again.	126
13. Ladysmith. Texas. Miracle Awakening.	144
14. Brad's Sea Monster. Jerry.	158
15. Tale of Two Doctors. My Fair Lady	169

16. The End of the Affair. Alice in Saudi Land.   178

17. More matrimony. Medea. Ram.   186

18. None of the doctors sent bills. A crowd in the ER.   191

19. The Tontine. Thailand. Asthma.   198

20. The Music Doc. Lizbet. Santa Clotilda.   203

21. Wild Men of Borneo. Longhouse living.   218

22. Sibu. Bario. Miri. Sandakan. Brunei.   233

23. New Zealand. Roots in Schagen. Paper trail.   244

24. Welfare Indians. Appearances. China Train.   256

25. Parisian Accent. Safari and the Skull Cracker.   267

26. The Rakes Progress. Burma, Paying it Forward.   273

27. Butch Cassidy Patagonia. Patagonia Penguins.   281

28. Last Tango at World's End. Revolution in China.   287

29. Tontine 2010. Hippcrates. Cambodia.   294

30. Ruins of Angkor Wat. Young Girl in Dantes Inferno.   303

31. ER in Laos. Marx Royal Ballet. Asian Patterns .   307

32. Dreams of the South Pacific. Epilogue.   313

33. Epilogue   320

Chapter 1

The nearest thing to writing a novel is traveling in a strange country.

Paul Theroux

The water buffalo.

The time is March 2002, the place is the Amazon Jungle in Peru. I had retired, but I still enjoyed working as a doctor. Up in Canada I was well paid, but in odd places I would work for the fun of it as a volunteer locum tenens, filling in for doctors on vacation. A small plane took me from Lima, Peru over the snowy Andes to the small town of Iquitos. No roads, reached only by small planes and the big Amazon river. That meant a boat, and there was every sort available. All shabby, dirty, some with ancient one lung engines. Except the Amazon Queen, with patches of bright red paint. The view from the upper deck was of the thick green jungle that rolled down to the river's edge. Many miles down the Amazon from the small town of Iquitos, Yanamono was a small village on a narrow river that flowed into the mighty Amazon.

I was looking after a woman doctor's clinic while she was on vacation. I was on call night and day and on weekends but that's how it is in small places. Life was simple. I lived in her house, which was built native style with a thatched roof. There was no electricity, no fans or air conditioning, no TV, and there was an outhouse at the back of the house. There was a cold water shower at a nearby tourist lodge that offered "Back to Basics on the Amazon." The water came from a stream in the forest which somehow stayed at sub zero temperatures, or so it seemed. It took me many tries to stay under the cold water with my body superheated from the high temp and humidity. The shock of the frigid water nearly put me into cardiac arrest, but after a week of removing the sweat with a hand towel I finally crept under the cold shower, inch by inch. Fingers first, then the arm, finally the rest of the warm body. After three months in the Amazon I was taking three cold showers a day, and boasting about it.

The doctor's house was only about thirty yards from the river, next to the edge of the jungle. I was never lonely. Before I took over the lady doctor, Dr. L., showed me her house. She was tall, intense, maybe a little hyper. Her clinic was not far from the tourist lodge, and sometimes sightseers would be brought to see what this single woman had created out of nothing. She was a good talker. I often heard her potted history for the tourists.

"I came down here as a tourist twelve years ago, and fell in love with the simple way of life and the beauty of the Amazon rain forest. I started up a clinic in one room of the lodge where you are staying."

She was a good doctor, and smart. And kind hearted. Good looking, not a young woman. She had been seasoned by two marriages and a couple of tragedies. In her house where I would live while she was on vacation. I found that I would never be lonely.

"If you see a white rope hanging down from the thatch, don't pull on it," she said. "It's a small boa constrictor. He's a good friend, treat him kindly, which means leave him alone."

"A snake lives in the roof?" I was not thrilled.

"He's only a baby one," she said. "About an inch and a half thick. He couldn't even swallow a child. The big ones could swallow me, but this one just keeps down the mice."

"Just eats mice. That makes me feel so much better," I said. "Anyone else live here?"

"Well, there is Charley," she said. "He is a rather large tarantula. Absolutely harmless. Please don't frighten him."

"If he jumps and frightens me, that's when they bite, right?"

"The bite is not lethal, for humans."

"What about the poisonous hairs they can flick at you? They are harmless too, right?"

"All the hairs will do is irritate the skin, and Charley never does that anyway. He is usually parked on the middle of the inside of the back door in the morning. When you get up, he will disappear."

She sounded a little offended at my critical questions of her friends. I made my tone soft and kind.

"At night, does he wander around, climb up the mosquito netting and get into bed with you?"

She laughed. "Don't be silly. That has never happened."

The back door was the way out to the outhouse, and I soon got into the habit of opening it very gently and slowly so as not to disturb the large, brown, hairy Charley in his usual perch. On the other side I found the bats. They were parked on the outside of the back door, hanging sleepily. Now bats carry rabies, and since we had no shots for rabies, I would extend my umbrella to its full length and prod them gently until they flapped away.

One evening I was reading by the light of the kerosene lamp when there was a knock on the door.

"Dotor, dotor, es muy grave." Doctor, there is serious trouble.

"What's the matter?"
"There is little girl bleeding badly. You need to come." In the dark outside was a night watchman from the clinic, with his flashlight. He turned, and headed back to the clinic. I picked up my bag. I carried a book, the Merck Manual, a stethoscope, a couple of flashlights, and my umbrella. It was the Amazon rain forest and it rained every day. I pulled on my gumboots and I set out for the clinic. Unfortunately this was about a mile from the doctors house. In the morning I would get to the clinic by eight thirty, walk back for lunch, walk back for the afternoon clinic, and at 5:00 walk back after the afternoon clinic.

During the day it was a pleasant walk, even on the muddy trail. On the right was the reddish brown Amazon River flowing quickly, and here the Amazon was about two miles wide. In the middle of the field was a path through very long grass. This I avoided carefully because of the many poisonous snakes hiding there. There were several palm trees with smooth trunks and a couple of rubber trees. These had the black scars of wounds from machetes, to drain the liquid rubber, but this had stopped many years ago. On the left was the jungle, where the buffaloes roamed. During the day they would stay in the cool of the jungle, but at night they would sometimes come out to the field.

On this particular night I had the whole walk to myself until about two hundred yards from the clinic. Then there were the buffalo, about fifteen feet to the left of the path. Big shiny black beasts with black eyes, huge curved horns, and a mean disposition. In Africa the water buffalo is afraid of no one. Even a lion will not to take on a fully grown healthy water buffalo. Dr. L. had said the buffalo would never harm me.

"I've been here for twelve years and they've never bothered me" she had said. So this night I walked past the buffalo as if I didn't have a care in the world. They looked threatening, and I gave myself a little pep talk. Animals can smell fear so I was convincing myself.

"I am not afraid. Absolutely not. What a lovely night for a walk."

One of the big black beasts looked at me suspiciously. It was a full moon, and I could see it was a male. A big, black bull water buffalo. It raised its nose and sniffed suspiciously, then carried on munching away at the grass.

Juvencio, one of the clinic nurses greeted me. A bit short, like most Yagua, with an intelligent smile.

"It's a little girl, three years old, from down river. Her brother was playing with his father's loaded shotgun, and it went off."

In the clinic a little girl was lying on one of the examining tables, naked, face down, her bottom up. She started crying when I came in. She was terrified, so I stood still and I just looked. She calmed down. Running up her leg to her bottom was a large gaping laceration. She was ripped open from behind the knee to a little to the right of her anus. She very nearly had a new one. I was amazed. The blast had missed everything important. There was no damage to major nerves, arteries, veins, or bone. It was a lucky break for both of us. Our guardian angels had been doing good work that night. If any of those vital structures had been involved she could have been in serious trouble. It was simply a matter of putting her leg and her bottom back together again.

The cut was about sixteen inches long and about three inches deep and it was a fairly straightforward job but it took a long time. I had to do the repair in several layers, with about sixty stitches. She whimpered when I injected the local anesthetic, but her mother comforted her. When I finished she was back in one piece again. She would have a scar, and a perfectly functioning rear end. I started about eight o'clock and it was eleven by the time I finished. The nurse dressed the wound, and I told the mother to bring the little girl back to be checked in the morning. She did, and I can show you the movie sometime. I picked up my bag, put on my gumboots, and headed back to my little house.

When I got to the field the buffaloes had moved. They were now on the path, and I had to walk right through the herd to avoid the long grass, and the snakes. I had antivenin at the clinic, but snake poison is extremely painful before it is neutralized. I moved very carefully, staying on the path, walking slowly between the big animals. I was giving myself a bigger pep talk.

"Come on, now. You've been an actor on stage, screen and radio. You can convince them that you are harmless, too dumb to be scared. No, absolutely not. You are not afraid, just a nice walk in the moonlight. I am not afraid."

Happily they ignored me, and when I got through I breathed a big sigh of relief. I kept on walking and I thought that it was the end of it. Then, suddenly there was the thunder of hooves, and I turned around. The big black bull buffalo was charging straight at me. I had no options. The river wasn't too far but he could run faster than me. There was no trees I could climb, he weighed half a ton more than me, and I had no bullfighter's cape.

Then for some reason I got angry. I had just as much right as he did to be on the path. I had just spent three hours stitching up a young child as an unpaid volunteer and I didn't deserve this. I pulled out my umbrella, opened it to its full length, waved it at the buffalo, and I started yelling as loudly as I could.

"Get away from me you big black skinned, black hearted, black enameled jumped up never came down $*#&."
I started using cuss words from East London cockney English, very bad words from my childhood that I did not know were still there. Something worked. The buffalo stopped about five feet away from me. He stood, looking at me. I looked back at him, still very angry. It seemed an eternity. A stand off. Then

I knew exactly what to do.

    As a young man I had been to many bullfights in Spain, and I had studied the bullfighter's techniques. I straightened my shoulders, and held my head up proudly. I rested my umbrella on my shoulder and turned around with a flourish. I showed my back to the bull and marched off. I had never seen a bull charge a fearless toreros back. I didn't look back, and kept on marching. Again, something worked, because there was no drumming of hooves and I made it safely back to my little house. Later, when I couldn't sleep, I analyzed the problem. It was all about sex. I decided that he was used to the smell, the pheromones, of the woman doctor. He could smell that my male genes were a challenge to his status as the alpha male.

    My male genes nearly got me killed. A little bit of luck had saved me.

Unwanted

I was not a wanted child, or perhaps my mother couldn't look after me. The foster home where I lived was not a pleasant one. The foster mother, tall and thin, spoke with a bogus kindly tone, rationalizing.

    "There are no presents under the tree for you, but that is only fair. You have no money to buy any presents for the real children, do you?"

    When she showed me up to the attic, again there was the bogus kindness..

    "Up here it is warm, the hot air rises, and you will have all the privacy you want." As if a five year old boy craved privacy among the spiders.

Somehow my mother must have rescued me, and I remember her undemanding loving kindness. Then my father came back into our lives when my sister was born. Being Dutch he was a strict disciplinarian, big and strong and discipline was physical. I clashed violently with him. The conflicts were very painful.

At the time I never knew that Dutch and English genes were at war inside me. My family tree was later traced back to Pieter Gerritn de Jonge Rotgans, born 1640 in Terschelling, a small island in the North Sea, not far from Holland. (Many years later I dropped the 'T' in my name, spelling 'Rogans' as I pronounced it.) He was my great (to the nth degree) grandfather. Eight generations later my father Cornelis Rotgans was born in 1881 in Schagen, North Holland. He was the last pure Dutchman in our line. I was the Ninth Generation, half Dutch and half English.

I inherited the genes for itchy feet from my father. He left Holland early in life and worked as a cook, then as a chef in France, Spain, Belgium etc, learning the cuisine and the language of each country. He finally settled in England, acquiring a permanent wife and family. He left behind an unofficial wife and child in Holland, and a couple of previous wives in England before being anchored by my mother.

He never told me or my sister about his siblings. About forty five years later, when I was close to retirement, on a whim I wrote to the Postmaster of the town where my father was born, Schagen in North Holland, and found out that there had been three brothers and three sisters. All were dead by then, and so were all of their children except one. Cousin Simon was a sign painter in North Holland and he answered my letter. He sent photos of the other uncles and aunts, but by the time I had organized a visit to meet him, a family gene had killed him. He was about sixty.

I went to Holland, and met his widow Geer, and another lady with the family name. Nel Fijnheer-Rotgans. I had written to genealogical institutes in Holland, and as this was her hobby she had come across my letter. She had traced the Rotgans name back to the mid sixteen hundreds, and found three family trees all converging to that point in time. They may have had a common ancestor, but she never found one. She published an anthology of her family tree, going back to Jacob Sieuwertsz. Date of birth 'onbekend,' Unknown. He had a son Lourens Jacobsz who had six children including a son Jacob Lourisz, born in 1690.

She traced the lineage to the present day, and also noted the links in the other two family trees. I am the ninth generation springing from the seed of :-
Pieter Gerritn de Jonge Rotgans, b 1640
    Child 1 Siebe Pietenoz
    Child 2 Cornelis Pietenoz
    Child 3 Neeltje Pietenoz

When I met Geer and Nel we went back over my and Simon's ancestors. We were helped by Nel Fijnheer-Rotgans.. A 'Rotgans' was a hunter of red necked geese, which landed on the dykes and pecked at the straw that strengthened the mud. We found that many of the males had died at about age 60. Death certificates in Holland were somewhat secretive, and it took some digging to find out the cause of Cousin Simon's death. It had been colon cancer, which is a sneaky disease and often shows no symptoms until it is too late. Many years later I met the widow of another cousin who had jumped ship in Adelaide, Australia. His widow Coby told me that Cousin Berthy also had died of colon cancer at age 56. Their three daughters now go for regular colonoscopies, which is the only way to detect an early case of colon cancer.

    Like many emigrants my father had a spark that saw him leave home for a strange and insecure land and hopefully a better life. He became a head chef with a staff of hundreds, a luxury car and a motor bike. The fast life led to accidents, which disabled him, and his fortunes changed for the worst. I followed a similar track. I also left the security of home for distant lands, first Canada and then the U.S.. The road led upwards at first, then I was crippled by hugely bad life-style choices, mainly matrimonial disasters. The genes were running true.

I have no pictures of him as a child, but he had an imposing presence as a man. Smart bowler hat, black coat and waistcoat, and a large corporation. I imagined him as a teenager in 1896, in old fashioned clothes, skating on the frozen canals in Schagen.

The Dutch and the English had a lot in common. Both are intelligent people, adventurous explorers, expert sailors and navigators. The Brits formed the East India Company in 1600, and started in spices, but India became far more profitable. The Dutch East India Company was started in 1602, and concentrated on spices but also colonized Borneo and other islands in southeast Asia. They were rivals from the start, and in the 1600s there were three Anglo Dutch wars. In the second war, in 1666, Terschelling was burnt to the ground. So, Great Great Great Grandad Pieter, aged 26 was probably on one side watching his house burned by the Brits, while one of my mothers ancestors was possibly in the Royal Navy, doing the burning. Over the years the word 'Dutch' has come to be used in English scornfully. A Dutch Uncle is harsh and stern, a Dutch Treat is not a treat, Dutch courage comes from heavy drinking, Double Dutch means gibberish, and a Dutch Wife is found in hot climes, a cloth bolster to put between a man's sweating legs to stop them becoming glued together.

Deeper differences marked their attitudes towards colonies. The Dutch and other Europeans merely wanted profits. The English, probably because of their puritanical streak strove to do better, and sometimes succeeded. The

British Colonial Office was charged with making the colonies ready, sooner or later for self government, as well as making them profitable. Some colonies were impatient and fought for freedom, like the bunch in North America, but they were the exception. Many retained ties with England and are still part of the British Commonwealth.

My father, like the long line of Dutch Uncles before him was harsh and strict, and with similar genes we clashed continually. I am sure I was not an easy boy to raise. One day I really got under his skin. From his days as a chef he had a big carving knife that he sharpened lovingly. I got him so angry that day that he came after me with that knife. I was about nine, but by then he had had another disabling stroke. His left arm didn't work properly, but his legs were good enough to chase me into the back garden. Luckily there was a wartime Anderson shelter in the garden, its top half above ground. I could run round this faster than he could chase me. Otherwise I would have become steak tartar.

Another vivid memory was of one day, just as I was going to school, when he lost control of his bowels, and everything ran down his legs. I can still smell the foul brown liquid. Mother had gone to work, my sister Betty had gone to school, so I cleaned him up. Took down his trousers, and wiped him clean with a wet cloth. No big deal for mothers. They do that several times a day for a baby, but I wasn't a mother.

He loved my sister. She was much cuter than me, more loving to her father. She tells how he waited for her by the open front door, in his wheelchair. I can't remember seeing him in a wheelchair. It may be denial, or just my bad memory. She went on to a long happy marriage with two children in Canada. I know she showed him more kindness than I did.

Mickey Sparrow's Gang

As kids, growing up in the streets of London, we made our own entertainment. There was no television, maybe a radio at home, and very occasionally we had a few pennies for the 'pictures,' the movies. Wendell Road Park had a couple of swings, but it was more exciting to climb to the tops of the very tall trees. The view was of the rooftops of thousands of other row houses, but high in the tree there was an exhilaration, a sense of freedom and adventure. The thought of danger from falling never entered our minds.

In the photos my mother gave me my short pants were neat, my shirt looked clean, but after climbing trees I am sure that they were fashionably torn and dirty. We urchins had our own dress codes.

There was a local gang of urchins in short pants, and one day I ran into them and shyly asked if I could join. The leader was Mickey Sparrow, taller than the rest, who had the spark of personality and smarts that made him a leader, and they followed him blindly.

"You'd have to pass the test," he said. The condescension in his voice showed he doubted I could.

"It really hurts," he added.

After years of war there were many bomb damaged houses, abandoned but still standing, jagged scars from the bombs looking like rows of broken teeth. One still had live electricity, and we shuffled down into the basement. Dark, deserted, it was littered with junk covered by spiders webs, stuff that previous visitors had found worthless.

'Them wires," said Mickey, pointing to bare, exposed

wires in a corner, "They got high volts. You gotta hold em and not let go if you want to get in wiv us."

The British wiring has 220 volts, compared to the 110 volts in the US and other countries. At the same amperage you get twice the kick. If your hands were dry and dirty, as ours always were, it probably would not electrocute you, but it would be like a kick from a bad tempered mule.

Somehow I knew this, but I tried to hide my fear as I walked nonchalantly to the wires. Trying hard to look casual, I was in no hurry. I reached out, slowly, and gripped them. The shock was terrifying, paralyzing, and powerful, flashing through every part of me. I was stuck, I couldn't move. It was only Mickey's voice counting up to ten that woke me up, and I wrenched free.

The reward, sort of, came the next day. We had seen the young girl, about our age, in the neighborhood pushing her small pram, which held her doll. We were not at all interested in girls. She was pretty in a skinny sort of way, but many of us had sisters, and they were all horrible and different, but Mickey looked at the pram. It might be useful for something, like a go cart. The girl plucked up her courage and asked "Can I join your gang? It looks like a very strong gang, and I can help with things."

None of the members wanted a girl, and there was no way any of us could see her in that dark basement, with the spiders, let alone touch the high voltage wires. Yet thinking of her in the dark was somehow just a little exciting. Mickey, thinking about using the pram, said,

"You'd have to pass a test. You couldn't do it."

"Oh yes I could." Maybe she had a bit of boldness in her.

"Come on then," said Mickey. He started pushing the pram, swerving it from side to side, trying it out. He led us up the road. Mickey obviously had something in mind. The girl followed, with her head up. Then the gang, mostly rebellious. We didn't want no girls.

At the end of the street there was another deserted house, with a patch of grass behind some hedges, which shielded it from the street.

"Okay," said Mickey. "This is it. Take your ... things off and lie down."

She was puzzled, but Mickey had a way of telling people what to do and they did it.

"Show us your thing."

Again she obeyed, and spread her legs. It was different, a bit intriguing but it wasn't impressive. Just a flat thing, with a crease down the middle, not at all like our male appendages.

"Now you lot," said Mickey.' You all gotta do it. We are a gang."

My hormones had not yet started raging. None of us had reached puberty, none of us was aroused, but obediently we lay on top of her and rubbed our loins into hers. Someone peed on her, and then we all tried to do that. Not even Mickey managed anything, and when she got up she was as virginal as when we had started. But as we walked back, she pushed the pram proudly. She felt like a woman now. We felt we had reached a plateau, we were more like men than we had been before. Mickey Sparrow and his gang swaggered proudly. Later, when we had discussed this with older siblings, we wondered about having made a baby, and we watched her closely for weeks. We had learnt a little about sex that day, just enough to worry about.

That was the end of our gang's adventures with the opposite sex. We didn't really want her in the gang. She refused to let us modify her pram into a go-cart, and she faded away. We had been way ahead of our hormones.

Chapter Two

Historic Accident

This is not really part of my story but it is an interesting medical titbit that coincided with my early days in London. When I was playing on the streets in London, as a scruffy boy in short pants, I never knew that elsewhere in that city the most important discovery in medical history had recently been made, by accident.

A brilliant scientist was tidying his lab before leaving for his vacation. One experiment involved bacteria he was growing. They had been spread in thin streaks on a layer of a gel, agar, which contained nutrients and vitamins. The bugs would feed and grow and be ready when he returned for him to drop on small discs soaked in various chemicals. He would then see which, if any chemicals stopped the bugs growing.

The agar was spread thinly on the bottom of three inch dishes called petri dishes, which would be covered with close fitting glass lids to stop any dust or other contaminants floating in. The scientist made two crucial errors that changed the history of the world. Perhaps he was just being a typical absent minded professor, but he forgot to put the covers on several dishes, and just as important, he left a small window open. These two omissions led to the production of an incredibly powerful antibiotic, penicillin, and to a Nobel Prize for the scientist, Alexander Fleming. Decades later when a London urchin (me) had become a medical doctor he was able to inject 2.4 million units of penicillin into buttocks to cure diseases, like the one that had infected Henry the Eighth. The curse that had survived through the centuries, syphilis.

Fleming's beginnings were humble, the son of a farmer. He received a small legacy that freed him to try to become a doctor. He had no formal education, and had to take an exam to get into med school. He passed it at the top of the list. He became an outstanding doctor. He was calm, efficient, reserved, and "He never said more than he had to." Married at 34, one son. He was a Scot, not given to emotions. Many photos show only a quiet, self effacing smile.

When he returned from vacation in 1928, Dr. Fleming found that the uncovered dishes were spotted with dust and molds and he was about to throw them out when he saw that one small spot of mold had grown and was surrounded by a perfectly clear circle of agar. It had killed all of the bacteria. Immediately he saw the significance and began to culture and subculture the mold until he had isolated the active ingredient. This he named 'penicillin' but when he tried to produce it in quantities he failed miserably. He kept on trying but six years later, in 1934, he announced "I have given up on Penicillin." If it had been left to Fleming, penicillin might have died then. In his early enthusiasm he had written papers relating how powerful a bug killer this was, but he did not have the skills to uncover its' chemical structure, and make it in sufficient quantities to be useful. Born in 1881, he died in 1955, age 73, in London.

Years later, in 1938, his paper was read by another brilliant scientist, Howard Florey. Florey had started in his home city of Adelaide, Australia, by collecting degrees. He was good at sports, even better at his studies. First he qualified as a medical doctor with an MB, ChB. These indicated that he was a bachelor of medicine and surgery, and he could have worked as a physician, but he moved around collecting degrees as he had collected scholarships to study for his next degree. He went to England with a Rhodes Scholarship, collected a BA and an MA from Oxford, then went to Cambridge for a Ph.D. His first marriage was unhappy, partly because his wife was sickly, partly because he was hard to live with. They stayed together, perhaps for the two children until she died in 1966. His second marriage was happy, but only lasted until he died a year later. He was known as "The man that gets things done." Photos show a strong face with a square jaw. He could be kind, sometimes critical, destructively. Sometimes ruthless, solitary, selfish. He had few close friends. Born in 1898, he died in 1968, aged 69, in Oxford.

He was working in Oxford when he read Flemings paper, and started studying penicillin. He built a research team of top scientists, including German born Ernest Chain, a chemist with an interest in biochemistry. From a Jewish family, Chain had left Germany when the Nazis came to power. He had joined Florey's team and worked on the structure of penicillin. The mold was so powerful that even diluted 800 times, it still killed bugs, but nobody could make it in quantity. Chain unraveled the drugs structure, to aid in its' synthesis, but supplies were still limited. In one experiment eight mice were infected with lethal doses of streptococcus. 4 were given Penicillin. They lived, and the others died. The very small quantities of the drug limited many other experiments.

In 1941 Florey went to America. There he made a pitch to an official with the USDA, the US Department of Agriculture who immediately realized the importance of such a drug in wartime. War with Japan seemed imminent, funds were allocated, and mass production was eventually accomplished in time for D Day, and the huge number of

casualties that followed the invasion of Nazi occupied Europe.
In recognition of their work, Fleming, Florey and Chain shared a Nobel Prize in 1945. They were also knighted, and became 'Sirs.' Florey's work in tackling the development and mass production brought him something extra. He became a peer of the realm, as Baron Florey, of Adelaide. As an Australian he may have savored the very old joke "Once a Baron, always a Baron. Once a Knight, dead in a month." Perhaps I should apologize for this lèse majesté, because this was perhaps the most important discovery in history. It may not have had as widespread an effect as say, electricity, but it cured disease and healed people. One estimate was that it had saved 200 million lives before the advent of modern super drugs. In fact Baron Doctor Florey is said to have commented regretfully that he had contributed to the over-population of the world. Who knows what would have happened if Fleming had closed the window, and covered his petri dishes?

Evacuated and educated.

I was happy enough in my elementary school, chasing girls that sought refuge in their washrooms. One memory of a game of rounders in the school yard stands out. Rounders had been around since the 1700's, and in the early days it was called 'base-ball.' It was under that name that it crossed the Atlantic in the 1800's. The rules were similar.
I was the catcher. We had no protective gear, and when the batter threw his bat backwards it caught me hard on the forehead. I woke up in the office of the headmistress, and

she was soothing my head on her knees with a cool towel. She was not young and pretty but I forgave the batter on the spot.

Less clear was a more important event. One day at school we were told that instead of classes there would be an exam. This was the 'Eleven Plus' exam, which would divide us into the trade school or the university track. There had been no warning. In more modern times parents with money sent their little ones to cram school to be sure of getting on the right track. I didn't know it but I did well enough to be sent to a good grammar school, on the University track.

Another little bit of luck that was a major turning point in my life came next. Part of the school was evacuated out of London to escape the blitz. I was a scruffy cockney urchin about to get the rough edges rubbed off. During the blitz I was one of those sent to safety away from Hitler's bombs, to Slough. This was 25 miles North of London, in sleepy Buckinghamshire. I was billeted with a kind, educated older couple, Florence and Henry McDonnell, who were upper-middle-class people, in the small village of Wraysbury. He had been on the County Council, and they had a smart car. Mrs. Mac had been a nurse. Dignified, with a quiet authority. On the very first night she said "I have run a bath for you upstairs."

She marched me up to the bathroom, and inspected every inch of my clothing for any unwanted debris or crawling beasties. She wasn't going to take a chance on this scruffy London refugee. Then she said "Put your clothes here."

I was too intimidated to object. I stripped and slowly climbed into the bath. The water was steaming and boiling hot. She found no nits or other parasites and then she scrubbed me from head to foot. It wasn't only embarrassment that had colored my skin. I had been parboiled, and when I got out I was deep red. She hadn't tested the water, and I had been too scared to complain. She was a kind woman, and was most apologetic.

They taught me polite table manners, how to dress correctly, but more importantly they talked 'proper.' I had a mild Cockney accent. In the 1950s distinctions between the classes was well and truly marked by such accents. Even a mild accent would mark you as being from a different, and inferior class. With time I couldn't help imitating their upper-class diction. This was a huge asset later. It helped me climb to dizzy heights in the Army, amongst the upper middle class officer type chaps. Mr. Mac had a wonderful supply of books, with popular authors like Rider Haggard and Conan Doyle, and shelves of books about the sea, his favorite obsession. After that I never stopped reading. This greatly broadened my vocabulary and supplemented my education, but it was 'talking proper' that made a huge difference in rigidly class conscious England. Bernard Shaw noted in Pygmalion that as soon as an Englishman opens his mouth to speak he makes some other Englishman despise him. Either looking up at the snob or a 'toff,' or down at the lower class. I doubt very much that I would have climbed the next rung up the social scale without the right accent.

Our little evacuated school had only one class and only a few teachers had been evacuated on a trial basis. The acting headmaster Graham Sutton taught several subjects, and had a unique teaching technique. When a student was slow to answer he would stand beside them, and drop his ham sized fist heavily onto the student's head. I don't think it helped, but it did make us struggle to answer questions quickly. I doubt that the concussions did any permanent damage.

Our history teacher was somewhat hard of hearing, and one of our diversions, when the long lists of the Kings of England was putting us to sleep was to cry out,

"Doodlebug, sir. Doodlebug."

When Hitler sent his flying bombs to scare London he sometimes didn't get the fuses right. They were the first jet aircraft, with no pilot but a payload of explosives, and switches timed to cut off the fuel when they were over London. You would hear the menacing monotone drone, on and on, until the switch cut out. There was dead silence as the buzz-bomb hurtled to the ground, then an earth shaking 'Crump.' Sometimes they over flew right over London and made a beeline for us. For an imaginary doodlebug the routine was to yell out and climb under the desk, which provided a welcome break from all of the boring King Henrys. If Hitler and his gang really messed up, and a whole flock of buzz-bombs was headed our way, the school would go outside and climb down into the underground shelter. A long tunnel dug into the playing field, covered with corrugated steel and piled high with earth. Our class took up one small corner of the school, and the rest was occupied by a girl's school. They had the major part of the long shelter, which was segregated from our segment by a brick wall. The powers that be had overlooked an emergency exit which led into the girls tunnel, and several enterprising boys had come back after an attack with tall tales of passion. I was never one of these. I had far too many inhibitions.

For a bit of excitement I started hitching rides on the back of US army trucks when I cycled to school, which was five miles from our village. The build up to D Day had flooded the country with GI's and their trucks, and our game was to grab the back of one as it slowed for a corner, then hold on for dear life. The truck would pick up speed, and by the time it was racing along our narrow lanes at 50 miles an hour it was too dangerous to let go, however scared you were. At that speed without the truck to hang on to I would have wobbled and crashed. I always hung on grimly, and arrived at school early.

Puberty hit with a vengeance, and although my fantasy life was stimulating to the extreme I was shackled by paralyzing shyness. In my bedroom there was a picture of a classical statue of a naked woman, brought back by my congenial hosts from a trip to Greece. She was missing both arms, but she had delightful breasts. Her thighs were seductively draped, and she often appeared in my dreams and fantasies.

I was developing an interest in the anatomy of the gentler sex, so different from my own. Driven by my curiosity and my hormones I came close to my first exploration of its delights in Wraysbury. One of the village girls was pretty, adventurous and quite precocious, and she took a fancy to me. The haystack was easy to climb and she led me to a hollow in the top where we were quite concealed. She lay back, we wrestled playfully, but I was far too shy to go very far. She tried another strategy.

"Let's go swimming," she said. The river Thames was close by. We went to her house, and her parents were away. She said,

"This should fit you. You change in here, I will change in my bedroom."

I put on the swim trunks and the house was quite still.

"Judy?" I called.

"I'm here, I'm nearly ready." she said. "I don't have any clothes on." And her bedroom door was wide open.

She did try again a couple of times but with my terminal shyness she gave up. My celibacy would last for many more years before I got any further. Real action would come much later. I seemed to have luck in finding opportunities, but I never had the confidence to consummate the process.

Chapter Three

Balcony View

When I returned to London I brought my monumental lack of confidence with me. I was at a boys only school, and my only outside interest was in matters aqueous. I did a lot of swimming, and became a sea cadet. My life saving courses gained me a bronze and then a silver medal. This helped a bit as I progressed through school, and became Captain of Swimming, and a prefect.

I was fascinated by ropes and knots, Morse code signaling, and boat handling. I gradually rose to become the head sea cadet. This was fun, and looked good on my resumé later.

I was still disturbed by raging hormones. One day I overcame my shyness, and went to classes in ballroom dancing, which at least let me get my hands on a girl. The tango was great for body contact.

"Put this record between you," said the teacher. It was a breakable kind, and she put it between our abdomens as she squeezed us together. "Don't let it fall. Get closer."

As I clutched the girl close to me the music and the tango rhythm became hot and steamy. So did I. Partly delightful, but so embarrassing, and I blushed.

That was as far as I got. I just couldn't talk to girls. That I was interested was evident when I began going to the ballet. This did not seem to be a very masculine pastime, but the scenery was delightful. Beautiful graceful young women with revealing, scanty clothes. In England at the time there was no Playboy or Hustler. But here there were short tutus, close fitting low cut tops, and muscular males grabbing these pretty girls and tossing them about. I became a confirmed balletomane, with an imagination in moving 3D and color. And I was a regular in the balcony of the Covent Garden Opera House where the Sadler's Wells Ballet performed. I saw the premier performance of Prokofiev's *Cinderella* with Margot Fonteyn in black, and again with Moira Shearer in red. The music sounded weird for the first few times, but the girls held my attention and I came to love the strange melodies after many repetitions. I became familiar with all of the classic ballets, from *'The Three Cornered Hat'* by Falla to *'Swan Lake'* and *'The Sleeping Beauty'* with Margot Fonteyn and Robert Helpman. Afterwards I would walk to the tube station, and dance athletically all the way down the many flights of stairs to the train level. I got all of their autographs, including Ninette de Valois by hanging around the stage door after a performance.

    The stage door widened my experience in other ways. I was anxious to see the fit, strong male dancers, but when they came out they were holding hands. This was a far cry from the idyllic setting of *Les Sylphides*, with one man and twenty gorgeous girls. I watched them walk away down the alley, hand in hand. It was not until I became a film extra that I really understood what they did with each other, but I do not have any male autographs in my collection.

Officer of Engineers

I never thought that being drafted for two years would be another little bit of luck. If I had been smart I could have tried to dodge it, but my life would have been completely different. After I finished school I was still completely without ambition. I went hitchhiking in France, sleeping in fields and on the floor of deserted cinemas amongst the cigarette butts. I dithered with odd jobs, and might have become a professional potato peeler if King George had not needed my help. College was never in my mind. Neither of my parents had been to college, and I didn't know anyone that had. Without an exemption for college I was told that I was going to be in the military for two years. I thought about where I would rather go - to the Army, the Navy or the Air Force? England is a very small place, nowhere is very far from the sea, and my zodiac sign is Cancer the crab, a water sign. For years at school I had been a leading Sea Cadet, and messing around in small boats was one of the few things that had sparked my interest. I could tie knots and steer boats like a pro. Naturally I put down the Navy. I put my second choice down as Air Force. My last choice, I wrote was 'The Army, Heaven forbid.'

When I got to my induction interview it was over in a few seconds. The officer looked at me, and there was a paper in his hand.

"So the Army is your last choice, heaven forbid." He was an Army officer. "Aren't you lucky? The Army needs you."

That piece of paper haunted me through basic training, and I was posted to the Royal Army Service Corps, the

RASC. This was only one step above the Pioneer Corps, with their picks and shovels.

Basic training

As with most armies basic training was designed to break down the raw recruit and rebuild him as a soldier. Basic training was indeed basic. Intended to turn a chaos of lower class and lower middle class uneducated teenagers into the raw material of soldiers who could march, double time, loaded with heavy field packs up hill and down dale but above all to obey orders instantly, without thinking. If a sane man was ordered to attack an enemy shooting bullets aimed to kill, the rational reaction would be "Hell no, I don't want to die," and he would turn tail and run.

A lot of basic training was made up of "Double time, up that hill you dozey lot. Move it."

Training NCOs were picked for aggressiveness and encouraged to shout sadistically.

"What do you think you're on, your Daddy's yacht? Pick those feet up, double time, About Face, Left Turn, On the Spot Double Time." To mock, shame, to humiliate the recruit, to tear him down to raw material and then rebuild him into an automaton willing and eager to obey instantly. Luckily the Service Corps would not be cannon fodder.

The Service Corps transported supplies, from toilet paper to typewriters for the Army. By a happy chance they had a small branch that moved things across water, and I was sent to a waterborne training company on the Isle of Wight, a small resort island, not far from Southampton.

"Right. Take her out to sea, and be smart about it." We were in an open thirty two foot harbor launch. The corporal was testing me to see if I really could handle a boat.

"Cast off aft, cast off forward," I ordered, and steered the boat out of the crowded harbor. At last there was something I could do.

"Steer 210 degrees," ordered the corporal, then watched as I changed course. Turning a boat in a choppy sea was not the same as steering wheels over a pavement. A boat turns around a point one third of her length behind the bow, and over steering was a common fault with beginners. But I was not a novice, and I handled her with confidence, quartering the waves like a pro.

"Right. Back to harbor, full speed ahead."

I knew that racing back at high speed was another test. If I waited too long I would run into the rocks, but throttling down too soon would leave me embarrassingly short. I did it just right.

When they found that I really could handle boats, they made me an instructor. Every morning at 8 am I mustered a gang of eight landlubbers and showed them the ropes. Then I loaded them into the launch and chugged out to sea. Turning right, I followed the coast, dispensing pearls of wisdom and nautical lore until about noon when we arrived at a sheltered cove. On shore there were pretty little white huts, and prettier young maidens. This was Butlin's Holiday Camp, a vacation resort full of young people dedicated to having fun in the sun.

"Lunchtime,' I announced. "Then you will change into swimming gear and reconnoiter the disposition off hostiles and friendlies."

The recruits had thought I had a screw loose when I had told them to bring swimsuits and towels.

"You, Jones are in charge of the boat while we go ashore and reconnoiter. Make sure the anchor doesn't drag and tomorrow you will be part of the landing party."

This had to be the cushiest job in the Army. I was my own boss, the coxswain. I enjoyed many happy hours of reconnaissance assessing the disposition of possible opposing forces on the beach. They were all lightly armored with only flimsy swimsuits to protect them. For some strange reason, however, I listened to one of the more ambitious members of the company.

"Every so often there is a USB, a Unit Selection Board. You get the morning off, it's a piece of cake, and if you pass you might even become an officer."

I knew very little about officers. They told other people what to do, and they were paid a lot more money. Between an ordinary soldier and an officer there was a huge chasm in the Army hierarchy. It was unthinkable, but why not? It turned out to be a short ten minute interview with the company commander.

The bored major with his short military moustache behind his desk asked a bunch of silly questions. Of the six that tried two did not pass and I was one of them.

"What did he ask you?"

I was puzzled as I quizzed one of the bunch that passed.

"Did you stroke his dog?"

"What dog?"

"By the side of his desk. He's very fond of that dog."

Next month there was another USB. I marched in smartly, stamped my feet in the British fashion, and before I even sat down I bent forward.

"What a wonderful dog, sir. What is his name?"

The next step was WOSB, the War Office Selection Board. This was not so simple. It was the real thing, on the Aldershot Plains. Three days of penetrating interviews and totally impossible tasks.

"You are in charge of this team. You have to get all of your men across this raging river."

Two chalk lines on the ground were about 8 foot apart. "There's your gear. Get on with it."

The 'gear' was a pile of very short planks and several lengths of rope. There was no possible way to construct any sort of bridge. We would all have drowned if it had been a raging river. What our tormentors were watching for was how well we led the team if we were chosen to be in charge and how enthusiastically we contributed if we were part of the team.

Some of the tests were more sadistic than others, some of the interview questions were deliberately insulting and personal to gauge our reaction to stress, and at the end of three days, exhausted, we were given shabby little pieces of paper. I still have mine.

'Course number 682, candidate number 44, number 11 War Office Selection Board.'

"To Private number 22333323 Rotgans J.A.," and there were three little boxes.

Option C. was 'Not recommended.' B was 'Not recommended at present but your commanding officer will be called upon for a report in three months time.' 'A' was 'Recommended for OCS training.' On mine B and C were scratched off. I was going to Officer Cadet School.

This was another major turning point in my life. Another little bit of luck. I left the fun of mucking around in small boats and started on three months of long hours, sleep deprived nights, and intensive training on how to behave as an Officer of Engineers. I was not told why I was promoted from the Service Corps to the more prestigious Royal Engineers. I was learning not to ask questions in the Army.

We may have been Officers in Training, but the drill sergeants made it very plain that until we passed the final test we were still the lowest form of animal life, and they treated us accordingly. They made the drill sergeants of Basic Training look like gentle nursemaids. If we even looked in the eyes of the drill sergeant he would send us doubling around the square, with rifles high above our heads, until we dropped from exhaustion. The sergeant major was short, fat and mean. On his bald head there was a small triangular scar where a tormented trainee had stabbed him with a bayonet.

"His skull is so thick that it never reached his brain," was the rumor. Perhaps there was no brain to damage. He closely resembled a Neanderthal with a short fuse and a bad attitude.

In between lectures on Bailey Bridges and Explosives there were five mile runs in full gear, and endless hours of close order drill on the parade ground. We took turns yelling the commands, and soon found out that getting drill commands from an amateur caused utter chaos.

All good things must come to an end, and I was at Moss Brothers, gentleman's tailors in London, buying my officer's Sam Browne Belt, peaked officers hat, and a swagger stick. I reported for duty as a second leftenant to Number Three T.R.R.E, the Third Training Regiment, Royal Engineers in Aldershot.

A bungalow and a batman.

The officers were mainly wild, young, heavy drinking, and prone to destructive games in the officers mess. I lived in a bungalow with one other officer, a great step up from the raw wooden barracks where forty men snored. I also shared a batman, who pressed my uniforms and shined my shoes, another perk of being an officer and a gentleman. I had come a long way from the scruffy urchin who had been scrubbed by Mrs. Mac. I never did really appreciate her or her husband, and I deeply regret never thanking them properly.

An officer has a God-like power of command in battle, and in class conscious Britain he was also at the top, a social number-one to the soldier's number four or five. The class distinction is despised but deeply ingrained, and officers were treated with fear and respect. Now I was one.

There were rumors that an adventurous few might be posted to Malaya, where bullets were flying. I thought it would be a crime if I was to collide with a bullet before I had extended my acquaintance with the opposite sex.

I had a lot to learn about being an officer and leading men. I was a brand-new idiot, still wet behind the ears, I was given a platoon of 120 men to transform from raw recruits into engineer soldiers known as Sappers. When they were trained a squad could slam together a Bailey Bridge in record time that could carry tanks across a river. Each panel weighed 600 pounds, and needed the coordinated efforts of six men to fit into other panels as the bridge was thrust across a gap.

As the officer in charge I was officially responsible, but in the beginning I knew less than the lowest NCO. The noncommissioned officers are the backbone of the Army and they all knew I was almost as ignorant of everything as the rawest recruits. Nominally I was the boss, but in fact they were teaching me. They obeyed and showed respect, partly because they were brainwashed to obey and partly because if the bridge collapsed they would also be blamed.

There had been no lectures in OCS on how to learn from senior NCOs. The dummies, who couldn't learn, had probably washed out of OCS and the survivors who ended up with a commission were deemed to be smart enough to learn on the job. I learned how to give orders, and have orders obeyed. Not the best training for a husband and a father. Later, as a father, I was still an idiot, and an extremely bossy one.

I also learnt to drink beer, and how to blow up bridges. A couple of other subalterns and I were given periods off from our lofty commands and sent to reconnoiter the bridges of the Aldershot to London railway line. Afterwards, we would adjourn to a country pub, and over a beer or two we would compare sketches and our placements of high explosives. Quite a congenial way to learn how to deal with dynamite and beer.

      I still have one RECCE PROFORMA. which records my estimation of how much dynamite to use and where to put it on one railway bridge of four spans, each twenty foot long. It was at map reference 662529, of a load class 100 - railway engines were heavy. My sketch and calculations were on a form AF W4012 (rev) and records the bulk high explosive needed for the various charges. The cutting, borehole, footing and crater charges came to a total of 2980 lb. of H.E. but it does not record where we had our pub lunch and beer.

      Teaching the same classes to platoon after platoon of raw recruits gradually lost its attraction, and I sought other fields. I volunteered for the parachute regiment and was accepted. I even went out and bought my red beret, but my posting was canceled by our Commanding Officer. Either I was too good to lose, or he didn't want the trouble of breaking in a new training officer. I next volunteered for active duty, any place where bullets were flying. Several of my trained Sappers were being sent to Malaya to fight the communists in the 'Emergency' and that sounded like fun. Not only was I not allowed to go, but I had to learn how to 'Search Native Villages' from a book so that I could teach this to the Sappers. They went on to the Jungle Warfare School. Foolishly, I was jealous. The only conflicts I had were with my superior officers.

      Not far from the camp was a lake, and several small sail boats. I was in Heaven. I was getting ready to hoist a sail when the N.C.O. in charge came running.

      "Sir, you've gotta be checked out in those first."

"Don't worry. This is one thing I know something about."

When I was sailing back I noticed a jeep waiting for me. A bad tempered adjutant was fuming.

"Rotgans, you took that boat out without permission, without being checked out in sailing. You are on my report tomorrow at eight."

He gave me a tongue lashing that described in detail my many failings, and his doubts that I was really officer material in the first place, and I was forbidden forever from even looking at a boat for the remainder of my enlistment.

Another serious crime was marking my initials in wet cement with my swagger stick. When I went on report into the Commanding Officer's office, he was grooming his military moustache. A small cupboard on the wall contained a mirror and several combs, scissors and brushes. He was too busy brushing his moustache to focus on a good tongue lashing. My chances of being posted to anywhere interesting dwindled from minimal to zero.

The success of 35,000 British troops in Malaya has been unfairly compared to the defeat of half a million US troops in Vietnam. The North Vietnamese had enormous support from Russia and China, and a mutual border with China which allowed supplies to flow freely. The Malayan National Liberation Army was isolated from outside communist support and were in pockets in the middle of Malaya, and they were not popular with the locals from whom they extorted food.

The British began a 'Hearts and Minds Campaign' in which they supplied food and medical aid to the Malays and the indigenous tribes. Plus many non belligerent Malays had fought with the British against the Japanese, while the French in Vietnam had collaborated with the Japanese when Vietnam was occupied. The Brits were trusted by the locals, while the French and Americans and other round eyed foreigners, were totally distrusted. All of these factors and others made a crucial difference in the outcome of the two wars.

I found out that while I had no plans for life after my two years were up, my brother officers did. Most were going on to college to study engineering, to design and build real bridges in civilian life. I had given no thought to the future. I had drifted through school, I had been drafted because I wasn't smart enough to dodge. I'd always had ideas about running away to sea. The voyages of Captain Cook, exploring Australia, and the South Sea Islands had made a great impression. Especially when he got to Tahiti and was welcomed by the beautiful bare breasted maidens who swam out to greet his ship. However that was a distant pipe dream, but I thought that if the others in our crowd could have fun at college maybe I could also.

It had not been in the scheme of things. My parents had never finished high school. My father had worked his way up to become a chef. He had little formal education.

I applied to Oxford, Cambridge, London, and Reading universities. An unexplained mental growth spurt in the final years of school had led to fairly good marks on the school leaving exam, and I was accepted by three out of the four. I chose London because I could live at home, and because there was no money for fancy places like Oxford and Cambridge. The main advantages of Oxford and Cambridge were the friends you made, who could really help your career later on, but I didn't know that.

The Merchant Navy.

My days as an Officer of Engineers were over. It was a bit of a shock to leave the officers mess, where we were treated like members of the upper crust, to come back to my roots, a small two bedroom flat with my family in one of a row of identical houses in London. I had been far away, physically and socially. I had long since forgotten about Mickey Sparrow and his gang. I was still terminally shy with girls at mess dances and I was still an innocent.

College was due to start in September. In February I was discharged from the Army and ran away to sea. This had been one of my very few dreams, sparked perhaps by the bare breasted maidens in the South Seas. I knew enough from sea cadet days to function as a seaman and my trade in the Royal Army Service Corps had been Seaman B3 before my miraculous elevation to officer rank. In the office of the Seaman's Union I asked if I could take the exam for Able Seaman. However, the Trade Unions had the British merchant navy in their iron grip.

"You can't ship out without going through the training course, mate."

"How long is that?"

"Six months."

'Why can't I just take the test? I know I can pass."

"You gotta do the course, mate. Union rules."

There was a shorter course of six weeks that would let me work in the Engine room. Getting hot and dirty did not match my vision of facing into the wind, the smell of the salt spray lashing my face as we headed for the South Seas. I modified my dream, and ended up in a somewhat grimy Liverpool learning how to shovel coal. The Beatles were still in short pants, but dances at the Atheneum relieved the tedium.

A ship's boiler is about 20 feet long, 10 feet wide, with a wide grating sitting low about 8 feet wide on which the coal burns. The hot gases circulate through narrow pipes surrounded by hot water. Coal arrived in huge lumps, which were chiseled into small pieces by a trimmer. The firemen then loaded their shovels and aimed a stream of coal through a hatch about 10 inches deep by 20 inches wide. The art of shoveling coal was to spread the pieces evenly along the length and width of the grate so that they would burn evenly. The hatch was at eye level, and directing a stream of coal through it to spread the coal in a uniform layer was an art that required fine judgement combined with tireless muscles. At the end of six weeks I was an expert. I could spray the coal through the small opening and make it land exactly where I wanted it to.

I passed the final test, and was issued my contribution book as a member 732017 of the National Union of Seamen, a probationary member of the Deck and Engine Department.

In Southampton I signed on as a trimmer on the Cunard liner *Scythia*, sailing to Montreal, and we headed out to sea. It was highly exciting to be on a big ship, going out to sea. There wasn't a lump of coal anywhere. She had three boilers fired by jets of burning diesel oil. There were firemen, but they were not shoveling coal. Their only job during their watch was to change the diesel jets, once. There was no coal for the trimmers to trim, but union rules fiercely protected jobs for everyone. There were three firemen, and three trimmers, and a lot of time was spent playing cards. These were the glory days of British socialism fiercely protecting jobs for union members.

I became the Peggy of the firemen's mess. I kept the dining table clean, got the food from the galley, and cleaned up afterwards. I learnt how to wash and wipe a pile of dishes eight at a time. I was on track to becoming a professional dishwasher. I was my own boss in a fairly cushy job. Except when the winds blew wild in the North Atlantic. The galley was about 100 yards from the firemen's mess, and the working alleyway was 12 feet wide. It was hard enough to navigate empty-handed when the ship was bucking and rolling. It was a real challenge to carry a huge tray of sizzling pork chops as the ship tried everything to make you slip and slide and smash into the steel walls. If you had a sensitive stomach and tossed your cookies into the tray of food, life became harder. The firemen were a tough bunch with few pleasures and they looked forward to enjoying their meals. Better for me to face an angry cook in the galley.

In Montreal there were no bare breasted maidens to welcome us. Instead I was introduced to the interior of the boiler, and the soot from burnt diesel oil.

"They've had two days to cool down," said the Chief Fireman. "In you go, and take these poles, with the wire brushes on the end. Clean out all the pipes. I'll be checking every one of them."

The boilers were still as hot as Hades, maybe a taste of things to come in my next life. Removing the soot was an exceedingly hot and dirty job. Soot penetrated every pore of our bodies, and was inhaled deep into the lungs. We became as black as coal. It was fully a week later before our skin was white again, and we stopped coughing up black mucus. My dreams of running away to sea had always landed me on the sandy shores of a tropical island, being welcomed by dusky skinned maidens, clad in tantalizing grass skirts, arms open to embrace me. They would have run screaming from the black, very dirty animal I had become. Happy dreams, and harsh reality. I would gladly have changed places with Capt. Cook's sailors, even though cannibals ate many of them when their welcome to the paradise of the South Seas ran out.

Being away from female company made the firemen unusually interested in the anatomy of other males. As a rookie I received many intriguing invitations.

"Come and see the Golden Rivet, mate. Solid gold it is, the last one they put in."

There was allegedly one in every ship. It would be located in the bowels of the ship beneath a narrow opening in which a young lad could be trapped and his pants pulled down. I did avoid the Golden Rivet, but I fell victim to the Phantom Gobbler. You awoke in the middle of an erotic dream to find your male member deep in the mouth of a shadowy figure, who disappeared quickly when you woke up.

In the roller coaster of life I had climbed close to the top of the social scale as an officer and a gentleman, only to slide down again into the engine room of *RMS Scythia*. Strangely, the pay was exactly the same. Twenty pounds a month plus food and shelter, but in the engine room there was no batman and no salutes.

I did yearn occasionally for the good life, and once I gave in to temptation. The fireman's mess was literally below the lowest paying customers cabins, and world's apart. Dressed in my best clothes I sneaked up to the First Class lounge and quietly busied myself writing a letter. The change of atmosphere was a tonic. A genteel quietness, and soft leather armchairs to sink into. A million miles away from the grimy camaraderie below decks. My messmates had warned me of the consequences.

"You'll be caught, mate. You'll be up in front of the Captain in the morning. You'll be logged. They will dock your pay."

I had always wanted to meet the Captain and I welcomed the new experience of being 'logged.' Having my name recorded for punishment in the ship's log, and the details of the punishment recorded therein. Surely they wouldn't keel haul me - I couldn't see them slowing the ship down for that, and surely being clapped in irons would be against union rules.

I took another deep breath of the rarefied upper class ambience, folded my letter, and leisurely strolled out of the lounge, confident that I was home free. Sadly, I was mistaken.

"Excuse me, sir, could you come with me?"

The crew member that was lying in wait was built like a tank. No taller than I was, but twice as wide and heavy, and all muscle. Firmly, with a grip of iron he led me down to a room labeled 'Master at Arms.' This was the ship's Chief Police Officer. Obviously someone had sensed that I was not one of the fare paying passengers. In the movie *'Titanic'* Leonardo de Caprio gets the same treatment from a nasty looking ship's policeman. In today's British Merchant Navy nobody carried a gun, but the menace was still there. Being a devout coward and a terrible liar I quickly confessed.

"Captain's Log, tomorrow, ten o'clock. Don't be late."

Naturally, I was punctual.

The Master at Arms read the charges.

"Trimmer Rotgans, sir. Trespassing in the First Class lounge."

The captain looked bored. Obviously a man of authority, rather like my Commanding Officer in the Royal Engineers.

"Why ..." he looked at the charge sheet, "Trimmer Rotgans?"

"No excuse, sir. Just trying to get a change of air."

He could tell from my accent that even though I was sailing before the mast I had had an education. I saw a flicker of interest as he debated whether or not to enquire into this breach of discipline, but he was busy.

"Logged one day's pay."

It would be deducted from my wages at the end of the month, and my crime would be recorded in the ship's log, and my pay book. I was marked as a minor criminal. Luckily my career in the Merchant Navy came to an end soon afterwards when I enrolled in the University of London as a student. I had found little luck, and less love when I ran away to sea. My day dreams never remotely resembled the reality of life at sea. But I did log many thousands of miles traveling over the waves. I had 'been to sea.' Voyages I had only read of in books now had meat on the bones, and with a selective memory, they were only the best bits. I could do more reading and dream more dreams. It had not been time wasted.

Chapter Four

University of London, City and Guilds, Imperial College.

My income became a lot less when I went to college in September but I was climbing back up the social scale again and life became fun. Many engineering college functions were formal, and one of my first investments was a used dinner jacket, cost five pounds. It had been made in Calcutta many years before, judging by the label and the style. There were Dinners in Hall, black-tie affairs, and formal balls where our partners had a much harder job choosing their long formal gowns. We merely swabbed off the beer stains from the last party and adjusted our black ties.

The last of the ex-servicemen who went to college after the war had just left. In war they had faced sudden death and disease, and college regulations were chicken feed for them. They set the rough and tumble standards which we felt we had to live up to, even if it meant dismantling the Dean's small car and reassembling it at the top of the bell tower.

The Metropolitan police, the Bobbies, of London were worthy opponents during 'rags,' the impromptu contests between students running wild and the police, outnumbered 10 to 1, who were trying to abrogate the freedom of assembly of the students. Police tactics were to isolate a small bunch of students and beat the hell out of them. This sometimes worked but it was a small price to pay for the ultimate souvenir, the dome shaped helmet of the London Bobby. When he felt it being knocked off a Bobby's reaction was vicious and violent, but many a helmet ended up on Albert's head.

The Albert Memorial was right next to our college and had an ornate statue of Queen Victoria's beloved Prince Albert. After a successful rag students would slowly climb the wide stairs leading up to the memorial, murmuring prayers that were not found in the Church of England Book of Common Prayer. Members of the mountaineering club would then scale the statue, and the Bobby's helmet was solemnly placed on Albert's head.

One student rag was aimed at kidnaping three pretty French girls. They had been invited from Paris to lead Reading University's rag day procession. The female students of Reading took umbrage at this, and paraded down the Whitehall tastefully clad in as little as possible. They delivered a petition to number 10 Downing St., but the prime minister did not come out to view the show.

The French girls heard of the fracas and did not come, but this was not known to a couple of hundred engineering students who marched to Victoria station. We met the boat train, bent on kidnaping the French girls. We found two very pretty young women with extremely sexy French accents.

"No, messieurs, we are not French. We are from Belgium."

We were not fooled, and we loaded them onto a large baggage trolley. Mounted on an improvised throne of borrowed packing cases, we pulled them through the streets of London, from Victoria station to our college in South Kensington. We were harassed by squads of Bobbies, who were hopelessly outnumbered as usual, and they inflicted the usual painful damage on several sets of ribs. However we made a triumphal march to our college and it was only when the girls produced their passports, proving they were really from Belgium that we delivered them by trolley to their hotel.

My memories are less vivid of the classes, but one Prof has stuck in my mind, Professor Pippard, of Structural Engineering. Designing columns to take an axial load always gave me problems, in spite of his expert tuition. He had been doing it for decades, back to the early days of flight. He had designed aircraft frames when they were made of wood, covered with fabric.

I was not usually a joiner, but I did get interested in judo. The ancient Japanese martial art that taught you how to throw an attacker over your head did appeal to me. I had never been in a fight in my life, and I was not looking for one, but it seemed to be a good idea to be able to use an opponents weight and momentum to my advantage. I was soon practicing falling. From a squatting position I suddenly straightened my legs, flew up and back and landed on the mat, the tatami, making a violent bang with my forearms. This took the energy out of the fall and soon became second nature. One day I slipped on a wet pavement, fell backwards, and my reflex action was to smash my arms onto the solid stone slabs when I landed. My bruised arms hurt like Hades, but nothing was broken. I rationalized that I may have saved myself from a fractured skull.

As a team we competed with other institutions such as the military college at Sandhurst, and the Metropolitan Police. I developed a new twist to a hip throw, an osotogari. My body language and hip movements feinted to the left, then I switched and did the throw over my other hip. It worked every time. The military cadets had been toughened by endless pushups and jogging, but they were all caught off guard by my double osotogari.

My biggest satisfaction came in a match with the police. I was fighting a veteran judo trained cop. He had thick strong arms and a body made of solid concrete, about forty pounds heavier than me.

"He has been in the team for fifteen years, and he has never been thrown," one of his team mates said. As we maneuvered for position, he seemed as solid as a rock. A truly immovable object. I gripped his judo jacket and tried to pull, but nothing moved. But, the whole art of judo is to use your opponents movement and energy. I feinted to the left, and as he moved to block I switched and did the throw in the direction he was moving. It worked. There was a crash, and a very surprised cop looked up at me from the mat. I never did try this out in the field. When we clashed with the Bobbies in a rag, I let colleagues in the rugby club do the heavy work. In theory, it would have worked. In practice I was a devout coward.

My terminal shyness was still a problem, and at twenty one I was still an innocent. Then, one day, swimming in the Serpentine in Hyde Park I saw a lovely young woman sitting on her towel, reading a large textbook full of anatomical diagrams. I walked past her on my way to a swim, dropped my towel, and said

"Hi Doc. Could you watch my towel for minute?"

Not exactly a prize-winning line, but it worked. Julia was a medical student at the Royal Free Hospital medical school, which had been the first medical school in England to admit women. She was attractive, highly intelligent, and totally liberated in every way. We connected, and we did not stop talking as we walked out of Hyde Park together. We collected our bicycles. Very few students in London had cars. I escorted her to her flat.

"Come on up," she said.

She was much more confident and relaxed than I. Maybe naturally so, maybe from her experience with dead bodies and live patients. I was very restrained and gentle. I didn't know what I was doing, even though my excitement was rising painfully. I was still quite shy, and we came together slowly, melting into each other, softly, lovingly.

My lack of skill as a lover was more than compensated for by my high level of enthusiasm.

I was rather busy that year. I was thinking about Julia every minute of every day. I was also a full time engineering student, learning the physics, math, and the properties of materials that would be integrated into a structure that might be stressed as part of a building, a bridge, or a soaring tower reaching for the sky. The judo team had regular battles with expert opponents, and that was the year that I became a film extra. Several days a week I would have to rise early to get to the film studios. To my surprise, somehow I did well in all activities.

Was it a naturally high level of testosterone that gave me a boost, or did the presence of a highly stimulating companion push my endocrine glands to outperform themselves?

Google says that the highest levels of testosterone are found in trial lawyers. They are associated with energy, dominance, and focused attention, and in high ranking males who do more breeding. It did seem that levels of high performance were associated with periods of intense stimulation. I have searched, but I have not found any scientific studies that have answered the question satisfactorily. I certainly did well that year with my studies, in spite of the extra burdens from an active love life and early morning trips to the film studios.

Julia was quite intrigued when I had to leave at 5 Am to get to the studio. We enjoyed each other tremendously all summer.

I occasionally had to miss a week of filming when engineering field trips were scheduled that counted towards our grades. On one field trip we collected an amazing selection of road signs, which we then used to redirect traffic deeper and deeper into narrow country roads. These were flanked by solid stone walls, making it impossible for a car to turn around at the end and an uproarious traffic jam was had by all.

At one camp at totem pole was erected, and anchored in a hole dug deep into the ground. It was adorned with all of our names neatly printed in engineering draftsman style and included Roy Ferris at number 11, Barry Hatch at number 14, John McDermont at number 24, Roger Powell at number 32, and J. A. Rotgans at number 34. I can't find the name of Katie Dent, the only representative in our class from the fairer sex. Female engineers were rare in those days, and we unkindly compared her face with that of Winston Churchill.

"Stick a cigar in and she is the spitting image," but we treated her with respect and kindness. She had a delightful personality, and we wouldn't have hurt her feelings for anything. I was basically kind, but quite stupid when it came to women. My first love and I parted because of my foolish inexperience.

We were lying in bed when she asked,

"Do you think my breasts are too small?"

"No, certainly not. They are just right."

"Tell me honestly. Aren't they a little flat?"

That was the moment that I learnt that flattery trumps honesty with a woman.

"Well," I said. "Is there some cream or something that you could rub in that would help?"

For my second year at college I had the luck to get a place in the college residence. My tiny bedroom was within staggering distance of the college bar, and there was no shortage of congenial companions who liked to party hard and save studying for brief interludes just before exams. It was hard work carrying kegs of ale up to the third floor, but they made a satisfying racket when they were rolled empty down the concrete stairway.

My love life recovered, and I had a new girl friend. Jill was as pretty as she was petite. Her physical size was important, because in my room there was just one very narrow single bed. Luckily we were living on the fruits of love and they were definitely not fattening. It was a little more complicated when I stayed overnight at her nurses residence. Then I had to wake before dawn and climb out of the window before matron began her rounds. We had many happy times together, including a trip when we hitch hiked down to the Balearic Islands, and wandered happily around Majorca, Minorca and Ibiza. There was only one thing we did not agree on. She wanted to get married, and I was not ready for the bonds of matrimony. That year I was certainly not short on luck, love, or travel.

Getting into Movies.

Roy Ferris was a classmate, and he came from a theatrical family. He was in movies, and knew all the inside rules. He regaled us with tales of the film studios around London and the famous and beautiful stars that he rubbed shoulders with daily.

"Can I get into that game?" I asked.

"It's a closed shop. You have to be a member of the union."

Then he told me that the FAA, the Film Artistes Association was reluctantly taking in new members. That of course made less work for the existing members, but the producers had been insistent. A recent call for 'students' had been answered mainly by geriatric members.

"Look on the back page of Variety. It will be a small ad."

It was, only two lines. "FAA audition. March 3rd. 10 AM, Finchley Street."

I was one of the first in line. All around me they were quietly boasting about "When I was in Hamlet," or "Larry Olivier and I were in ..." I kept quiet. I had never even been in a school play. If this was the competition I hadn't got a chance.

"Next."

I walked into a cold, bare room. There were three small tables, and three hard unsmiling men.

"You understand that there is no guarantee of getting any work of any kind?" said the first.

The second one said "If you get a call and you don't show, you'll be blacklisted. Understand?"

The third asked "You got your own dress duds?"

"Excuse me?"

"Smart suits, dinner jackets, that stuff."

I thought of my beer stained tuxedo and nodded.

"Yes, I have my own stuff."

"Right. Give them your details." The third man pointed to a small office and my audition was over. They took the first fifty in line and I became a brand-new member of the FAA.

"Call Film Casting tomorrow afternoon, Gerard 5680. They will tell you if they want you."

I got to know the girls at Film Casting quite well. The routine was always the same.

"John Rogans checking in.

There would be "Anyone want John Rogans?" Then "Nothing right now dear. Call back later."

When I was lucky there would be,

"John, Gabby wants you."

I think Gabby developed a soft spot for me. I got a lot of calls, and made very good money.

Then would start another adventure into fantasy land. The next day I would gather my books and slide rule, get into costume, go through makeup, and wait. We always spent more time in the dressing room than on the set, and I always got my work done on time.

Hurley

Sometimes I had to bend the truth, and Film Casting knew it, but it didn't matter.

"John, can you play Hurley?"

"Yes, Gabby, like a pro." I had never heard of it, but I was always eager to work, and I counted on bluffing my way through.

"Alright dear. Be at Pinewood Studios tomorrow at seven, they will have the gear."

As soon as I hung up I was off to the public library to find out what in Heaven's name Hurley was. Something like grass hockey, played a lot in Ireland, and I scribbled down the rules. The next morning I was put into sporting gear complete with running cleats, all ready to go, sitting at the side of a field in the back lot of Pinewood Studios.

Of course I never got to play Hurley. We extras sat on the sidelines while two expert teams from Ireland ran up and down, with the star in the middle scoring the winning goal. The director had no intention of wasting film on us ignoramuses, but he couldn't employ non union people without paying a union member for each non union player. This again was England in the great days of the trade unions.

Boer War

Sometimes there were moments of heartbreaking sorrow and Oscar worthy acting. I will never forget climbing up the gang plank of a troopship, in the uniform of one of Queen Victoria's soldiers going off to fight and maybe die in the Boer War. With my pith helmet, khaki uniform, rifle and kitbag, I went onto the ship that would take me to Africa and maybe death. The crowd was weeping.

The next day I didn't have the helmet and gear, or the rifle and pith helmet. The crowd was weeping on cue, with me in it, sobbing my heart out as I waved myself goodbye. Oh that was acting, such acting.

German guard

Colditz Castle was an outdoor set at Shepperton Studios for the movie *Colditz Story*. I was in the German Army with a funny helmet, poking my rifle into British POWs to get them out of bed.

"Raus, raus, schnell, schnell." Get up, and be quick. "Raus, raus, schnell, schnell."

At the end of shooting we were always paid in cash, and I got time and a third pay because it was a night shot, plus extra money for saying lines, plus extra money for lines in a foreign language. The basic days pay was 2 pounds 12 shillings. For a night call it was 3 pounds 9 shillings and a 4 pence. Plus an extra pound for speaking, plus an extra pound for speaking in a foreign language, German. 5 pounds 9 shillings and 4 pence was more than many working men made in a week. My pay in the Army and the Merchant Navy was closer to one pound a day. The next night I took my girl friend to the best restaurant in London. I was now one of the best paid students in London University.

Pilot

It was a varied life. After escaping from the German POW camp I was a dashing young pilot in the RAF in the Battle of Britain. I was quite good looking and in those days I had hair. I was allegedly in the same squadron as Douglas Bader, the pushy pilot who lost both legs in a car crash but was determined to fly again, and get back into the RAF. By sheer determination he did, and flew in combat with two tin legs. Even the Germans admired his determination. He was shot down, ruining one of his metal legs. Through the Swiss the Germans got a message to the RAF, of safe conduct if they would supply a new tin leg. A lone Spitfire flew over, and Bader had his two tin legs again.

    We were on location at Bigham Hill aerodrome when he came to visit in his Rolls Royce. In the film he was played by Kenneth Moore, a very congenial fellow with a great sense of humor, who even played cards with us lowly extras. Bader was now a successful businessman, still pushy, hard driving, and no sense of humor at all. I preferred the screen version. The movie was *Reach For the Sky*.

Peasant to Knight.

From pilot I went to peasant, a medieval peasant, with rags on my feet and sacking for my clothing. We peasants were revolting, as you would be if you had to wear sacking. Oooh it was itchy. The movie was *The Black Knight* or in some countries *The Dark Avenger*. It was one of Errol Flynn's last films. He was aging, but he had quick hands and long arms and still could make a fast grab at a passing female. They loved it.

That movie brings back sad and embarrassing memories. For a short, glittering moment I was in line to be a knight in shining armor, one of the good guys going to fight with Flynn. Film Casting had asked,

'Can you ride a horse, John?"

"Yes Gabby, of course. Born in the saddle."

"Be at Twickenham on Wednesday and they will fit you out."

So I had a whole day to learn how to ride. I'd never been on a horse in my life but I was willing to try. Riding a horse paid more than three times the basic rate, and I was always jealous when I was in line at the cashiers window behind an extra who had ridden a horse. They walked away with a bundle of five pound notes.

I booked a riding lesson on Rotten Row in Hyde Park, and it lasted long enough for me to learn which side to mount, how to go forward, back and turn. I was all set. A bus took us from the studio to Tring, a small country village. In the dressing tents I climbed into the costume. First there were silver colored tights that hugged our legs, then heavy knitted woolen leggings sprayed with silver paint to look like chain mail. My armor was a mixture of real metal and rubber armor. Unfortunately the collar around my neck was the real thing. At a break when I lifted up my coffee cup my arm section jogged the shoulder section which jogged the metal neck collar and nearly knocked me out. It was not a good start, and things did not get better. To get to the shooting area we had to walk through the village. I had never worn tights before. I had seen them on ballet dancers and frankly I thought they looked a bit obscene on the males, especially as the dancers always added some padding to exaggerate their masculine equipment. Mine were skin tight, and as I walked through the village I felt that everything I had was on display. It was a long walk, and highly embarrassing. But worse was yet to come.

They put me on a big old horse, and my aluminum sword hung down at my side. Then they handed me up a long lance, with a red pennant at the end. My test ride started slowly, but the pennant flapped in front of the horses face, and the sword slapped his flank as we bounced up and down and soon he was off. He had been a police horse, and he had a mouth as hard as iron. I pulled up with all my might but I couldn't get him to stop. Luckily there were trees around the field, not a low hedge or I'm sure he would have been over and I would have been off. When I finally got back, it was obvious to the assistant director that Errol Flynn would have to ride without me. It had been a meteoric ride up the social scale, from peasant to knight and back again in a few short days. That's show business.

Gabby forgave me, and I made good money all the way through engineering school. A lot of time was spent in dressing rooms, and while the others played cards I worked on my books and my slide rule just enough to get through the courses.

I became quite blasé about working beside Laurence Olivier or Ava Gardner, and I never had any ambition to become a star. There was a casting couch for male actors, and a lot of people in the film business were always looking for fresh meat and that discouraged any theatrical ambitions. I was young and good-looking, and I had many offers. I refused them all, and I sometimes wonder how things would have turned out if I had been more receptive. This was long before the days of HIV AIDS. I had no ambitions for stardom, not even for the big money that went with it.

In *Sink the Bismarck* I was a young German sailor, who had to jump out of his bunk when the torpedo hit. There were twenty extras in the scene, I was the only straight one. They were a kind bunch, otherwise I wouldn't have dared to nod off in my bunk. My only regret was a missed opportunity in *Around the World in 80 Days* I looked enough like David Niven that several times an assistant director came over to me.

"Mr. Niven, you're wanted on the set."

However David Niven already had a stand-in and a double so what would have been the point of trying to get noticed? It would have been fun to travel with him and the film crew to all the exciting distant locations in that movie, but my unimaginative mind was still amazed that I was an engineering student, in one of the best colleges in the world, which was more than I had ever hoped for. But, I was tempted. On that movie every day there were stars from both sides of the Atlantic begging producer Mike Todd to give them just a small part.

I still have my membership card for the Film Artistes Association, Registered Number 1990 T., registered under the Trade Union Acts 1871 to 1940. I kept paying my dues, long after I had run away from England I would check in if I was passing through London. I would call Gerard 5680,

"John Rogans checking in." There was usually

"Gabby wants you."

"John, where have you been?"

On one visit I had come over with my new bride to visit her parents. Staying in London briefly I naturally checked in with Film Casting. The next morning I was at the English branch of MGM Studios, North of London, to be an American naval officer. By then I had grown my military mustache again in an effort to look mature enough to be a supervising engineer. The art director on the film was not sure.

"I'll call the technical director," he said.

The American expert said,

"Those are officially allowed, but the U.S. Navy doesn't like them. If you want to work, lose the fuzz."

When I got back my new wife did a classic double take. But I took her out on the town, and the mustache quickly grew back again.

Chapter Five

Spain

One summer late in Engineering school I took three months off from filming to work as an engineering exchange student in Spain. This had always been the country of my dreams, romantic, exciting, so different from stodgy England. I acquired a small book, 'Teach yourself to read, write, and speak Spanish in 10 days.' I did just that, and it saved my bacon. I became a junior assistant to the Municipal Engineer of Cordova, in Andalucia in southern Spain. Nobody in the office spoke English, and only the chief engineer spoke French. It was sink or swim in immersion Spanish, and I had a ball. Again I was a lucky wanderer, but not so lucky in love. My salary was nominal, only a few pesetas but engineers were quite high on the social scale. I was treated royally. There was a room at the best hotel in town, wine with every meal, and a weekly ticket to the bullfights, in the shade. There was just one distraction.

One of the secretaries looked exactly like the sexy Ava Gardner I had seen when she was working in *Bhowani Junction* on the set next to *80 Days*. Ava had looked very sexy even with her face covered with artificial sweat running down it in Pinewood's make-believe jungle. Maria Helena looked just as gorgeous. Large dark eyes, smiling and invitingly set in an olive colored face beautiful in its oval symmetry. The rest of her was a tribute to God's handiwork, and it was lust at first sight. I hovered around her desk every day, asking questions in my charming broken Spanish, but I got nowhere. Nice girls did not talk to men in the conservative South of Spain, especially to suspicious young foreigners like this Englishman with his tongue hanging out. Even approved courting was done through the iron grill outside the window, the reja. The suitor would be outside the house, whispering sweet nothings through the ornamental burglar bars. I never got as far as the reja. Then just when I thought I was making no progress at all, she would give me a small smile.

But then I was rudely uprooted. I was sent to the mountains to supervise some surveying on one of the hydro electric dams. I had to leave my luxury hotel and move into a stone hut high in the hills. My day started at dawn. By 11 o'clock it was 110°, and heat waves rising shimmered in the telescope of my transit, blurring my view. After lunch the siesta lasted until things had cooled down. My gourmet meals were replaced with chickens and rabbits, the only food available. Rabbit stew, omelettes, and fried chicken appeared in various forms three times a day, washed down with a bottle of red fluid. Usually this was 'vino tinto,' ink wine, and that's exactly what it tasted like.

I finished the surveying as fast as I could, and my exile ended. I was back in my comfortable hotel, and at the office

I think Maria had missed me. My heart skipped a beat when she said,
"There is a feria coming to town this weekend. Would you like to meet me there?"

I was early at the fairgrounds, waiting eagerly, when I saw Maria coming. My pulse raced, but then my heart sank. She was not alone.

"This is my aunt, Señora Teresa Ramirez Hernandez, and my cousins Lucia and Rosita."

When she introduced me she knew that all engineers were addressed with the honorific 'Don' so I was Don Juan. That didn't help one bit. The reception was cool. And expensive. When I took Maria on a fairground ride I had to buy five tickets. Plus it was hot, and I didn't begrudge the five ice creams but I was a broken man. My dreams of gently holding Maria's hand were shattered by the cousins and Tia Teresa.

I shouldn't complain. I had traveled to the land of my dreams. My boss had introduced me to local weddings where I danced all night, and to most of the local industries. My tour of a vineyard led finally to the cave where hundreds of barrels of wine were stored, and my host had insisted that I sample the white and the red, the young and the old, until I lost all inhibitions. I do not remember how I got back to the hotel, but judging by the hangover the next day I must have had a wonderful time. I had seen the mosque in Cordoba, the second largest in the world. Over the wide Guadalquivir River the new bridge was very similar in design to the ancient Roman bridge down river, in flattering imitation. The castanets of the flamenco dancers, in fiery flaring red skirts still click in my ears. True romance with the lovely Maria had been an impossible dream from the start.

I was almost glad to head back to stodgy England and pick up the threads of my life. The movie studios, the occasional lecture, enough studying to get through exams, and a charming young girl friend whose only fault was a burning desire to get married.

    Dear Jill, she was delightful in every way. She was English type pretty, peaches and cream complexion, intelligent and we seemed to be deeply in love, but she had this fixation about matrimony. She was also smart enough to know a losing horse. When I graduated, and still had not popped the question she made a clean break, and left for Montreal, Canada.

Love

I think I have been in love a few times, in its various forms. It seems to me that love starts in one part of the body and migrates. I am sure that for the male it usually starts with lust. Of our two basic appetites, for self preservation and preservation of the species, the latter is far stronger. When experimental rats are given a choice of pedals to press, they will not press the one that gives food, but the one that activates an electrode placed to produce sexual pleasure. Then they starve to death.

    When a man sees a beautiful woman, he may think he is admiring her outer beauty and inner grace, but at some level of his mind he is programmed to view her as a potential mate worthy of passing along his genes. In other words he thinks of sex.

    It is only later that he finds in her qualities to admire and adore. Love has risen anatomically and he feels sensations in the regions of his heart. This does not make sense in a physiological fashion, but we have been so trained by poets that when we find delightful and adorable qualities in our loved one we feel a warm sensation in the middle of the chest.

Physical and visceral love often fade. If we are lucky and the object of our love really has an inner beauty, and we are worthy of it, lust is replaced gradually by loving kindness. This works partly at the level of the brain and the mind, and can also stoke the fires at the lower levels. We are constantly changing physically and mentally, and it is unrealistic to believe that any form of love can last forever. I have often asked people that have been married for 50 or 60 years "Have you ever thought of leaving him?" The answer was always the same.

"Many times, maybe once a year."

All had thought of separating, even if this would be physically or economically crippling. All of this in spite of the powerful feelings that inspire so many songs and poems about love.

Oh the painful foolishness of love. The constant obsession, thinking about the loved one every minute of every day. Being reminded of her by a sound, or a sight or a smell. Wanting to tell her of all the small things that remind you of her. When the words of a sickly popular songs sound so true.

William Shakespeare is a hard act to follow. He was such a genius with words, how can a mere mortal compare to his odes to love? But did he love children? Google says he had three, but something is missing. I can't find him talking about loving his children. And this is strange not just because he was a man. Women are genetically programmed to blabber baby talk when they see a small infant. A mother has such a strong bond to the child she has carried inside her for months that it lasts her whole lifetime. Seventy years, eighty years on she still thinks of 'my baby' and is ready to sacrifice everything for her 'child.' However badly the 'child' behaves, hurts her, ignores her, steals from her, murders others, she will always love him.

The father is not immune, although his bond is nowhere near as strong. Mother Nature has made mothers indispensable, but not so fathers. Her commitment is lifelong. His can be extremely brief, limited to the rapid passage of tadpole shaped sperm. Eight squirts, 0.8 seconds apart, total time taken 6.4 seconds. Even if he knows that one of his seeds has taken root, he can walk away without a backward glance. Especially during the breaking in period when the little animal seems to have no personality and insists on making piercing noises and foul smells at both ends. This can take up to two years, but gradually there builds a loving attachment between father and child. For me, father and son, then two years later father and daughter. I was sure that I loved their mother. Attractive, intelligent, working so hard to try to please her mate. She was a good woman, and a great mother. Yet as my son became a personality, I would feel my insides turn to jello when he smiled at me or reached up to give me a hug and a sloppy kiss. That would make me melt. I felt something for his mother, but not this. Exactly the same thing happened with my daughter. This was love taken up to a higher plane. I wonder why Will Shakespeare left that part out.

Chapter Six

Graduation

I was one of the few who did not show up for graduation ceremonies. I was at Ealing studios dancing from 8 am to 5 pm every day with an attractive young actress, Penelope Newington. The movie was quite unremarkable, called *Touch and Go*. I was still suffering from the humiliation of Spain and I didn't give Penelope a second thought. The chemistry was just not there. As we danced, cheek to cheek, under the soft lights with sweet music playing, my mind was on Jill.

    I qualified in July 1955, but did not pursue an engineering career right away. The money was better in films, until November, when the sun went in and work at the studios became scarce. I reluctantly joined a firm of consulting engineers, Freeman, Fox and Partners, and once again I was at the bottom of the ladder. Both senior partners were real knights of the realm. It was in class ridden England, and if one of them visited the drawing office where we junior engineers slaved everyone stood up and said "Good morning, Sir Ralph." My stomach turned. We did not have to pluck our forelocks, but in the real world we were definitely peasants to these knights.

    I stuck it out for six months. The following April I shipped out of Southampton, this time as a passenger, bound from Montreal. Jill had written, and I was coming.

    The cost of an airline ticket was exactly the same as one on the Holland America line, which bought ten days of good Dutch food, as much as you could eat, cheap drinks, and the girls were exciting. It was party time all across the Atlantic, a dramatic contrast to my previous sooty voyages.

    By the time I arrived, Jill was already married. We had a couple of dinners, a passionate farewell, and my career as a civil engineer really began.

Labrador

Jobs were plentiful, but one in particular looked like fun. Supervising the building of five radar stations in Northern Labrador. The headquarters were at Hopedale, a native village on the coast. Supplies came in by ship and seaplane until the sea froze, then by planes on skis and in helicopters landing on the ice.

    A VIP, the zone engineer Zane Parks looked at my application. He was a small, busy man behind an acre of polished desk.

    "You've had six months experience?" He was not impressed. My prospects looked dim. He turned a page. It was time for another little bit of luck.

"You were in the Royal Engineers?" He sounded more interested.

"I was in the Canadian Royal engineers," he said.

"Did you build Bailey Bridges, and handle explosives?"

I nodded. He smiled. I was in.

"Those were good days. Okay. We are the consultants, and you'll have a contractor's engineer on your site. We will have engineers for every two sites along the line. It goes right across Canada, known as the McGill fence. It will give us and the US an extra 2 seconds warning of Russian missiles coming in. Any questions?"

I had a few hundred, but I was too excited to ask. Only "When do I leave?" It sounded like a great adventure. I was sure I could handle the responsibility, and the money was seven times what I had been earning in London.

"There is still broken ice in the bay. They will radio when there is a clear passage for a sea plane to land. I hope you're okay with astro surveying? There are no good maps and you'll have to fix your position by the sun and the stars. Very accurately, so that the microwave dishes point where they are supposed to point."

I kept silent. I had devoutly believed in the conservation of energy, especially when studying for final exams. I had reviewed 10 years of previous exam questions, and there hadn't been a single one on astro surveying. I hadn't even gone to the lectures. I had been correct, and no questions came up on the exam but now I would have to learn in a hurry. I went out and bought a book on celestial navigation.

I checked the radio messages every day. There was always the ice, until about three weeks later.

"It's a possible. A Canso amphibian is going to make a run and have a look. If there is too much ice, he'll turn around."

I was on the plane, which was fully loaded with cases

of supplies.

"What's in these?" I asked the pilot.

"Dynamite. You'll be blasting the road out of the granite to get up the mountain." He saw my face.

"If we bump into any ice, it won't explode. The detonators are on the next flight."

The Labrador coast was barren rock, with gullies of snow remaining, and ice in the inlets. Officially above the tree line, there were just a few stunted pine trees. In the bay there were scattered chunks of white ice. My heart fell. I wanted so badly to start work. The pilot flew around a few times.

"I think we can get in without hitting any ice. I hope."

My brain told me that dynamite didn't normally explode on impact, but I was sitting on 2000 pounds of it. Surely there wouldn't be any old stuff, would there? When dynamite got very old the nitroglycerin could liquefy and leak and form a deadly pocket of highly unstable explosive, liquid nitro. All these cases were new, weren't they?

The thin aluminum hull of the seaplane landed with multiple crashes on the rock hard waves of water, but nothing broke, nothing went Bang and my career as a construction engineer had begun.

The next two years were a ball. I was the head honcho, with 250 men in my camp, of laborers and assorted trades, and huge garages for the heavy equipment. These also came in handy to keep small helicopters warm in winter nights at 50 below zero. I needed to be mobile so Frank the supervisor taught me to drive in a three ton truck. In England I'd had a bike. Here I was given my own Jeep, and when the snow became too deep in September we ran around in Bombardier snowmobiles. It was great fun.

There were problems that came up the chain of command. When a construction foreman on one of the sites had a problem he checked with his engineer who radioed the supervising construction foreman in my camp. A tricky problem might occasionally be passed to the contractor's engineer, a smart, civilized fellow from Montreal, who had had a lot of construction experience. If he was stumped he'd come to me for a decision. The man with the least experience.

In the beginning I didn't have a clue, so I usually called a conference. There was my own supervisor, the contractor's engineer, his supervising construction foreman, and possibly the site engineer was flown in. As chairman of the meeting I outlined the problem and asked for ideas. It was a game of blind man's bluff, and I had to conceal my utter ignorance and pick on the idea most likely to work. All of the stations got built, I wasn't fired, so somehow the game was successful.

It wasn't always easy. Part of the station was a 200 foot tall tower and when it was ready for the final inspection guess who had to climb and check every level right to the top. At ground level there was a ten knot wind and the temperature of at least 30 to 40 degrees below zero. As I climbed higher the wind increased and the temperature fell. We didn't know about wind chill in those days but by the time I got to the top I was chilled to the bone in spite of my Arctic clothing. I would guess it was in the order of 100 degrees below zero. The ladder was not protected with a cage and climbing had to be slow and careful. I knew from the drawings that the ladder rungs were rods of steel one inch in diameter. The plans did not show the one inch thick collar of ice all around which made the rungs three inches thick and very slippery. This made us very careful. Nobody ever fell off. I was too busy curling my mittens over the ice to be scared.

Pouring concrete at temperatures of 40 below zero is not recommended or covered by the textbooks. We learned. We covered the new concrete with tarpaulins and pumped in lots of hot air for a couple of days.

It was when the station was almost finished that a new challenge popped up. Power in the stations was provided by three diesel engines, and a team of mechanics was flown up from Montreal to check these out. They flew up in a de Haviland Otter, fitted with skis to land on the ice of the harbor. Then a blizzard blew in, dumping about ten feet of snow over the camp, and over the road up the mountain.

"But we've got to get them running," said the senior mechanic. I explained "There is too much snow. The snowmobiles would just slide sideways down the mountain. You'll have to wait until the dozers have cleared the road."

They grumbled. "We can't sit on our butts all day. There must be a way." I looked at their well fed bellies, their cigarettes, and I said "I can lead you up on snow shoes if you like."

An hour later, the expedition was ready to start. We all had many layers of clothing, snow shoes, poles, and there was a rope leading from my waist to the waists of the three Montreal mechanics.

"We are Canadians," they said. "We pioneered this country. No problem."

So led by the tenderfoot from London we set off up the mountain. I knew the road intimately, and I didn't mind stopping often to let them catch their breath or shed a coat.

It took hours, and even I was tired. They seemed close to death. But, they recovered, and they knew their stuff, and started the engines. By the time all three were running smoothly, a snowmobile had made it up to the top. All four of us squeezed into its little cabin, and we skidded down the mountain. I'm sure they had tall tales to tell when they were safely back in Montreal.

I was well paid. Everyone worked sixty hours a week, and supervisors got an overtime allowance. Plus a northern allowance, and a hardship allowance, and it came to big money. Especially as there was nothing to spend it on. At the end of my stay I had a pile of money in the bank.

Entertainment was a bit of a problem. I had a

shortwave radio, there was no television, but there were occasional movies flown in for the construction crew. There was beer to go with superb grub that kept the men happy. Discipline was never a problem. They were piling up too much money to risk getting fired.

  The only real clash was with a road foreman. Before we could work on the site I had to build a road up the mountain. Surveying the route meant tramping through the brush, drawing a sketch, then cutting down trees along the route, then excavating any high spots. This meant drilling and blasting solid granite much of the time. The drilling crew would bring up the air compressor, and drill holes with jackhammers. The powderman came next, dropped down sticks of dynamite with a detonator connected to a red wire that snaked up the hole, over the rock to the firing point. The area was covered with a blasting mat, of old ropes woven together. Everyone would take cover, the powderman would retreat to his safe shelter and yell "Fire!" three times.

  All of this I had covered in engineering school or the army, and there was no problem, except with the road foreman. Guns were forbidden in the camp, but somehow he had smuggled in a rifle, and liked to take pot shots at small animals. We had a polite discussion and I reminded him of the rules, but he kept on playing with his gun, and the discussion became a confrontation. In a private session I explained that either the rifle would go or he would.

  Things were quiet for a while, no rifle was seen, then one sunny day I was walking up the road. The foreman was sitting on a rock.

  "No problems," he said. "The crews are working fine."

  I kept on walking, and as I got close to the site I noticed all was quiet. No noisy air compressor, no rattle of jackhammers. I rounded a bend and saw that the site was deserted. The blasting mat was in place, and when I got closer

I could see under my feet the red wires trailing away to the powderman's shelter. Then I heard,
"Fire!"
I froze. There was no place to run and I was right on the edge of the rock to be blasted. I would soon be flying up with the mat and sharp splinters of granite.
"Fire!"
Then I found my voice.
"Stop! Stop!" Weak at first, getting stronger.
"STOP ! STOP !"
The silence seemed to last forever. I wondered if I was facing the life hereafter. Then I saw the head of the powderman above a rock. He saw me, and went pale. The foreman was on the next plane out.

The powderman carried on, but his yells were quite a bit louder, and his head would pop up after each yell. The road was finished without incident, and I was a proud father of the very first road that I had carved out of a mountain.

The native village across the bay was out of bounds, except that I had to go there occasionally to hire new labor from the Eskimos. This was long before they were called Inuit. They were paid the grand sum of $1.10 per hour. The white population consisted of a two-man detachment of the RCMP, a Department of Transport radio operator, a Moravian missionary and his wife, and a young woman, the Moravian schoolteacher for the village children. The only white woman for two hundred miles.

I became a frequent visitor to the missionary's dinner table. I invited them to the camp and fed them superb steaks from my kitchen. I had the school hand bell re-built by my machine shop, but the schoolteacher never allowed herself to be alone with me. It was rumored that she had been raped by the Russians as a child, and I never even got to hold her hand.

The Mounties were far more friendly. Ray Isaac and Randy Zink were young, superbly fit, and rather bored. They were responsible for an area the size of England, but there was very little crime.

They often took me out on patrol, in their harbor launch in summer, and by dog team in the winter. We invented ice cream and Scotch parties. They cranked out home made ice cream and I supplied the Scotch. On patrol we caught many fish, and netted a seal or two. A delicacy on the mission dinner table was often steak and kidney pie, with deer steak and seal kidneys. Delicious. It was wonderful luck to get this plum of a job.

In my spare time I wandered over the rocks of Labrador prospecting for minerals. I found only a small patch of commercial grade asbestos. Twenty years later and ninety miles to the North two prospectors in a helicopter saw a metallic sheen on the rock. It became the most valuable strike of nickel, gold, and copper ever found. They both became multimillionaires. I was ahead of my time. Plus ninety miles as the crow flies was double that clambering up and down smooth rocky ravines in the short summer season, and being eaten alive by monster mosquitoes could be fatal.

On balance I had a big serving of luck, I broadened my horizons in the frozen North, and the only thing lacking was a little bit of love. Still, two out of three ain't bad, and if I had been really desperate I could even have had the third ingredient.

The Code of the North

On one winter patrol the morning was bright and brilliantly sunny. At 50 below all the condensation in the air freezes and falls to earth taking any dust with it and the visibility is startlingly clear. You can see for miles, even if it is all white.

White snow in the low hills, and white snow on the ice covering the ocean. The dogs were jumping and yelping, eager to go. They were bred to work and a trip like this was complete happiness for them. They pulled so hard that they had to be slowed down at times, or they would end the day with their paws bloody, and red bundles of snow clinging to the fur. They were harnessed in the Eastern Eskimo fashion, on separate traces, not like the Alaska double trace where the dogs are lined up behind each other. The wooden sled, the komatik, was covered with supplies, and as well as the Mounties and me there was an Eskimo guide. This was long before it became politically incorrect to call them Eskimoes. They are now Inuit, 'The People."Ray and Jason said it would be about three days, down to a small Eskimo village on the coast.

"We will be camping on the snow, but with a thick bed of pine needles and a good sleeping bag, we'll be alright. There is only one family left in the village, and they will be glad to see us. We'll tell you about Eskimo hospitality later."

Our village sat on a promontory of granite that stuck out into the ocean. The mission building was a three story affair, a tall pointed roof New England style, with the Minister's residence on the ground floor. Guest rooms on the next floor, and at the top were two three hole thunder rooms. The only heating was in the residence. On the third floor there were leaks between the planks, and the wind at that elevation was strong and cold. Nobody lingered there long. Waste froze before it hit the ground, and it was spring before it thawed. The church and the school were close by.

Then came the prefab house shipped in for the Mounties, next a jumble of roughly made native huts. In front of most huts was a komatik and a team of boisterous sled dogs. Without their chains they would have been racing after us. At the tip of the point of land we passed the Department of Transport radio station.

The village became smaller behind us. The huge expanse of snow covered sea ice stretched without boundaries to the North and East as we headed South. On our right the tides had driven the ice up into a scattered jumble of jagged white blocks.

We set out over the frozen ocean, running by the sled. Nobody sat and let the dogs do all the work. Maybe they do that in Alaska but not in Labrador. When the snow was deep the going was slow, and we had to jog along in snowshoes. On ice where the snow had blown away the running was easier and the miles went by quickly.

When the sun went down we were glad to pull into a small bay and make camp for the night. We picked a low flat area of land up off the ice, and after tying up the dogs we collected driftwood for the fire and pine boughs for our bed. We laid these in a layer almost two feet thick on the snow, then put our sleeping bags over the boughs, then put up the guide's tent. This was made of old sugar bags and through the holes we could count the stars.

The stove was a tin can about eight inches wide, five inches deep and eighteen inches long. One end was open, and in one of the flat sides there was a round hole for the lengths of stove pipe that went up through a hole in the roof of the tent. The Mounties gave me a warning.

"If you need to go, do it now. If you get up in the middle of the night you'll never get warm again."

So I found a small tree then climbed into the tent as the fire got going. It burned furiously. We warmed up our cans of meat, which had been frozen solid and a billy can of snow crystals to make tea. It was delicious, and then we settled down.

Unfortunately the tea tasted so good that I drank too much, and in the middle of the night I just had to go. I was bursting, and I got out of the sleeping bag, out of the tent and did my business as quickly as possible. Luckily there was no wind. If fingers or nose or anything else was exposed to the wind at a temperature of 60 below, there would be instant frostbite of fingers and other parts. Delicate parts might freeze solid.

"Did you lose anything?" asked Ray when I scrambled back into the sleeping bag.

I tried to wrap the down bag tight around me, but for the rest of the night I was shivering and shaking with cold. I thought sympathetically about The Cremation of Sam McGee, where "It's the cursèd cold, and it's got right hold till I'm chilled clean through to the bone." Both the narrator and Sam had felt the Arctic cold, and Robert Service knew what he was talking about. So did I.

I was glad when the sun came up and we started moving around. I was soon running hard to get some warmth back into my frozen body. I have never ever been so cold as sleeping on the snow that night.

Two days later we saw a single plume of smoke, and around a headland we came to Makovick, the village. Only one cabin was occupied and two men were waiting outside. They somehow knew we were near. I'd been told that the two men shared a woman, and that started a lecture by Jason on the Code of the North. The Eskimoes listened to the missionaries, but didn't really change their customs. In a village any man might be the father of a child, and it didn't matter. All the children were loved equally. If a traveler came in from a cold journey they put him to bed with one of the wives to make sure he warmed up. If he contributed to the gene pool that was good, as it reduced the risk of inbreeding, and the child was certain to be well loved. The running was slowly defrosting me, but the Eskimo method sounded intriguing.

"Have a good story ready," said Jason. "When they offer you their wife to keep you warm, you don't want to offend them when you refuse."

"Refuse?"

My lewd mind had been dwelling on Eskimo Nell, a rude, crude ballad about a legendary sexual athlete. We sang it in the bar at college, along with other pornographic rugby songs. I had been away from civilization for nine months, and the Moravian schoolteacher had been a painful reminder of what I had been missing.

"Trust me, you will. And don't forget the little initials they may have, like Tb, VD and so on."

The Mounties were exempt, as they were the government's representatives, but the Code of the North definitely applied to me. Still, I thought there must be precautions one could take.

The men led us inside the cabin, where there was a wood stove and it was delightfully warm. There was a mouth watering smell from a pot of stew on the wood stove being stirred by a small woman. She turned and I shivered, but not from cold. She was burnt black by the sun and her face was lined with deep ridges. When she smiled I saw she had three teeth. Two on the bottom and one on the top.

As the cabin got warmer I discovered that another story about the Eskimoes was true. They didn't take their clothes off in the winter, and sometimes sewed themselves in, leaving flaps for necessities. This didn't matter in the cold, but as they warmed, and the sweat melted, it soon smelled worse than a locker room after a football game. In particular I was sure that the Eskimo lady had not changed her underwear in four months.

Sure enough, one of the men waved to the sleeping quarters, and through the guide he said for me to 'go and get warm.' With his wife. To refuse would have been a serious breach of the code. I realized now that I didn't want to hurt her feelings. So, after frowning with disappointment, I told them my story.

"I am so sorry, but I do have to decline your kind offer

of hospitality. On the first night on the trail, being a rookie, a cheechako, I made a stupid mistake. I drank too much tea. I had to get up in the middle of the night. There was a strong wind, and everything got frostbite. My fingers and nose weren't too bad, but down below it was much more sensitive, and the frostbite on my male member is now hurting so much I couldn't ... take advantage of your kind offer. Please forgive me."

      I don't know if he believed me but maybe he gave me credit for a good story. It seemed that there were no hard feelings. I was celibate all the time I was in Labrador, but I had honored the Code of the North

Chapter Seven

The Canary Islands

After a couple of years of isolation in the frozen north I took a break. England was cold in November. So was the south of France, and so also was the south of Spain. In Cadiz I found a boat going to the Canary Islands. I was hoping to get warm there. This was the beginning of another major turning point in my life.

We docked in Las Palmas, on the island of Gran Canaria, blessed by tropical breezes from nearby Africa. I checked into the penthouse of the best hotel in town. I could afford it. My bank account was bulging. There was another penthouse occupied by an older American lady, Catherine, whose husband was away at sea.

For a long time I fended her off, then one night she got me drunk, and my memory of that night became hazy. I thought a change would be a good idea and luckily it came from a bunch of men on the beach. One saw my beach bag with the logo 'Trans Canada Airways.'

"Hey Canada. Come and have a beer." They were a group of reporters from the *Vancouver Sun*. Bostock the Brave, Alex McGillivray, plus the Giraffe, and Jim Kirkwood. Jim was writing his Great American Novel, Alex organized everything. Bostock was an eccentric English chap, doing cartwheels on the sand, and the Giraffe had a dry wit that added many a smile. They had rented an apartment, and soon I was one of the gang, and safe from Catherine. We drank our way through every bar in town and camped out on the sand for a change of scenery. I have a vivid memory of the Giraffe in the morning sun lowering his pants to stick himself with insulin.

They had noticed, as had I, that in front of one hotel on the beach there was often a pretty young woman.

"She's always got her kids with her. She's married." complained Bostock. One day I was relaxing at a café nearby, and as a gesture of friendship I sent over a glass of ice cold Coke.

"Tell her it's from the Englishman," I told the waiter. When she smiled, and raised her glass, I wandered over to say 'Hi.' Auburn hair, a lovely smile, and two well behaved children.

"I'm Barbara," she said. "Also English. I'm here as a nanny." She gestured to the children."

And so began a liaison that was as hot and fierce as the tropical climate. We became besotted with each other, and I saw her every day. We often ended up in the apartment, and Bostock took it well.

"I always thought they were her kids, dammit. She's a lovely girl."

As I came to know her I found she was more than lovely. Very pretty, very smart in a bookish way, soft and warm, superbly loveable and loving. What was so delightfully amazing was the ardent bond between us. No magnetometer ever made could have measured our mutual attraction.

Naturally there were a couple of glitches. One afternoon she offered to cook. "I've been here so many times, it's my turn," she said.

"We were going to eat out," I said. "If you really want to cook, we had better hurry. The market is closing soon. And it's a holiday tomorrow."

Luckily we found some nice thin slices of veal, the last meat they had. On the balcony we opened up some beer, and Cindy - short for Cinderella, as we thought she worked too much - disappeared into the kitchen. After a while I went in to check.

She had lots of vegetables bubbling, and to my dismay she was also boiling the veal.

"Cindy, my dear, that is so tender it only needs frying gently." She grabbed the pot, and I went back to the balcony. I had few more beers, I went in again. The poor veal was now sizzling in the frying pan.

Nobody said much as we ate. We were too busy chewing.

"Nice veggies," said the Giraffe. "Have some more wine, my dear." He filled all of our glasses. The wine was powerful, the view of the turquoise sea was a picture, and life was good. She had tried her best, and we gave her credit. The Giraffe opened another bottle, we were all quite happy as we chewed.

She had good cry when I had to leave. After six months I was itching to get back to the adventure of engineering. I told her where I was going, we exchanged addresses, and she sobbed as I boarded my plane.

Vancouver

When I got back to Montreal, I turned down more radar stations, and a building job on a dam in Argentina.
"I'm going to Vancouver."
I had been thoroughly brainwashed. I was convincing a skeptical friend with my Las Palmas tales from the reporters. Alex had said,
"Wait until you've seen the coast of British Columbia. And the Gulf islands, fantastic. The best sailing in the world. Mountains? Grouse Mountain is only minutes from downtown Vancouver. You can ski in the morning, and sail in the afternoon. There is a party every night. It's a young, friendly party town."

I left Montreal in a small green Volkswagen Beetle, sharing the driving with an overweight operatic tenor who had a very large voice. He was going to a concert on the West Coast, and he practiced all the way. In the small car with that big voice my ear plugs did not help much.

My little bit of luck did not show up in Vancouver. I arrived just after 200 civil engineers had been laid off by the biggest consulting firm in town. Experienced men with families and mortgages were walking the streets.

"BC is a boom or bust place. You just came at the wrong time," they told me. I should have gone back to Montreal, but I was stubborn. I hunted for work, while I lived off my savings. Months went by, and it never occurred to me to draw Unemployment Insurance. I was a happy optimist. Something would turn up.

Vancouver was a fun city. Full of young professionals, many Brits, and there really was a party every night if you could afford it. My savings dwindled, I sold my stocks and shares, and just when I was looking at the bottom of the barrel I took a job as a taxi driver. Yellow Cab Number Nine. I got to keep forty five per cent of the take, ten percent was for maintenance, forty five percent for the owner. To make money you had to hustle, know which places were busy and when. Vancouver had little crime in those days, and there was little drama. No babies born in the back seat, no "Follow that car" chases, mostly small tips and a few large ones from VIPs looking over property around the city. When I got tired of this, I sold the first Life Insurance policy for the newly opened British Pacific Life Insurance Company. It was also my last sale. That was not my forte.

Next I fell in with a group of smooth talking salesmen who were tiring of selling aluminum siding, even though the profit was great. They wanted to diversify into selling swimming pools. They'd seen how easy it was to put in a pool in California, and they sent me down to San Francisco to learn the ropes. It was easy if you had the right location. A front end loader can dig a hole in sand easily, cement block walls went up quickly, and a thick blue plastic liner fitted snugly. Plus a 'diatomaceous earth' filter, which was chalk by a fancy name. When I got back to Vancouver I warned them that the scenic mountains all around were made of solid granite, and where there was not rock there was hardpan, which was just as hard. The system might work well in San Francisco and the Fraser River Delta, but they should stay away from the hills.

With the grand title of Supervising Engineer of Johnny Weissmuller Swimming Pools I scooped out several pools before I found that they had ventured into British Properties. This was an expensive development with many high priced homes who could easily afford their pools, but it was on the side of a mountain. I warned them that the price would exceed the amount in the contract, which made no provision for blasting out rock.

I should probably have got some sort of dynamite license, but I had blasted out a lot of rock in Labrador, and I knew what I was doing. With plenty of blasting mats I prevented flying rocks from bombing nearby expensive homes, and I built a couple of beautiful pools. They greatly exceeded the selling price but we parted company amicably just as the job market reached bottom and started upwards again.

In Swann Wooster Engineering I was a junior design engineer. I learnt how to design pulp mills, ocean terminals, and highways, then one day one of the senior partners came to me.

"John, here is a challenge for you. A plate girder bridge that will carry the heaviest locomotive in North America."

Preliminary designs had shown that the simplest and most economical construction would be several huge, deep steel plate girders, about 15 feet deep, of solid steel 2 inches thick. This was heavy stuff, and I had to calculate and recalculate the stresses and strains as I trimmed off any surplus steel. This would have been easy on a computer, but they were just coming in, and were still huge machines spitting out punch cards. I had to do all the calculations on my slide rule and drew by hand the engineering drawings. It took three months to finish, and I was so thoroughly fed up with the girders that I let someone else supervise construction. I had seen all I wanted to see.

A little later I was winding up a small design project when the partner bustled in again.

"Good news, John. We've got another plate girder design, and you are the expert." By the time I'd finished that one, and the one that followed, I'd spent nearly a year on plate girders. My drawing board had become a purgatory. Then followed a series of docking terminals for freighters and passenger ferries. BC was blessed with a lot of coastline, and a new ferries in new places needed terminals to dock at. These were built with piling, some vertical, and some angled at 40° to withstand the impact of a ferryboat. Our shock absorbers were originally layers of used auto tires, later replaced by large blocks of black rubber. The stresses and strains in all components had to be calculated carefully. Ferry captains were supposed to dock at three knots or less, but there was a hefty safety margin to allow for wind, waves, and whiskey. To this day, 50 years later, I still watch a ferry docking with a fascination and a critical eye. As always, the first project was a challenge, but by the third one the charm was long gone.

I was only one of many junior engineers. To rise and become a partner took luck, engineering skill and experience, but above all an ability to sell your talent to non-engineers who would be buying the structure. I already knew that I was not a salesman.

3276 West 11th. Avenue

My personal life became more interesting after I joined a group of two engineers and an architect, sharing a house at 3276 W. 11th Avenue in Vancouver. The leader was an intense, handsome Keith Payn. He was in the Water District, designing sewers, and on the days when he physically checked them out he returned with a slight fragrance to him. He was the spitting image of the film star Omar Sharif, and his talents and charms truly blossomed at 3276. He designed and built devices for washing beer bottles en masse when we brewed our beer. He went on to teach himself welding, even how to weld aluminum, which came in handy later when he did his own repair jobs on his plane.

Peter Stagg, the architect, set up a company to design and build campers to fit onto a pickup truck. Unfortunately, he was ahead of the times, and one of his employees siphoned off most of the profits.

The other engineer was an old classmate, Roy Ferris, the student from London, 6000 miles from where we had first met in engineering school and worked in movies. One of us had a delightful girlfriend who supplied us with the latest discoveries of a mining company, and we all dabbled on the stock market and became a little richer. None of us was married, and we had a ball.

John Mitchell was also a regular visitor. He was a married man, but I think he was still fascinated by the dissolute life we singles led. He was remarkable. He had been born in Singapore of upper class parents. While living in England he was caught by the draft, and the Army sent him through cooking school. He became a chef, and still cooked a wonderful meal. In Vancouver he became interested in brewing, fought regulating agencies and founded the very first micro brewery in Canada, in a pub in Horseshoe Bay, West Vancouver. That led to another, and he finally sold out at a nice profit. Books were written about him. His cooking, and his wonderful beer are things that I miss the most.

Jumping ahead many years we started a Tontine in 1999. Keith, Peter, John and me. We had lost touch with Roy. Instead of money, we bought a hugely expensive bottle of brandy, opened it to imbibe two ounces each at the founding ceremony, and the Tontine would meet if one of us dies. Two more ounces each. We carefully calculated, and the last one standing will have enough for many toasts to the good friends departed, and a world class hangover. At the time of writing this there are two survivors, Mitchell and I. It is lonely when your best friends die, and I do not want to be the last. Enough

about mortality. At 3276 we were young, and immortal, concentrating all of our efforts on living life to the fullest. Vancouver was indeed a party town, and our parties were highly successful. We put as much sugar into the beer mash as possible, and the alcohol content was higher than most wines. The young ladies would say,
"This is a delicious. Almost like a fruit punch. Yes, I will have another."
Everybody certainly had a good time, even if memories were hazy at breakfast.
My personal project was selection of a mate. There was no shortage of candidates. Cindy had come over from England and we had resumed our warm and energetic affair. However, somehow the love that had bound us so closely together did not survive the time and distance of separation. She was still a girl in a million, and when we had parted an Australian she had met in England came running. In retrospect, he was probably more mature and tolerant and no doubt made her a better husband.

I concluded that the most important decision I would ever make would be picking a partner for life, and the standard method was really no more than a high stakes game of blind man's bluff. How could you possibly evaluate the deeper strengths and weaknesses of a partner by the usual social interaction, however intimate? What would they be like under stress? I therefore developed land, sea, and air tests. They were modeled on the tests developed by psychologists to pick out potential officer material from promising candidates. WOSBs were designed to show the strengths and weakness of prospective candidates for the highly important job of leading men into battle. Choosing a partner to spend the rest of your life with surely deserved a similarly intense scrutiny.

The land test was simple. A camping weekend, when rain was in the forecast, with the tent in a gully between hills.

At two in the morning the rain turned the gully into a river, soaking our sleeping bags. When I 'accidentally' collapsed the tent poles we were well and truly wet and miserable, even including me as I observed the effects of stress on my test subject.

Next the sea test involved a small motor boat we owned. It was indeed yellow, and I warned the unsuspecting candidates that it really was a lemon. I would motor out from English Bay into the Straits of Georgia on a misty day. When we were out of sight of land I would secretly turn off the gas supply line. The boat would sputter and stop. Without gas my frantic efforts to start it would fail.

"We must be out of gas. I did check, but something's wrong. Keep an eye out for a tow." I would gently rock the boat. "I do hope the wind won't pick up. The forecast was good, mostly." Then I would open a stop cock just a little, and water would slowly trickle into the boat.

"Don't worry," I would say. "We do have life jackets, and someone's bound to come along. There are no sharks, and the killer whales usually feed on salmon or sea lions."

I would give a weakly convincing laugh.

"They really don't like warm blooded food." I paused for effect. "Most people won't go swimming out here, but that's just superstitious, psychological hang-ups, and old wives tales."

The air test proved to be too difficult to set up. They might come to the airfield and watch the parachute jumping, but I never persuaded any of them to get into a plane with no door.

These tests may have been highly devious, even cruel, but with a divorce rate of 50% tearing apart families, I thought this testing system might reduce that horrible statistic. Little did I know.

In later years I turned to science, and once had both of us go through a psych evaluation to check for compatibility.

This was more logical, far less work to set up, and I thought it would give a much more accurate prediction. If she hadn't walked out on the psychologist, it might have, but without her permission he could not reveal his assessment. I had plenty of good ideas, but I was close to giving up. Do you ever feel you just can't win?

Chapter Eight

'She'

At one fateful party a group of young women were rather special. They were all attractive, English, and all were doctors, working at the Vancouver General Hospital. I was greatly taken by a tall, slim, shy young lady. She had never known an engineer, and I think I swept her off her feet, unbalancing her. She might have been deceived by my youthful good looks. In those days I had hair, and she did not detect my manifold deficiencies. We started dating, and she was outstanding. I never even tried the usual land sea and air tests. Once we did go skiing down to Mount Baker in the Washington State. She was not a good skier, but I convinced her to come to the top. She did not like the look of the steep slope, so I tried to reassure her.

"Come on. Take it easy, go slowly, and you'll be alright. I'll be with you all the way."

She started, then tumbled down the rest of the first slope. Then I was truly remorseful.

"I am really sorry. If we climb back up now we could get on the ski lift to go down."

She wouldn't give up. She tumbled over her skis all the way down the mountain. She was brave and persistent. I don't think she had ever backed away from a challenge. When we got down to the final bunny slopes she was exhausted, and we started skiing gently to the lodge for lunch. When I looked back, she had disappeared. I clambered back up, rounded a corner and she was sitting on the snow, apparently resting.

"When you're ready, we can go for a hot chocolate," I said. She shook her head.

"I'm afraid I have broken my tibia and fibula. I heard them snap."

The ski patrol put on a temporary splint, and she insisted I drive back to Canada. She knew the orthopedic doctors in Vancouver.

This had been tougher than any test, and she was exceptional. Not a complaint, not a word of blame. She was still smiling, even during the bumpy ride in the back of my station wagon. Feeling guilty, I was happy and surprised when she agreed to marry me.

We wanted a quiet wedding. Just two witnesses. Both sets of parents were back in England. I still have the audio tape. As she walks down the aisle there is a strange slithering sound, then a thump. It was the cast dragging on the floor between her crutches.

She didn't object when we took the mascot of 3276 on our honeymoon. Bloodnok the dog was fairly large, a Rottweiler mix, but all of his genes were happy ones. He had been trained to tangle his lead around female legs and facilitate introductions in our bachelor house, but he loved camping. We drove, and camped down through Washington, Oregon, California, and into Baja Mexico. She was a good sport all the way. When we got back, we bought a sailboat, and I taught her to sail. I had always dreamed of sailing across the Pacific to Tahiti and other exotic places.

Some time later, as we were booking a vacation in Europe, I placed an ad in a British yachting magazine, offering to crew on a sailboat going back to Canada.

We forgot about the ad while we skied the Italian Alps. Huge mountains that took half a day to make one run down. She was an expert by now, and we had a great time. Then down to Milan where we bought a Lambretta motor scooter, and ambled up through Italy and into France. Provence an the charming country around Avignon tempted us to stay.

Large ocean, small boat

Back in England one of the replies to the ad was a dream come true.

"We have a new 20 ton cutter. We're going to the Caribbean, through the Panama Canal, to Honolulu, then back to Seattle."

That was right at our front door. But, it would take six months, and we had already been away too long. The only practical possibility was a 39 foot motor sailer, a converted Aberdeen fishing trawler. The skipper was a professor of Constitutional Law at the University of Cambridge. A highly competent sailor, he'd been given an award for his voyage the previous year to Sptizbergen, way above the Arctic Circle. The skipper might have resembled the original grumpy old man, but he was an excellent sailor. He even looked the part, with his black woolen cap and pepper and salt beard.

The boat was solid, old fashioned. Heavy, not built for speed. We averaged four and a half knots across the Atlantic, taking altogether six weeks. A twelve foot bowsprit stuck out in front to carry the jib sails. Then a double ended plank boat built to survive the brutal gales in the North Sea. She was a ketch, with a gaff rigged mainsail and a mizzen mast behind the box-like wheelhouse set amidships. This was custom fitted by the skipper with fold down seats that once rode in a London taxi.

    He had heard the call of the North. He was going to Montreal to teach for a couple years and naturally he was going via Iceland, Greenland, and Labrador. With luck, it would only take six weeks. For crew he had a couple of students, Alex and Tony, young and fit and keen but with little deep sea sailing experience. Alex told tales of the African continent, and of the years he had spent underground after graduating as a mining engineer. Tony had spent vacations in Lapland, sailing the Mediterranean in an eighteen footer, and wandering around Israel and the Middle East in a sports car.

    My wife was with me, and she would be the ship's doctor and head chef. We had our own sailboat waiting for us back in Vancouver, and it was my dream to sail her across the Pacific, to Hawaii, Tahiti, and the other exotic islands of the South Pacific. I wanted some deep water experience, so I signed on as first mate.

    The boat was sound, the skipper knew his stuff, and the course plotted looked like an interesting challenge. From a small port on England's East coast, stopping at Aberdeen for supplies. Then to Iceland, Greenland, and Canada. However, there were a few warning signs that I should have taken more seriously.

    The skipper's wife came to visit as we were fitting out. Petite, charming, intelligent, but she adamantly refused to sail with us. That was our first warning. When we got to Aberdeen to take on supplies, the Skipper said "I have ordered the bonded spirits. Three cases of gin. Should be enough, what?"

We had not been consulted. There were mutterings from the crew, and finally we ended up taking on rum, brandy, and scotch. A little later we were on our way, but made a detour to pull into the small harbor of Wick, Scotland. The approach was through a channel studded with black rocks pointing up through the water, and tricky rip currents marked ominously on the chart. I smiled happily.

"This looks just like some of the tricky passages in British Columbia. I can take her in."

"No, John, I'll steer. These waters are dangerous."

We argued. This was one of my conditions for signing on, to do the boat handling in challenging waters. But, he was the skipper, he won, just as he won every time when I reached for the sextant to take the mid-day reading that would fix our position. I had come to get deep water experience, and he blocked me all the time. When we got to Iceland I quietly informed him,

"We will be leaving the boat here, and catching a flight to Canada."

"Oh John, you can't do that. Whatever is the matter?"

His apologies were profuse, and he promised that everything would be different. Then he announced that we would stay in Reykjavik for twenty four hours and quickly move on. He had been there before.

"I have not been here, and I may never return," I said. "I will stay for four days, to explore."

I should have been suspicious when he gave in too easily. We did explore Iceland, saw the famous waterfall, the Gullfoss, and the hot springs. But hardly twelve hours out of port it was back to Captain Bligh when it became time for the next noon day shot with the sextant.

"I'll do that," he said when I objected.

The next leg took us to Julianehaab, Greenland, and I vowed we would get on a plane and we would part company. To my sad surprise, we learned from our radio that the port there was closed. The winter ice was late in retreating, and still blocked the harbor. We had to divert to Fredricshaab, population 400, accessible only by boat. No aircraft of any sort. There was nothing we could do, so we made the best of it.

By now She and I had become expert at cramming ourselves into the narrow bunks in the foc'sle, the triangular space at the bow of the boat. We had to lash ourselves in to stop the boat throwing us out in a rough sea. Moving around in the main cabin became a contest between us and the twisting, bucking, boat. However firmly we held on, the fiendish boat twisted our hand holds loose and we were thrown across the cabin into something hard and wooden with a sharp corner. By some miracle there were no bones broken, but our bruises were colorful and painful. Between Iceland and Greenland we found out just how incredibly rough it could be if were caught with our sails up by a full force gale.

After a few days in Reykjavik we set sail for Julianehaab, Greenland. Tony had become the radio operator, and then Julianehaab again told him,

"You can't come here. The weather has been cool and the harbor is still full of ice. You"ll have to go to Fredrickshaab, about 200 miles further up the coast."

Tony had also talked to weather station Alpha, a weather ship parked in the middle of the North Atlantic. They usually talked only to passing airliners flying the Polar route from North America to Europe. They were intrigued to hear from a sailboat, and when we sailed close enough for them to see us they said "Your boat is so small and the ocean is so big." Then they warned us "There's a big storm coming. You'd better get ready."

We started lashing everything down. We were sailing

with the wind behind us, carrying our square sails. These hung down from yards on either side of the mast, and we looked like a Viking ship. Suddenly there was a mighty Bang, as the storm hit without warning. The wind shifted from the East, and came roaring out of the North. We rushed to get the sails down. We got the starboard sail down, but the one on the port side was caught, and the wind wrapped it around the mast. The wind grew stronger, the sail flapped madly and something had to be done before it tore the mast away. Someone would have to go up the mast and fix things.

The Skipper, with his arthritis couldn't do it. Alex and Tony were young and fit and keen to try but wouldn't know what to do when they got to the top of the mast. I certainly didn't want my wife to try, and that left just one volunteer, me.

The seas had built up and the boat was rolling and pitching. Later, the waves got to be about sixty feet high, taller than the boat was long. A solid wall of gray water would speed at us, we would start to climb, then the wave would break over us before we dove down the other side. We were rolling about forty five degrees from side to side and there were times when it felt she was going to keep on going and going, and roll over. If we survived a capsize we wouldn't last long. There were small icebergs around and the water seemed cooler than freezing. Why bother with life jackets when we would last only a few minutes in the water and it would be impossible to turn the boat around?

The rain was pelting down and the wind whipped the tops off the waves, covering us with freezing spray. I put on a couple of sweaters and oil skin suit, a southwester for my head and clipped on a belt with a safety harness. This was a short length of rope with a snap hook on the end. I left the shelter of the wheelhouse and crawled towards the mast. To hold up the mast were stays fore and aft, and shrouds on each side, a pair of galvanized wire cables. Between the two cables were short lengths of wooden slats, called ratlins. I climbed these like a ladder. At the top of the mast I snapped my safety hook on to one of the cables and started to wrap the flapping sail with a length of rope I had taken up.

One important rule when you are up a mast is 'One hand for the boat, to do the work, and one hand for yourself.' I held tight to the shroud with my left hand and started work with my right hand. The sail was flapping noisily, whipping around like a wild animal. Slowly I got the rope around it and pulled and gradually got the sail tied up. I had learned to tie one handed knots long ago, but this was a challenge. The rolling was bad enough at deck level. Forty five degrees one way, then forty five degrees the other way. At the top of the mast it was exciting. When the mast was cutting through the sky one way I was plastered to the shrouds, spread thin like a fly smeared on a fly screen. When it whipped away from me it tore my feet from the ratlin and I flew horizontally, holding on with my left hand and fastened by my safety line, working all the time on the sail.

Finally the top of the sail was lashed, much smaller now, and I unhooked my clasp and climbed down a few steps to get at the bottom half of the sail. The aerial ballet continued, flying through the air, my body flapping in the breeze. Finally it was done. The sail was lashed into a tight bundle with much less wind resistance and I could climb down. I reached down to unhook my safety clasp.

Then I said to myself,

"Oh dear."

The snap-on clasp was hanging loose at the end of the small safety rope, swinging with the boat. Somehow it had come off, and I had been flying through the air held on just by my hand. A cold hand, no gloves, fingers frozen. I had seen circus performers doing stunts like that. I had never been too impressed, as they usually had a safety net. I didn't have a net. If I had fallen I would have smashed onto the deck and bounced into the water, or fallen directly into the freezing cold wet stuff.

I clambered down and scrambled to the wheelhouse. My only thought was to get a hefty glass of brandy inside me to warm me up. I was too wet and cold to be scared. I wasn't being brave or noble, it was just survival. If the mast had gone the wheelhouse could have been ripped off and we all would have had a cold, watery death.

In those days I was a civil engineer, and everything had to be proven scientifically. A bridge can't be built with only faith that it would stand up, and I was having a lot of trouble believing in God. I couldn't prove He existed, or that He didn't exist. There had been a bunch of books about angels, with guardian angels doing wonderful things. Again, there was no proof, but it was an appealing idea.

Years later a person with psychic powers told me that I didn't have just one guardian angel. I had three. I think I know why. On that day in the North Atlantic, to keep me glued onto the top of the mast, I think they must all have been very busy.

After Greenland we went through Iceberg Alley. We got up close and personal to many monsters of ice, much bigger and harder than our little boat. When I saw 'Titanic' years later it was deja vu, and I was shivering in my seat. It reminded me of some of our fun and games.

In the end we were glad that we completed the crossing. I might have missed one of the best meals of my life.

We arrived in Canada just where Newfoundland looks at the southern tip of Labrador across the Straits of Belle Isle. The fishing was fantastic, and we just drifted, jigging with a large, chromed lure at the end of a long line. Every time we jigged we caught a big cod. In a flash the fish was cleaned and into a pot with water and salt. After weeks of mainly canned food we feasted on fresh cod garnished with butter, and boiled potatoes. I still remember that as one of my all time favorite gourmet meals. We started sailing up the St. Lawrence River, past the scent of pine trees coming from Anticosti Island. The skipper was headed for Montreal. She and I got off at Seven Islands, the first port that had an airport. It would have been easy sailing up the river, but we had had enough.

In Montreal we enjoyed our 15 seconds of fame. We were interviewed on TV, then we picked up our motor scooter from the shipping agent and headed across Canada.

It took precious little time to adjust to walking on dry ground that didn't bump and twist beneath our feet, or to eating normal food in a normal way, without a fork suddenly jerked by the boat lurching, aiming straight for an eye. How quickly we forgot, and we were heading back to beautiful British Colombia on Trans Canada Highway number one, still under construction. The 150 cc scooter was loaded with two rucksacks, sleeping bags, tents and cooking gear. For the last 1,000 miles we added two cats in a specially made box, picked up where they had been left on the BC and Alberta border where we had been living. We headed for the coast, sunny peaceful Vancouver, and after a short rest, maybe plan our trip across the Pacific in our own small sailboat. Sheila didn't say anything, but I think her enthusiasm was waning.

Guardian Angels For Real ?

I've had more luck imagining and 'communicating' with Guardian Angels than I did with communicating with God. I've been trying to imagine him for fifty years, and failed. He is too immense, and it blows my mind.

About thirty years ago when a psychic told me that I needed three guardian angels to handle the scrapes I got into one of them was a lady with white hair. She sounded just like Mrs. Mac, who took me in as an evacuee in War II. She had the personality of an angel, all loving, always smiling. When German bombers got lost and dropped bombs near our small village we had no shelter to run to. She took me into her bed when the 'Crump, crump' of bombs landing got close. There was no physical contact, but my imagination was alive. Perhaps that is why I see her when I try to meditate. Once in Las Vegas, to impress my partner, I predicted that Mrs. Mac would save me a parking space on the second floor of the garage, near the crossover to the hotel. I asked Mrs. Mac, and there they were, four days in a row, an open space in the crowded garage, right next to the crossover.

My interest in matters paranormal dated back to when I was a medical student. I had a doctor friend Janet, dating from my time with 'She.' One night Janet said "John, you must come over. I've just had the most unbelievable experience." I listened, and went over. The psychic 'reading' that she described was peculiar. Janet said that I was described as a platonic friend, which I was, and that we often paired up, then Janet said

"He described you completely, color of hair, eyes, many other things but he got your name wrong. Said you were John Rogers."

I pulled out my wallet.

"Here is a receipt from the cleaners. I never try to use Rotgans, it gets them confused, so I say put down 'John Rogers.'" For simplicity I later took out the 'T.' "But Janet, this could all just be telepathy, and he was reading my mind."

"That's not all. He said we would soon be three, joined by a nine year old boy, called Paul, wearing a funny cap." She looked at me quizzically. "Have you got any accidental offspring anywhere? Was he foretelling the future?"

"No Janet." I smiled. "Not that I know of. We will have to wait and see."

Three months later the phone rang.

"This is Big Brothers, Big Sisters. We have a boy for you." Then I remembered that I had signed up as a volunteer. "He is nine years old, lives with his mother, nice family."

We ended up including Paul, (Yes, that was his name) in our excursions. He went to a private school, and sometimes wore a British looking cap. There was no way that this could have been telepathy, so was it clairvoyance? I had to meet this psychic. I phoned, just gave my first name, and met him in his home in East Vancouver.

"Do you want to do the tea leaves thing?" he asked. "It's not necessary."

'Reading the tea leaves' left behind in a cup of British tea was a time honored custom in England. It must be disappearing with modern tea bags. I said that wasn't necessary.

He then graphically described the three areas I was actively involved in. He could see the dissecting table at med school, the summer slide rule of engineering, and the lonely hours of trying to write a great novel. All of this was telepathy, but he did some predictions as well. He allowed me to tape the session, but I never found his prophecies impressive. I still couldn't explain 'Paul.'

Or 'God.' I did think of Mrs. Mac many times, but trying to do the same with God was a different story.

To receive and answer billions of prayers every day from all over the world seemed to be absolutely inconceivable. Especially with Muslims praying five times a day. A mind boggling total. Perhaps it might be possible for a supercomputer, but this was long before Big Blue and Dr. Watson. My brain is not capable of such divine imagination. Maybe I should try harder next Sunday.

Chapter 9

Transmogrification

When we married, I was becoming disillusioned with engineering. It attracted independent, smart young men, but promotion was slow and uncertain. Working on site, on fascinating outdoor constructions in South America or the Far East was fun and adventure for a young man but it was no place for a woman, and there was isolation and frustration. In a design office in the city only one or two made it to the top. The majority grew old bent over their drawing boards. Every year a few cashed in their savings, opened an office, and set up shop as independent design engineers. Only about one in ten survived, and the rest went back to being employees, or on to try another career.

      I had been writing articles and stories for years, and I briefly took time out to try writing full-time, leaning on She to pay the bills. As always, She was a good sport and didn't complain. Until I told her about my latest bright idea.

"Doctors are always needed in the community. You help people when they're sick, they smile when they see you around town. Nobody knows me. All the engineers could go on strike and nobody would notice. No one would care." She smiled sympathetically. Then I dropped my bombshell.

"I'm going back to school to become a doctor." She stopped smiling.

"That would mean six, seven years or more, with long hours, hard work, and little money," She said. She had been there, done that. She knew.

There was another factor in the equation. My deadly personality trait of being very critical was hard to live with. Living with constant negative put-downs was destructive to the ego. It had become worse while I struggled with the frustration of life as an engineer. Plus going to med school wouldn't be easy. There was the painful possibility that I might fail, and then what? I would have spent all my savings for nothing.

The divorce was civilized. She kept the house and custody of the cats and dogs. I couldn't look after them anyway, because I kept the sailboat and lived on it while I struggled into med school.

That was a challenge, as there were hundreds competing for the 60 openings every year. They took only the best, plus me. Maybe engineers did have a superior intellect. There were three engineers in a class of 60. Maybe being married to a doctor had helped. By the time I got in, my marital status had changed, but I am sure it had given me an edge.

Premed included two second-year courses of organic and inorganic chemistry. I hadn't touched a test tube in 17 years, since high school. There was also a course in English, and I managed to get into second-year Creative Writing, where we spent months discussing poetry. Specifically a month on a two line poem by Robert Frost. "The old dog barked backward without getting up. I can remember when he was a pup." For a month! How I suffered, but I passed. Plus zoology. I studied hard. I hadn't seen anything yet.

Med school was much harder than engineering school, where you can usually work things out from first principles. I kept all the formulae I needed to memorize every year in thin notebooks. One skinny notebook a year in engineering school was all I needed. In med school we had to memorize a pile of three inch textbooks every year. The stuff I had to memorize filled two feet of small notebooks. Every year. Once I came across a study of the IQs of the various students at college. Engineers had the highest, with med students at number two. Naturally I believed this, and concluded that engineers had been smart enough to make their field user friendly. Memorizing was not my strong point, I was getting older, and I came close to failing. No wonder most Canadian med students worked hard and played little.

It was harder for me, the old man of the class. By the time I had finished internship I was forty years old, halfway through my life. My brain was crowded with half a lifetime of memories and experiences, and it was much harder for me to pack in hundreds of new facts. I envied the young child with a brain like blotting paper, soaking up everything without trying hard. From first year anatomy onwards I suffered every time we had an exam, especially the orals.

For an engineer, the knee is a simple hinge that bends in one plane only, simplicity itself. Little does he know or care of the many muscles that attach to the upper and lower bones. Gastrocnemius, adductor magnus, plantaris above with semimembranous, popliteus and soleus below, to mention but a few. Then there are the shock absorbers between the bones, the menisci both medial and lateral, and the host of tough ligaments that prevent a knee from bending sideways in a football tackle. Just as important are the nerves, arteries and veins that thread between the various muscles. These might be colored yellow, red and blue in an anatomy atlas. In a dissected cadaver specimen they were all grey and smelled strongly of formaldehyde. Fourteen large pages of the atlas with multiple drawings show how all of these pieces of the knee related to each other. All relations between the pieces had to be committed to memory. Woe betide the student who could not identify any part of this complex web of muscle, ligament, vessel and bone.

These feats of memory were repeated in histology, biochemistry, pathology, and hematology long before the larger clinical courses appeared. Obstetrics, pediatrics, cardiology, neurology, orthopedics, psychiatry and others each had three inch thick textbooks to be memorized.

The London cabby spends two to three years learning all of the streets in London, and the shortest routes between A's and B's. CAT scans show that in his brain his posterior hippocampus almost doubles in size. The medical student has been less well studied, but significant changes do occur in the size of his posterior and lateral parietal cortex.

Does memorizing this mountain of information make him a better man, or a better doctor? Better informed perhaps, but his basic temperament probably stays the same. A lifetime of assessing patients and telling them what to do may make him more opinionated and assertive. He usually knows a lot more than the average man about many things, but only time will tell if wisdom comes with the knowledge.

Engineering students in England envied the boisterous med students. In Canada the engineering students had fun, while med students strained their brains. In England a med student could repeat a year that he had failed, sometimes several times. In Canada and the US, one repeat was allowed. After that, fail a course again and you were out. Luckily I found a hard-core bunch of people like me who drank too much on weekends, and skied down hills too fast. We organized several happy, drunken gatherings yet still managed to pass most exams. One played his guitar with such vigor that his fingers bled. They all went on to become physicians and surgeons, respected in their communities.

The House of Lords

I started med school with money in the bank, a sailboat, and an almost new car. I finished absolutely broke, with a pile of student loans, no sailboat, and a crumpled VW bug. But I had a great time, especially in the House of Lords, 3695 W. 34th Ave. This was a bachelor house with an excellent cook who came in during the week. Mrs. Jarvis arrived about 4.30 pm, started the meal, cleaned part of the house everyday, and at 5.30 a delicious meal was on the table. We took turns in treating girlfriends to dine with us, and they took care of our needs on weekends.

Lord Plunger of Poole was Tony, an accountant, who eventually went back to school, got his MBA, and then into government. He was totally immune to cold and jumped into icy waters every New Years Day. I claimed that the Polar Bear Plunge had affected his mind, as he was quite crazy in many ways, but he was one of the kindest, most gentle men I have ever known. I was Lord Carver. Lord Dipper of Wick was George, intense, with suave, middle European moves. His surname was Russian. He was fond of saying "I will pass it through the crucible of my perception." Somehow he reminded me of Joseph Conrad, the brooding author of the Heart of Darkness. A Polish sea captain who became a great writer in English, which was his second language. There was Auntie, quiet but very pleasant, Graham Stollard was a city planner, Bruce, known as BJ, perpetually avoiding matrimony and Don, a highly intelligent barman, another good man. On the cruise boats going up to Alaska he would take in order from a table of 20, and wrote nothing down and made no mistakes. Many years later his first inkling that anything was wrong was when he did make a mistake or two in a tray full of drinks. He died slowly of Alzheimer's. I only wished I had had his memory at it's peak.

Lord Plunger had a slightly sensitive stomach, and if I wanted an extra helping of the dinner delicacy I would describe the body parts that I had been dissecting that day. When Tony turned green, I took his plate.

In later years a big interest in his life was theology, and he took so many courses that I think he had the equivalent of a D.Div.. This totally suited his personality, which was always kind, helpful, loving. I must give him a call, and see if he is entitled to 'Reverend,' or takes over sometimes at his church. It wouldn't surprise me a bit.

Chapter Ten

Yellowpoint

One Christmas was memorable. I had passed mid term exams, but I was still not a single man. The divorce laws were tortuous. I had already 'provided the evidence.' A private detective had brought a young woman to the house and pocketed his $200. I awkwardly sat with her in the front room for two hours with the lights dimmed. Then she left, and joined the watching detective. 'Evidence' of adultery was the only acceptable grounds for divorce.

    In the meantime, I was getting on with life, and that included spending several delightful weekends at Yellowpoint Lodge, happy hunting grounds for Vancouver's swinging singles. It was on the coast of Vancouver Island and experienced bachelors would gather early on Friday evenings to scan the quarry as they arrived. I met a most delightful and loving young woman. We seemed to bond closely as we walked the woods and the beach, searched tidal pools for baby crabs and marooned fish, and we became an item. I still had the Lambretta motor scooter and I have fond memories of camping in remote spots on Vancouver Island. A bonus was that coming back home we could go to the front of the line at the ferry.

Yellowpoint was normally closed in winter, but for one Christmas as an experiment it stayed open. There was no tennis or volleyball with snow on the ground but plenty of walks in the pine woods, or along the shore collecting shells and chasing crabs. The huge walk-in fireplace always had logs blazing, and the meals were delicious. With only eight guests it would be a cozy bunch that gathered afterwards to play silly games like Password. My partner was delightful, pretty, and a very loving person. Possibly the most loving person I have ever known. I probably made a mistake when I didn't marry her. However, the two late arrivals could have ruined everything. The last couple to arrive was 'She's' divorce lawyer and his wife.

During that night there was a six feet fall of very heavy wet snow, breaking branches and blocking the only road out. Definitely not Lambretta weather. One branch snapped directly above the place where I had parked my car. It fell, making a foot deep dent in the roof of my VW. My companion and I were marooned, obviously in flagrante delicto, and we couldn't escape. However, there was plenty of good food and drink and firewood, and we were extremely comfortable castaways. The lawyer was a congenial chap, and he knew that I had 'provided evidence,' he didn't need any more, and our parlor games were harmonious.

Driving back was a bit cramped, with the caved in roof pushing my head down until my nose was level with the steering wheel. In Vancouver the question became,

"How many Lords can you pack into a Volkswagen?"

All of them. We squeezed in, lying with our backs on the seats and pushing up with our feet. Forty seven years later Tony still has a clear memory of that combined operation.

The first two years of med school had summer breaks. I was still a professional engineer, and I was well paid by my old firm of consultants. After that, we worked through the summer on our clinical rotations, and my bank account slowly melted away.

One summer I had a rotation that took me into a different world. I spent a couple of months giving physical exams to all the mentally challenged ladies at Riverview Mental Hospital. It included pap tests and breast exams. It was the first time that anyone, medical or otherwise had laid a male hand on them in over 20 years. Fortunately I insisted on having a nurse with me, because several of the women told me a day or two after our intimate encounter they had had 'our babies' during the night.

"Could I name one of the boys after you, Doctor?" was a frequent request.

The closer we came to graduating, the harder we worked. Sixteen hours days, on call all night, sleeping in green scrubs, tumbling out of the duty bed to rush to the ER in the wee hours, and then to try to be fresh and alert for 7 am surgeries or medical rounds. "It is good training, and we all did it" was the attitude of the professors teaching us.

I was too tired to go to graduation, to put on a cap and gown and recite the Hippocratic Oath. I knew it well anyway, and the piece of paper came in the mail

"The University of BC has conferred the degree of Doctor of Medicine on John Albert Rogans, May 1970 etc."

The MD gets a wife.

Soon I was busy being a married man. We married in my year of internship. Jean was wife number two and number three for me, out of four. I was husband number two and four for Jean. She was petite, blonde, vivacious, and had many other qualities that emerged as our marriage progressed. She was from New England, which may have been significant later. She brought with her a son, age 7, and Jason was not at all sure about having another man in his father's place. Especially this bossy former engineer, coming home from work in an interne's white uniform. All very strange. Jason was quiet, not at all aggressive, and it was easy to miss his inner strengths.

    We had a small sailboat that we enjoyed on my infrequent weekends off. He wasn't sure that he liked getting swiped by sails that flapped hard in the wind. A favorite destination was Snug Cove on Bowen Island, not too far from West Vancouver for a day sail. Our chunky little sloop could make it there in a couple of hours, if the wind was right. We would tie up to the dock on the island, and explore before a picnic lunch. Then it was time to leave for the gentle sail back, except for one time.

    In the cove we were sheltered from the wind, but I had been watching the sea outside the entrance. White caps were showing, which usually meant a stiff breeze, 25 knots or more.

    We hurried through lunch, and motored out as we hoisted the sails. All was well until we left the shelter of the cove. We were barely clear of the headlands when we were hit hard, and the sails which were still loose started flapping viciously.

    "Take the helm, quick" I said to Jean. "I'll get the sails down." I didn't want the sails to have a big patch torn away by the wind. We started rocking and pitching, more violently than ever before. Jean didn't like this one bit. And she was several months pregnant with our first child. She sat on the deck of the cockpit and would not move. She didn't scream, but just completely retired from the battle. We had to get the sails down, or they could carry the mast away. We needed to turn into the wind to do this, but if I left the tiller, the wind would swing her around broadside to the waves and wind. We could lose the sails, the mast, even the boat.

"Jason, come and take the tiller." He gave me one of his 'that is not logical' looks.

"I've never done that before."

"I'll show you how. Come on." I tried to sound calm and confident, although I was getting a bit worried. He reluctantly came and sat by me.

"Hold the tiller, and aim for that mountain with the double peaks."

Jason quietly considered how best to do this, and I left him to it. As I was lowering the sails, and lashing them into small bundles I could see his frown of concentration. He didn't look in the least bit scared. He held her steady on her course.

"Well done Jason. That was good work."

We were not close, but I had to admire his grit. I turned around carefully and headed back into Snug Cove. I put Jean and Jason onto the small ferry that went to West Vancouver.

"The wind will go down tonight. I'll bring her over then." Jean was not happy about leaving me, but her other option was to stay and do a moonlight run with me, assuming the wind had dropped. This did not appeal to her, and I waved as the ferry sailed away.

The wind did drop at dusk, and I motored back. I tied on a lifeline, like a good single-handed deep sea yachtsman. I had time to brood. If I had known that Jason would later be thinking about a degree in engineering, I would have taken the time to try and talk him out of it. Later, when he realized that a bachelors degree was not enough, he considered more engineering and even briefly medicine. Finally he took an engineering Ph.D.

Bradley

On January 19th, 1971 around about noon in the OB ward of Vancouver General Hospital, Bradley Cornelius burst into the world. Noisy, demanding, messy, and his parents loved every bit of him. He changed little in the next few decades. He was a much wanted child, even later when he would finger paint the walls with the brown paste he had access to from his diapers. Quite fearless. He constantly abused our 100 pound German Shepherd, and she loved him. After internship I worked briefly in Prince Rupert, BC, and a few memories stand out.

Bradley decided that his mother should come and comfort him at any hour of the day or night, and if she didn't come he yelled.

"There's something wrong with him," Jean would say, and get out of bed. Sometimes he cried and cried and she got me out of bed. I would give him a quick exam, then pronounce,

"He's fine", and I would carry him to the far corner of the big house we were renting and closed the door. He cried himself to sleep and we slept.

He explored the lakes and woods sitting in my back pack, followed by his step-brother Jason. I had already found that beneath Jason's Doctor Spock exterior there was a complex and capable human being, and he was soon jumping from one wet slippery log to another.

Chapter Eleven

No pulse.

I was the new junior partner to a brilliant doctor who had visited our class in our final year. He might have picked me because I was the oldest, maybe with experience of the big world. Certainly not for my grades, which would have impressed nobody. Now I was giving the anesthetic while he and a surgeon were ready to remove a gallbladder. Doctor H. enjoyed surgery and the surgeon Doctor James was there only because it was a major case and rules required it. Putting the patient to sleep for them to cut was the main reason my boss wanted a partner.

    I was shaking in my boots. I tried not to show it, but giving anesthetics terrified me.

    "I haven't even done a rotation in anesthesia," I had protested.

    "All the books are here. I have given hundreds. When one of your patients needs cutting, I will pass the gas while you cut. You will soon pick it up. It's just like falling off a log."

"Passing the gas" was far from the simple affair he had claimed. There were potent drugs to raise or lower the blood pressure, others to adjust the heart rate and the respirations, to relax the muscles just a bit or paralyze them completely. There was no room for error. The wrong drug or the wrong dose could kill, very quickly, and each drug had its own idiosyncracies and side effects. The patient's life was literally in my hands. Every beat of the heart and every breath he took was my personal responsibility.

I had studied long and hard to commit to memory the drugs and doses. There would be no time for looking things up if anything went wrong. And today I was giving a new drug, the latest and the greatest for producing complete anesthesia. In me it was producing complete panic, which I was trying hard to mask.

One of the wrinkles of this new drug, Innovar, was that it upset the heart rhythm if given too quickly.

"Give the dose of two cc's over two minutes," was the ominous warning that came with the vial. I had drawn up exactly two cc's with the utmost precision, and now I was ready to inject this alarming poison into the live patient. Doctor H was already on my case for plodding along so slowly and holding up the show.

"Come on John, we haven't got all day. We have been ready to cut for hours."

At least ten minutes, I thought.

James the surgeon was smiling tolerantly. He was aware that I was new at this game.

"Don't mind us, John. Just do it your way."

I did a last minute check on pressure, pulse and respirations. We had no fancy monitors that went 'beep,' and I adjusted the bezel ring on my watch so that the zero mark was aligned with the minute hand to mark the start of the drug's action. For the heart I had a stethoscope head taped over the apex where the heart sounds would be heard most clearly. Rubber tubing fitted to it ran from the chest to my right ear. I could hear every variation in rate and rhythm instantly.

"Anesthetic going in now," I announced as I started to press the plunger of the syringe.

"About time too," remarked Dr. H nastily.

'Two minutes' was the time recommended, but I pushed slowly and took four, just to be on the safe side. I didn't want to have to deal with any deadly irregularity, an arrhythmia, that could possibly be fatal. I was also using a potent anesthetic gas. Even mixed with oxygen it had already caused some nasty skips and extra beats in both the patient and me.

For the cutters, standing idly in their green scrubs, scalpels in hands, the four minutes must have seemed like an eternity.

"John, I am ready to cut, and unless you can give me a good reason not to, I will," said James.

'A good reason' was not long coming. Suddenly I realized that I could hear no heart beat in my left ear.

"Damn," I thought. "They have moved my monitor. Idiot butchers."

I slid my hand under the green surgical drapes that covered everything except the oblong opening where they would cut to stick their hands into the patient's body. I traced the rubber tubing until I reached the stethoscope head.

It was still there, firmly held in place by the adhesive tape. What the .... Then I realized that I heard nothing in my ear was because there was nothing to hear. The patient's heart had stopped. Completely. I felt for the carotid pulse, but there was no pulse to feel.

My heart also stopped. I should have been dizzy but I was too busy.

"Which stimulant should I use?" I ran them through my mind. Ticking off the pros and cons my brain raced. Then I was forced to admit that CPR was the method of choice, except that it would reveal that I had killed the patient, and I knew that Dr. H would blow a gasket. I would be out of a job. There was no contract, junior docs with no experience were ten a penny, and it wouldn't look good on my resumé.

By now even Doctor James was looking impatient. I soon had to own up.

"I would really like to cut, John. Anytime soon would be good," he said.

"You would be cutting into a dead patient. I am afraid his heart has stopped. Do you think you could thump him on the chest? "

"What? You bloody fool." Dr. H's face was red between the white mask and the green cap.

"I told you not to fool around with new drugs until they have been out for two years." And he had, and it was good advice that I followed ever afterwards. Doctor James didn't say a word. He raised a big fist and gave one hard blow to the patients chest, at the apex of the heart. An old fashioned way to shock a heart into action but it did work sometimes.

I heard a faint "lub dup", and as James kept on massaging the heart I could feel a pulse in the carotid. After a long minute I said,

"Hold it, let's see if beats on its own."

I heard the "lub dup" of a normal heart, and the carotid pulse was strong and normal again. I had been squeezing the ambubag and he was well ventilated, so all was well. And I had not peed my pants, though the urge was strong.

Obviously the nasty side effect was transitory, leaving only a permanent scar on my psyche. After another couple of minutes I looked up.

"I would advise we wait a day or two. Let him recover completely."

"Nonsense," blurted Doctor H. "He's fine. Let's get on with it."

"John, you're the one passing gas." said Doctor James. "If you don't feel comfortable, we can wait. I think he's okay, but it's your call."

The surgery went smoothly, and recovery from the anesthetic was routine. The patient did ask why his chest felt sore, and I explained that anesthetic drugs sometimes had that effect. It was not routine for the anesthesiologist to visit the patient every few hours after surgery, but in the end both of us were happy.

Passing gas was just like falling off a log - a very slippery log over a deep canyon, lined with hard sharp rocks. I never did get used to it. I could always think of the nasty things that could go wrong, and the time there was dead silence in my ear.

Matheson, Northern Ontario

Next we crossed Canada to take a position in Matheson, population 3,200, way up in Northern Ontario. Almost as far North as Labrador, and just as cold. The record one night was 63 degrees below zero. There was a great opportunity to take over a solo General Practice. Bradley enjoyed it, and was soon riding fearlessly behind me on a snowmobile, or pushing hard on his small cross country skis along the frozen Black River. Taking a deep breath at 50 below zero could be hard on the lungs, but he coughed up the frozen bits without stopping. It was hardest on Jean, who had to dress this small restless person in many layers of clothing until he was as wide as he was tall. If he fell, he rolled. He would sit briefly on a frozen river or lake, then get back up for more. It was the same when cross country skiing on the frozen Black River. Bradley's enthusiasm was much greater than his skill, and after falling down a hundred times he ended up with a frozen rear end. Not a good place to get frost bite, something to watch out for.

He couldn't stop teasing the small black dog. Jean's Schipperke was a Belgian barge dog bred to hunt rats in small places. It was twelve inches tall and twelve inches long, and had as much aggression as a great big German Shepherd, but Bradley loved to play rough. One day while we were having lunch he was teasing her without mercy, and he backed her into a corner. When she couldn't go back any more she became anxious, then lunged. He yelled in pain, stood up clutching himself. When I came to see what had happened there was a small tear in his shorts where the legs came together, and a spot of blood.

I took him into his bedroom and found he had a small cut, about half an inch long, not on his most important member but on his scrotum. I checked, there was no serious bleeding, no damage to any vital structures, so I put on a dry dressing and finished my lunch. Then I took him to the office. I called to the nurse.

"Hi, Grace, could you set up a suture tray in room two, and take this patient in and clean the wound."

"No, Dad," he moaned. "Not the nurse."

"Don't be silly Brad. They have seen it all before."

"I don't care. They haven't seen mine."

"Oh. Alright." I cleaned the wound, checked it carefully, put in some anesthetic and sutured the wound. I gave him a lecture while I sewed.

"You won't tease the dog after this, will you?"

"No, Dad. No I won't,' and I think he meant it at the time.

A week later I took him down again to get the stitches out.

"Grace, please open up a suture removal set in room two, and clean the wound."

"No, Dad, no, not the nurse." But he knew I was kidding, the sutures came out and all was well. There were no lasting effects as he proved many years later when he fathered three children. It was no big deal by comparison with world events, it was, so to speak quite a little thing, but at the time it certainly meant a lot to him.

Several years later when I was working the Emergency Room in Brownsville, Texas a young boy, about twelve was finishing in the bathroom of his school when the school bell rang for the next period. He hurried and pulled up his zipper, too quickly. He yelled, in pain, as the teeth of the zipper dug into tender flesh. Reluctantly, and with acute, terminal embarrassment he let the school nurse look at it. She joggled the teeth of the zipper, causing him to yelp again. She obviously didn't know the zipper trick. She put him in a car and took him to the emergency room.

I was the ER doc. Work in the ER is 95 percent routine and 5 percent panic, like OB. We had our moments, our share of major trauma, gun shot wounds leaking blood, massive heart attacks, but this was not one of those. The ER nurse checked the boy out, then came to get me.

"Doc, see if you want an instrument tray in there."
She obviously didn't know the zipper trick either. The boy was nervous and highly embarrassed to have to continually expose his private places. I looked carefully, then turned to the nurse.

"Please get me the large bandage scissors."
"The big bandage scissors? With the blunt ends?"
"Yes please."

She brought me the scissors, which we usually used to cut off clothing like blue jeans from accident victims. As I stood there holding the big scissors, the boy looked worried.

"You're not going to use those on me, are you?"

"Well, sort of, but I guarantee it won't hurt."

I got the nurse to lift his anatomy out of the way. I took hold of the zipper below the disaster with my left hand and cut through the fabric, and the zipper, with the scissors cutting just below my fingers. Then it was a simple matter to separate the zipper painlessly from below, clean him up and put on a band-aid. It would not make the nightly news, but to that boy at that time, little things did mean a lot.

My practice in Matheson was fifty miles from any specialist. During and after a blizzard this made transfer by ambulance impossible. I was on my own except for another GP, and there were problems. In the small, 32 bed hospital the loyalties of the nurses was divided equally between us. However, when it was my turn I couldn't refuse a call, and all the nurses cooperated..

"Doc, there's a big snake here that needs stitches. We've put him in the Xray room." He was the pet of a strange lady passing through town, and she had lost him two days previously. That evening he had wriggled out from between the mattress and the box springs where he had been hiding, and the energetic movement of the lady as she had entertained visitors had made many cuts into his skin. There was no vet, the roads were blocked. I was a bit reluctant. His muscular body was 12 inches thick, and he could have crushed me with ease. However, he was amazingly docile as I sewed him up.

There was the young blonde school teacher who went into atrial fibrillation. I had to get her back to normal in a hurry. She was fully awake, there was no time to put her to sleep, so I stuck in some valium, slapped on the defibrillator and gave her 50 joules. Her body jumped. "That felt like a kick from a mule. A nasty angry mule." she said afterwards, but she was alive.

She was an attractive blonde, with a bosom straight out of Playboy. But, there was no attraction. If I didn't do the right thing, she would have been a dead blonde. People often fantasize about a doctors frequent access to a pretty woman's unclothed beauty. But, there is nothing sexy about feeling deep into a vagina and finding feet or a bottom when you were expecting a head. In the city, a breech delivery was always a call for an obstetrician. Often this malpresentation was expected beforehand, but not always. If it was also her first baby, like the one I delivered, her pelvis had not been stretched . The larger head following the smaller body might get trapped, and a dead baby was a possibility.

The scariest cases were young people with severe, deadly asthma, or old people gasping their last in congestive heart failure. Both could die if they were not treated correctly and quickly. Or there was an urgent call over the radio when I was out on the snowmobile.

"We have a fifteen year old boy in a full code," meaning in cardiac arrest. His heart was in bad trouble and I got there too late. Autopsy showed a congenital heart defect, previously unsuspected. His heart had given out suddenly while he was out skating on a frozen lake.

The cases that broke my heart were the children, especially the very small ones. I was in the ER when a slightly plump young lady with black hair rushed in carrying an infant.

"Doctor, please help me. He is not breathing."

The tiny infant was only a few weeks old, and warm, but I could hear no heart beat, and his chest was absolutely still. I started CPR, squeezing the chest and blowing into his mouth. There was no mask small enough so I put my mouth on his and blew. The ER nurse was hovering waiting to help.

"Make her sit down. Get her a paper bag."

The mother was starting to hyperventilate, and rebreathing her own carbon dioxide would help. I was not helping her baby one bit. After twenty minutes he was a little more pink, but there was no signs of breathing or heart beat.

I would have loved to have given the mother some hope, but I couldn't.

"I'm very sorry, but he is not responding."

"He was happy and normal when I put him down. Please keep trying."

I had known that she would say that, so I kept up CPR for another twenty minutes. Finally I stood up, and shook my head. I had known from the beginning that it was S.I.D.S., Sudden Infant Death Syndrome, the unexplained death of a perfectly normal baby. There were several theories, but it was truly a tragic mystery. Maybe the tongue fell back and blocked the windpipe, or they vomited while lying on their back. Recommendations these days include laying the baby on its side, but a few cases still happen.

The next day I had a horrendous sore throat. Red, swollen, and very painful but that was minor compared to the grief and guilt that the mother felt. I tried to convince her that it was definitely not her fault, but to suddenly lose the little baby she had carried inside her for nine months, for no apparent reason, was devastating.

Chapter Twelve

Routine delivery

Delivering babies could be a delight. It usually resulted in two happy, healthy patients, and a doctor who had been imagining the worst as the baby came down the birth canal. But usually all ended well. I never delivered any babies on the Amazon. They had been doing that themselves for many years. Obstetrics, like the ER, is ninety-five percent routine, and five percent panic, and you never know which one is coming next. Mother Nature has been pushing out human babies for tens of thousands of years. How many patients Mother Nature lost is not known, and she isn't telling, but even for a woman that had had a dozen healthy normal deliveries, there were always potential troubles and tragedies. Especially with a primip, having her first scary experience of childbirth. The OB nurse was calling me.

"Doctor, Mrs. Watson is here. She is a primip, due in three days, 23 years old, vitals okay, cervix effacing. Fetal heart 140, regular. She looks good. Will you be over?"

I was one of two doctors that cared for the three thousand people. Routine care, minor surgery and anesthetics, and routine deliveries were all ours. The nearest town with a specialist was fifty miles away.

The baby would have to dilate the birth canal for the first time, and that could take hours. But, it was six am, I had just finished with the ER patient they had called me for, so I could check her and go home for breakfast before starting the day.

"I'll be right there."

Patricia was a small, slim young woman, and had been modest and calm during her pre-natal visits. She was calm now, except when she gritted her teeth during the early contractions. All was fine. The baby was in a perfectly normal position, heart rate and rhythm normal, cervix fully effaced. The mother was healthy and happy. With just a touch of anxiety about the strange adventure that was starting, but that was normal also.

"Everything is just fine, Pat," I reassured her, smiling. She smiled back. Delivering a baby seems to bring out the best in the doctor and the patient, even the ones that screamed their heads off during the last stage.

"I will be back, and I won't be far away."

So started another normal day. After breakfast, I went around checking on my hospital patients, including Pat, then down into the basement where we had our offices. Patients were already gathering, and Grace, my nurse was putting the first one into an examining room. After about an hour I went upstairs to look at Pat. The OB nurse would have called me if there had been any problems, but frequent visits were comforting for both the doctor and the patient.

"She is dilating, doctor," said the OB nurse. "About two centimeters." Which meant another seven centimeters to go. "Flow is spotty, and she hasn't had anything for pain."

I checked her again just before I went home for lunch, to my house about half a block from the hospital. Her progress was steady, and she was eight centimeters by the time I finished seeing office patients. I stayed with her, as the last little bit could be very quick or very slow. And painful. I never understood how a woman could tolerate having a four inch diameter object pushed slowly through her vagina, accustomed until now to an object much smaller. On the first time it obviously hurt like hell.

I was told that Italian women were known as the ones with the loudest screams, which was because they were told that the louder the scream, the stronger the baby. Apparently Pat did not have any Italian blood in her, and her pain threshold must have been high. Right until the end she tried to swallow her screams, restraining them to the very end.

He was a happy, healthy boy and he had no inhibitions about making noises.

"Very strong lungs," said the OB nurse, beaming. However many they deliver, they are always as happy and proud as the mother.

Everything had been so healthy and normal that one of the junior nurses was allowed to share in the post partum care. The uterus was well contracted. I had massaged it well, and given her an injection of pitocin, and we expected it to bleed, but only a little. I went home to play with my children, then have a quiet evening. It was not to be.

At about 8.30, after the kids had played at having a bath, I dried myself off. Then I had a feeling, an urge to go over and check on Pat. The junior nurse gave her report. The senior OB nurse was away on doing something.

"She's doing well, doctor. Still has a mild to moderate flow, but vital signs stable, and the baby is doing well."

"Let's go up and see"

"Oh, she has the baby, trying to nurse, doctor."

"Let's see how that is going too."

As soon as I walked into the room I had a feeling that something was wrong. Pat was paler than she had been, and looked tired. The baby was full of energy, trying hard at the breast.

"Show me the last pad."

We went to the utility room and the nurse found the pad. It had a large blood stain that went all the way through.

"Have they all been like this?"

"Yes, doctor. All mild to moderate."

Pat was losing too much blood. No wonder she looked pale. Then started the worst hours of my life. She didn't respond to uterine massage, or any of my injections. I ordered fluids and blood, but the nurse couldn't find a vein. Neither could I. Her blood pressure was falling, her pulse rising, signs that she might be going into shock. So was I. I tried for a cutdown, opening the skin to look for a vein but failed. I called the only other doctor in the small town, who had had more surgical training than me, and he finally got a small vein open. The blood still had not arrived.

"We only have two donors with her type, and they are both out of town. Shall we call in the O negatives?"

We were too small to have our own blood bank, and usually calling in a donor didn't take long. Not tonight. Pat's blood pressure was still going down, and my guilty feelings were rising. Shock could be fatal. I was angry. I knew it had to be all my fault. She was bleeding too heavily, and women could die from a post partum hemorrhage. Usually from a small piece of placenta left inside the womb. All signs pointed to one guilty party, me. I had reassured everyone that everything was nice and normal, and now Pat was close to dying in front of my eyes.

"Phone Kirkland Lake ER. Tell them we have a post partum hemorrhage going bad, and ask them to call in Dr. M."

He was the obstetrician who later delivered my daughter, and he was good.

"Get her ready for transport, with an OB or surgical nurse, and an OB tray, a gynecology tray, a cutdown tray, plus oxygen and several bags of normal saline."

"But doctor, they will have to send an ambulance up from Kirkland Lake. We will have to wait. We don't have one here."

"We will use my van." It was a VW camper van. It would be crowded, but I didn't dare wait another hour for an ambulance to drive the fifty miles.

"But doctor, we can't do that. What if ..."

My trusty van started beautifully, as if it knew it was needed for something special. The familiar sound of its Volkswagen engine comforted me, and soon it was crammed with the patient, a nurse and all the gear. I had driven the van all the way across Canada, and she had never let me down.

It was a good road and empty, but I resisted the urge to step on the gas. Most ambulances have a recording device, sometimes even a governor for the engine to make sure that the driver kept within safe limits. With critical patients the temptation is go as fast as you can, but the extra speed gains little time, and is certainly more dangerous. The cargo is always too precious to take any chances with. I had left the baby behind with another nursing mother who had a surplus of mother's milk. I was tense as I drove. An Act-of-God type accident might happen at any time. I wasn't normally a praying type in spite of the Baptist exposure, but that night I drove with half of my mind while the other half was having a long chat with the Almighty.

"Not tonight, dear Lord, not tonight."

Either Lady Luck or the Lord or both were with me, and the ER at Kirkland Lake sprang into action when my green VW van pulled into the parking lot. Nurses and doctors swarmed around Pat, and I saw that one of them was a doctor I knew. I stopped one of the nurses.

"Is that Doctor T?"

"Yes. He is the head of our ICU."
"He's not an Obstetrician. Where is Doctor M.?"
"I don't know. I think he is out of town."

Doctor T. was a good man, but I didn't think he was an expert in complicated obstetrics. Inside the ER I went over to him.

"Hi," I said.
"Hi John. This is your patient, right?"
"She is, and she has been bleeding heavily for hours."
"I have sent a sample to the lab. Right now I am digging for a nice big vein to push in lots of saline. She is shocky."
"Is Doctor M. around?"
"Won't be back for a few days."
"Has he got a locum in to cover his practice?"
"Yes. Me."
"You did a rotation in OB?"
"No. Just a few updates in Toronto on complications in everything. I run the ICU, and we get all sorts."
"What are the options here?"
"She has probably bled out all of her clotting factors. She may need a hysterectomy."

Oh my God ! This is what my stupidity had led to. To take out the uterus of a fertile young mother, and make her feel like half of a woman. She would never be able to have any more babies. An aide brought over some papers.

"Here are the lab results. She only has one third of her blood volume left, and no clotting factors. We can fill her up, and just hope that she doesn't bleed to death when we do the hysterectomy."

Oh Dear God, don't let this be happening. I had made mistakes before, but never one as horrible as this one. How could I face her husband, and tell him it was all my fault? I felt physically sick. I backed away and took a deep breath to try to blow away some of the vicious guilt tearing at my

131

insides.

I bumped into a man I had never seen before. Short, tubby, with a Father Christmas beard and eyes that had obviously seen tragedies like this before.

"Don't have to take the uterus right away," he muttered. "Leave her open with artery clamps on the uterine arteries for twelve hours and see what happens."

"You have done that?"

"When you are all alone in the backwoods you are on your own."

He turned, and went to join a group that was working on a bad car accident victim. Maybe one of his patients. I moved back to the group around Pat, and stood beside Doctor T.

"The man with the beard. Do you know him?

Doctor T looked, and smiled.

"Santa Claus? He's been out in the woods too long."

"He had an idea."

"I'm not surprised. I think the air is thin up there near the North Pole."

"Maybe. But what do you think of this?"

I told him the old doctor's idea.

"You won't find that one in the books." Doctor T smiled condescendingly. "But ... some of his weird handiwork has come through here to have their sutures out, and I must admit, I've been surprised at the techniques, and the results."

He paused, deep in thought. I waited. Please God, let her keep her womb, Just for a little while, maybe, then see what happens.

Doctor T took a deep breath.

"I don't know, John. When a post partum hemorrhage has produced a D.I.C, (a disseminated intravascular coagulation) the bleeding can be massive, and the treatment complicated. I've been talking to experts down in Toronto, and they will call me back when they have done some brain

storming. I will just push antibiotics, platelets and blood until I hear from them. We might get by with a scraping, a D and C to clean out the uterus, which might be risky. I am waiting until I hear from them before I do anything drastic."
> "*Thank you God. If you are running this show, please stick around for the finale.*"

Someone did. Pat kept her womb, and later, in due course gave her son a lovely sister.

And so a simple country doctor survived another normal routine day. With a little help from his friends.

Julia

Julia was a much wanted baby. I loved Bradley dearly, but I also wanted a little girl to spoil. And I knew how to make one. I had noticed that married med students during internship who had a child always made a boy. Their seed was highly concentrated and intimate times with their spouses were infrequent. When they got out into practice, and there was more time for canoodling, that's when the girls came. Even Google knows this now. Check under sex selection, timing and frequency of intercourse.

Jean knew I wanted a girl when she became pregnant again, but she wouldn't tell me the results of the ultrasound. The OB was in Kirkland Lake, fifty miles away. She went into labor one afternoon, and it was her third baby. It might be very quick. I wasted no time as I drove her down..

"No, Doctor McFadden says you can't be in the delivery room. Your wife wants to surprise you." The nurse was adamant, and put me in a waiting room. By seven o'clock it was over and I was allowed in. Jean was propped up on pillows, looking tired, and happy.

"Over there," she said. The blanket was pink, and Julia Elizabeth had come into the world. She was exactly what I had wanted, even if she had the typical new born's appearance and looked a lot like Winston Churchill and very red and wrinkled. She grew up to be a beautiful young woman, and I became the most important person in her life for thirteen years. Until her teens and the days of peer pressure, but that was a long way off.

Office work was simple. All bills were sent to the government health plan, small computer cards with a minimum amount of info, and every two weeks a check arrived. I never paid much attention to financial things. When a visiting American paid with cash, I was embarrassed. This happened seldom, and I never knew what to do with the stuff. Plus it made me feel like a mercenary. Without money directly coloring the issue I could feel that I was helping people because they needed help, not for the money.

I had a total staff of one. Grace answered phones, prepared patients, and stayed in the room if the patient was female. She was a lovely person, outside and in. Young, attractive, and kind and loving with patients. When she became pregnant she would only have me as her doctor, not even an OB, and she objected when I asked her to get a nurse from the hospital floor upstairs to chaperone me when I examined her. My office was in the basement. She wanted only me.

"Doctor, I don't want anyone. I am shy, I don't want another woman knowing all about me. Not in this small town." She always wanted to be examined at the end of the afternoon, when all the patients had gone. She wanted to be examined in private. I objected. In a small town people would talk.

I always won out. One of the nurses would come down when Grace took any clothes off. She eventually delivered a normal healthy baby, without any complications, medical or ethical.

I learned a lot about life and death from the patients. I knew their problems and their families, and their crises and happy moments were very personal. Especially the sad endings.

Charles was an accountant until his lung cancer clawed at him and wouldn't let go. His face was thin, not yet sunken from weight loss, and his thin hair was combed carefully across his head. I found that I had to adopt a "Don't ask, don't tell" policy. He might be coughing hard, or hurting badly, but if I asked "Is there anything you want to ask me, any questions?" he would shake his head. He never asked what his diagnosis was, and I never mentioned it. He may have felt that by not mentioning it, it would go away. He was often in pain, and short of breath, but he never asked why.

I checked with his family. I told them what was going to happen, and I made sure that his affairs were in order. One morning as I was making rounds I went into his room. He was sitting up in bed, his eyes wide open, staring, and absolutely still. It must have just happened, and his death had gone unnoticed. In his last moment he knew he was close to death. His worst fear had arrived. I have never seen a look of terror like that. He looked as if he had been scared to death.

Most of the time I was happy and fulfilled. Looking after complete families, from the grandmother to the baby I had just delivered. At home Jean was a good mother busy raising two small children plus Jason, and she was happy most of the time. We had problems as did most couples, and while I was sometimes unwilling to admit my lack of perfection, I did agree to 'counseling.' Unfortunately I knew more about psychology than the psychiatrist, or I thought I did. I went on my merry way.

I spoke French a lot. I was on the school board, and since half of the population was French Canadian, if a new class was added in English there was an immediate demand for it to be added in French. My schoolboy French expanded, and my medical vocabulary increased. However, I never could understand some language peculiarities, such as why the intestines marched, but the vagina ran if there was a discharge. I gave up on the gender issue. Rock River and Rock Lake were both bodies of water, but one was masculine and the other feminine.

We had some good vacations, and the one we spent in Vermont was a great change and relaxation. We took cross-country skis, downhill skis as well, and just to be in a warm cabin by the fire and to look out on the blanket of pure white snow outside was pleasing to the soul.

One day Jean was shopping in town when she stopped for coffee in an impressive lodge. An old lady came and sat beside her, to talk and she reminisced about her children. It turned out that she was the owner of the lodge, and she was Maria von Trapp. She was the former nun made famous in ' The Sound of Music.' Such a small world. Jean had spent many years as a music teacher, and she was thrilled to meet the Maria who had sung all over America with the Von Trapp Family singers before settling in Vermont.

Not everyone in Matheson was scared of death, but William was an unusual young man. Quite, serious, almost intellectual. His schizophrenic delusions, however were the standard ones about the micro chip that the C.I.A. had implanted in his brain, and he told me about some of the messages he had received. I simply increased his medications. The nearest psychiatrist was two hundred miles away, and his family didn't want to make the drive every month. Plus, the era of sending psych patients out to be cared for in the community had arrived. They were turfed out of mental hospitals, to the care of a home team.

Sadly, the home team was just me. Sometimes I tried to get him admitted for his own protection, but it was not easy with socialized medicine.

When he started to 'forget' to take his medications I switched him to an injection, once a month. At least I knew that he had some protection. When he missed an appointment I would get the police to bring him in, which they did with tact and kindness. Then one day they couldn't find him. It was the season of autumn thunderstorms, and it had probably affected him.

"He went out walking in the rain," his mother said. "I couldn't stop him."

As I was also the local Coroner, the equivalent of a Medical Examiner, I had to be on call for any unusual deaths. There was nothing I could do except call the police, but they were already looking. Nearly two weeks later I was called out to assess a body tangled in the pilings of a wooden bridge, floating face downwards. I had the police pull the body to the bank and turn it over. It was Bill, bloated, and the smell of decay was strong. He must have just walked into the river, and not walked out again. His body had stayed submerged until gas formed and popped him to the surface again. I sent him for autopsy, but I knew the cause of death, and I felt guilty that I had not worked harder to set up a system to protect him from himself.

In Matheson as Coroner I was even empowered to hold court for an inquest, call witnesses and I was expected to deliver a verdict and make recommendations for preventing futures disasters.

One night it had been sixty three below zero, a record. Three electric cords ran to my car. One to the block heater, or the engine wouldn't turn over. One to the battery warmer and one to the interior warmer, or the frozen seats would crack when you sat on them. On that morning my office was filled with patients when my nurse said,

"There's a policeman in your office. He wants to see you about a body."

It was not a summons about any of my misdeeds. He

was a member of the Ontario Provincial Police, complete with gun and blue uniform.

"Doc, we have a death, and it doesn't look right."

Grace was not alarmed. She was gentle at warning the waiting patients about a delay. I pulled on my boots and heavy parka, and picked up my black bag. In the police cruiser he said "It's Jim Bacchus."

I knew Jim. He had seen me once. "There's a sore on my leg that won't go away, Doc. Been there for six months."

He was small, shy, and I knew he lived alone. It showed in his crumpled, dirty clothing. He was getting old, a little old man with thin gray hair.

"I need to see it, Jim." He didn't say anything but he gave me a look, and shook his head "No."

"Jim, I really do need to look if I'm going to help you."

Finally he took off his boots, then his trousers, and underneath was a long gray pair of woolen pants, his long johns. He took off a pair of socks and then the long johns. Underneath was another pair of socks and more long johns. When he finally got down to skin he did have an ulcer. I trimmed it and gave him medicine and said

"Come back in three weeks and let me look" but he never did. I saw him once a week at the Canadian Legion, where he usually had two beers, and lost two dollars on bingo once or twice a week. The only words I got out of him about his leg ulcer was "It's gone."

The police cruiser stopped. Across the road, behind banks of snow were a couple of houses with smoke rising from the chimneys. I followed the cop up a path in the deep snow to a shabby cabin. There was no smoke rising.

"A neighbor called us," explained the cop." There's been no smoke for two days."

The cabin was made of unpainted wood, and was about ten foot by twenty foot.

"It's strange. The door was locked from the inside", said the cop. It was dark, cold and gloomy and the cop lit a kerosene lamp. Inside there was a short divider, and on one side was a bed, untidy with crumpled blankets. Hanging on nails around the shabby room were dozens of grey socks and long johns. On the other side there was a small table with one chair and a black wood-burning stove, now cold.

Jim's small body was on the ground, on his side, his head in the middle of a pool of frozen blood. He was frozen solid, but he wasn't heavy and the cop gently lifted him up. Then I saw that the front of his head had been smashed in. It was a horrible wound, something that could have come from a heavy blow with a blunt object. Yet the door had been locked from the inside. I examined him as best I could then told the cop to get photos of everything and take an inventory.

"That looks like the cause of death," I said pointing to the head. "But we'll have to see what the autopsy report says."

On this side of the cabin were rough wooden shelves, and on them only three things. Old newspapers, plenty of split firewood for the stove, and rows and rows of cans of cat food. Plus a collection of empty wine bottles on the floor. From the police inventory later I learnt that there was no other food of any kind in the cabin. I was trying to read the label on a can when I heard a rustle. The kerosene lamps were flickering and I shone my flashlight up. On one of the rafters was a black cat, very still, looking at me. Then there was another movement, and I saw a brown tabby cat, and then another and another. All told there were fourteen cats, and they were hungry and scared. It looked as if they and Jim had lived on a diet of cat food. After all, the label promised that it provided a balanced diet of meat and vegetables and vitamins. Perhaps Jim figured if it was good enough for the cats it was good enough for him. A simple diet for a lonely bachelor, and cheap.

When the autopsy report came back I found that I was wrong. He hadn't died from a fractured skull or brain damage but from loss of blood. There were two other clues. His bladder was very full, about eight hundred cc. He must have been bursting. Head wounds bleed profusely. And his blood alcohol was very high. Obviously he had been drunk and the way I put it together he had got up to go the outhouse, tripped and fell and hit his head on the cast iron stove and lay unconscious and drunk on the floor. He bled to death, and his body froze when the stove went out.

What to do with fourteen cats? Luckily there was another Englishman in the town as foolish about animals as I was, and he was crazy about cats. He found homes for thirteen of them and kept one himself. I'll never forget the story of Jim, and the happy ending for his cats.

I always felt guilty when I was called to a suicide. Somehow I should have prevented it. I always tried to shield the family from the police. They had to rule out foul play, and their questions, though necessary, were painful to the family as their grown daughter was being cut down from the rafters where the rope had been tied.

I only saw one case where the body was hanging from a tree with a plastic bag over the face. A male, with his fly open, an obvious case of sexual asphyxiation gone wrong. The lack of oxygen was said to enhance the climax.

Exotic Spain again

One year we took a longer vacation, to Europe. In London we

rented a camper van complete with shower and toilet, and wandered through Holland and Belgium, then down through France. This was camping in comfort, superior to the delights I had when I hitchhiked through France and slept in a field in my small pup tent. We did sleep in a field, but we just drove in, parked behind the trees, and Jean turned on a propane stove as I walked the kids by the river.

The van, being English, had the steering wheel on the right. The foolish French roads often had a steep camber which put me way lowdown on the right, unable to see past the slow-moving French bus in front of us. Jean would say "Not now, something is coming" and I would wait before overtaking. She was a little too cautious, and sometimes after waiting for many minutes I pulled out to look. This was usually the time when a mad French driver in a speeding Citroen would be hurtling straight for us, horn blaring.

Bradley, almost three and very active was hard to manage in the moving van, until I bought a large plastic laundry basket. The sides were mainly holes, and turned upside down and tied in place it made a convenient holding cell.

In the south of Spain we met with my sister, her family, and my mother, who had all flown into the airport in Malaga. We all stayed in a beachfront hotel. Bradley did not need the language to charm the female staff, and they looked after him well. They prevented him drowning himself several times in the swimming pool when he had scooted out of sight of his jailers.

My mother was adamant about one thing.

"I am not going to a bull fight. They stick nasty things in the bull and torment him before they kill him. That's cruel."

The blast of the trumpets, and the march of the matadors, excited the crowd and even my mother. When they did do beastly things to the bull, she covered her eyes with her hands. The climax came, and the tension of thousands of people holding their breath could be felt as the bull was about to die. I glanced at my mother. Her fingers were apart, just a little and she was peeking through them.

"Oooh," she said afterwards. "That was so cruel. I want to go home." But, she stayed until the end.

We took a day trip to Morocco, and walked through the market in Tangiers. Grandma was pushing the baby carriage A crowd of street Arabs followed our little group. Bradley was securely fastened to the carriage. My sister Betty should have been similarly restrained. She had always been adventurous, and this mysterious city was a challenge.

"Here Jean. This looks like an interesting alley. Let's explore." She led the way and they ended up in a walled garden where many women were sitting, without veils, doing very little. Our guide said later that they had penetrated into the Caliph's harem, and they were lucky that they had not been detained on a permanent basis.

Back in Matheson, I was also the company doctor for a goldmine, in nearby Ramore. I always made a point of visiting places where patients were working. In this case I was fitted with a canvas coat, trousers, boots, and a miner's lamp on a helmet. Then I climbed into a small cage, shielded on the sides with a grating of iron bars. As we dropped down in free fall, leaving my stomach behind, we could see the bare rock flashing by. Three hundred feet down we came to the working tunnel. On the jagged rock wall there was no seam glinting with gold, just the marks where the rock had been drilled and blasted. I thanked my lucky stars but I had not become a miner, to have to work in this very dark tunnel. I could almost feel the immense mass of rock above my head pressing down. Luckily, I was never called down to amputate an arm trapped by a heavy rock slide, but my imagination worked overtime.

For vacations on long weekends we camped out in a cabin by a lake. In winter the lake was frozen except for a couple of holes that had been broken in the ice near the saunas used by mad Finns. After warming up in the sauna their naked pink bodies came running out to jump in the pools of ice cold water of the lake. A big wood burning stove kept us warm, but it had an insatiable appetite for split logs. I got up every few hours during the night to make sure it hadn't gone out. We dressed the children carefully, especially little Julia, age two. Every time I got up I checked that her little woolen cap came down to cover her tiny ears. And strangely, it was fun.

Chapter Thirteen

Ladysmith, BC.

After four years, with the children three and five years old, and me with itchy feet, we moved back to beautiful BC. I bought a solo practice in Ladysmith, on Vancouver Island from Doctor Wilkes Neville. On my first visit to meet him, he showed me around the office, introduced me to his one receptionist/nurse/billing agent, and by then it was almost noon.
    "John, we'll go next door before lunch." Two doors down was the local Royal Canadian Legion, with a bar. Wilkes didn't ask what I wanted.
    "Two specials, please" he told the man behind the bar. These turned out to be mainly large double Gins, with dashes of vermouth, bitters, and a couple of olives. I couldn't handle a second, but Wilkes could.
    He had been there for decades, he knew everything about everyone in town, and was much beloved by the local

Indian band.

"They made me an honorary chief." He smiled. "I'll show you the feathers, and I'll introduce you." There was no way that I could fill his shoes. He was larger than life.

We again had a sailboat, which was conveniently anchored about fifty feet off shore from our beachfront cottage. On weekends Bradley and I would take Emile and Christiane deKonincke for a sail. They were from Belgium. He was short and muscular, exuding self confidence. He was a teacher and counselor at the high school. She was slender, exceedingly friendly, and an absolutely superb master of continental cuisine. They had two huge Great Danes, as big as horses, both male. If I sat on the same sofa as Christine, one would jump up between us, and gently take my arm in his mouth.

"Watch out," he was telling me. "This is my territory. And this is my woman."

While we were sailing Jean stayed home with Julia in the cottage. If I was needed for an emergency she would hang a white sheet from a window. Christine always brought delicious snacks, like her crab soup delicately flavored with herbs and spices. Bradley loved to steer, but he was still a little bit short and had to stand on the seats to see over the cabin. He handled the tiller expertly. Emile and Christine were very good people, and delightful friends. They eventually moved north to the city of Nanaimo. He went back to school and became Dr. deKonincke, with his PhD in psychology. In their Nanaimo home one room was his study and consulting room where he saw patients. Sadly he later lost his vision. He had only five percent peripheral vision left but he could to still pour a good gin and tonic. He maintained his position as consultant to the local parole board, but they spent more time in their cabin on Gabriola Island. Here he felt free in the open space, and he had a rope rigged to guide him down to the beach. There he enjoyed walks tasting the familiar smells of the sea.

Sadly, he became a victim of health care rationing in Canada. I had visited him once, and over a gin and tonic he said

"John, what do you think of this?" He rolled up his trouser leg, and there was a deep ulcer, as big as a silver dollar.

"How long have you had that, Milo?"

"Almost a year."

He had not consulted a doctor. He poo hooed my suggestion that he do that right away, but after I left he did, and they put him straight into hospital to remove it and graft on a piece of skin from his backside.

Unfortunately his second stay in the Regional Hospital coincided with a government cutback of funds. The hospital had to fire all the experienced cleaning staff, and hired minimum wage personnel. They were not as well trained, and there was an outbreak of a nasty bug call C. Difficile. About twenty became very ill, and five died. Milo survived the infection, and I happened to come up to Canada for a visit just after he had been discharged.

He was as weak as a kitten, and still had remnants of the infection. Christine gave him his meds, but he stayed in a recliner downstairs next to a bathroom, which he needed often without warning. During the night he cat napped, and stayed in his recliner all day and all night. Shortly after my visit he relapsed, was put back in the hospital and died.

Another couple in Ladysmith were also teachers, and he in fact was a principal. His favorite pastime however was slightly illegal. He had found a path into deserted woods that took him to a pool, where a small river ran slowly. Salmon swam. up to spawn, and he landed many spring salmon weighing over a hundred pounds each. The steak cut from one of these monsters would be twenty inches deep and feed our family for days. Unfortunately, the pool was above high tide, where only Indians were allowed to fish legally, and he knew it. One day, acting no doubt on a tip, the Fish and Game Warden was waiting. The hook was barbed, not the smooth one required for catch and release, the only legal way for a white man to fish. It looked like a hefty fine, even jail, and he realized that he would probably lose his job. I don't know exactly what happened. He did not go to jail, but there were no more salmon steaks.

Ladysmith was between two pulp mills. When the wind was from the North the fumes, the smell of rotten eggs came from Harmac. When it was from the South it came from Crofton, and it was strong. There was no escaping them. The rotten egg smell was in every nook and cranny. I longed for a gas mask. During the one year that I spent in Ladysmith I found three kidney tumors, hypernephromas. These are rare. I hadn't seen one before, and I haven't seen one in the thirty years since I left. I checked with a classmate who was in the B.C. Cancer Institute. No, there was no greater incidence statistically around Ladysmith than anywhere in the Province.

When I went back years later I found that many friends had died from brain tumors. Again, the BCCI could find no connection with the pulp mills.

It wasn't the smell of rotten eggs that made me leave Ladysmith but a combination of factors. The socialized medicine scheme meant that the politicians held the purse strings, and they wanted to cut payments to doctors. So to make the doctors look bad there was a battle, and the politicians played rough. In 1969 they had published the gross incomes of all doctors on the front page of the Vancouver Sun. The 'gross' income looked obscene.

In a radiology clinic ten radiologists might be billed under one doctor's billing number, while the expenses of some thirty techs etc, plus mortgages and equipment costs were not listed. It looked as if one doc wanted the government to pay him over a million dollars a year. Obstetricians were paid less for a delivery than a nurse-midwife, even if they had seen the patient for all of her pre-natal visits. The politicians were in charge, and doctors were the bad guys, and had to be controlled. There was non stop bad mouthing, and the negative publicity began to alter patients attitudes towards doctors. I had been looking, and one U.S. recruiter phoned.

South to Texas

"John, we will fly you down, and you can look at some of our hospitals in Texas."

Rick Holdren was a friendly, persuasive recruiter for a hospital chain with its headquarters in Houston. The socialistic government in BC and it's a dirty war had triggered a massive brain drain of docs leaving for the US, including many Brit docs who had preciously fled the British National Health Scheme.

"Take your time, rent a car, and look around. We have places in Nacogdoches, Beaumont, all over."

I drove all over, but nothing was really appealing, not even in Beaumont close to the ocean. Then Rick pointed to the map and said "We have one down here. It's on the border, by the sea, but they speak a lot of Spanish." That got my attention. I had always had romantic fantasies about things Spanish since childhood.

A stairway rolled up to the door of the Braniff jet. Wide bodied and colored purple. When the door opened we were hit by a solid wave of heat. It was about 100 degrees, and 90 percent humidity, just an average day in June we found out later. This was Brownsville, at the southern tip of Texas. There were tropical palm trees all around. My body and soul warmed, with fond memories of Spain flooding in. Was this really America?

Illegally perhaps. There had been a land grab by the U.S. over an alleged intrusion from Mexican soldiers, about a hundred and fifty years before. It was really occupied Mexico. Eighty percent were Hispanic, and most preferred to speak Spanish. I felt at home. Especially when we drove across the bridge over the Rio Grande into Mexico for lunch. Serenaded by mariachis, sipping large green Margaritas, Canada and the snow and government medicine seemed a long way away.

Another factor behind the move was that my marriage was rocky. I thought a new location might help, and get me away from Jean's lawyers. How foolish. There were lots more lawyers in Texas than in BC, and they were much more aggressive.

Opening a solo practice was not too hard. I had learnt the ropes in Matheson long before, and the administrator, Bob Carey was very helpful.

"We will make sure you do well for the first year. There is an office vacant right next to the hospital. You can even walk to the doctor's dining room in the hospital for lunch."

Of the twenty percent who were Anglo, a few were Brits. I was not good at socializing, and we made friends slowly. But I organized the first game of cricket in South Texas. One of the pediatricians owed me a favor.

"Susanne, when your parents come over next month, could you ask them to bring a couple of cricket bats, and a set of bails?"

The natives didn't know that up until 1844 cricket was much more popular in the US than baseball. I was enthusiastic.

"There is a wide stretch of sand on South Padre Island that will be ideal for a wicket. I can make the stumps, and I already have a couple of leather cricket balls." Stumps were round sticks, 28 inches long, three inches apart, with short pieces of round stock, the two 'bails' balanced on top. One way to get a batsman out was to hit a stump with a ball and dislodge the bail. South Padre Island was about twenty five miles east of Brownsville, and a popular resort. One of the boundaries was the warm waters of the Gulf of Mexico. I can't remember who won the first and last game of cricket on South Padre Island, but it was certainly fun, and authentic. Except we had a barbecue instead of a tea break.

Mrs. Pompa's Miracle

She was a very lively lady for her age, somewhere in the late seventies, and I first met her in the First Baptist Day School in Brownsville. She was the "custodian," which involved her in everything, and she was a short little old lady, bent forward, in black and bubbling with energy who was in perpetual motion. Julia, four years old was in pre-kindergarten, and Brad, six, was in first grade. They loved her, and respected her and she doted on them all. She was proud of her memory.

"Bradley's has been with us now for a year next week. I know his birthday is not until January, but I am making him a little cake." She was telling me, not asking, but I said "Okay" anyway.

She usually went to a doctor in Matamoros, in Mexico across the river, but when she was felled by a massive stroke the family called me in.

The ER nurse gave me a bleak summary.

"The ER doc has checked her out, and she doesn't have a single reflex, anywhere. No response to commands or to pain. It must have been a big stroke."

I found the same. I could only give the family a small measure of hope.

"She has lost almost all of her brain function. Her heart and lungs are working well, but that's about it. The outlook is not good. Sometimes we see a small recovery, sometimes a lot. Sometimes none. I will put her in hospital here, and see what happens."

I didn't want to dash their hopes, so I didn't say that recovery was rare, and that most of those that did survive ranged from vegetables to spastic cripples.

I had tubes put into her stomach and bladder to feed and drain her and we took care of all of her bodily functions. After a couple of weeks, as she showed no signs of any progress I had to transfer her to a nursing home, and added physical therapy. This was mainly putting her limbs through a full range of motion to prevent the contractures of immobility.

The nursing home was clean, but in spite of daily wet mops and Pinesol the smell was still of stale urine. Most of the staff were a little overweight and Hispanic, as were the patients. Many patients were laid out neatly and never moved, as if positioned for their final journey. Televisions were turned on in many rooms, often the only changing element in patients lives from one week to another. Most had been stripped of their assets to qualify for the State paying their bills. Visitors were few, only the kindhearted who would talk to those who seemed to neither hear nor see. But they could. The rare case of spontaneous recovery would say "I could hear every word, but I couldn't move. Not even my eyes."

I would visit Mrs. Pompa about twice a week for a one sided conversation.

"Good morning, Mrs. Pompa. How are you

today?"Her breathing was regular, her pulse strong, but nothing else moved.

"It is still a hot day, with blue skies and a little wind."

Her eyes had been closed since admission, with ophthalmic cream to keep them lubricated.

"The world keeps on moving, whatever happens to us. They do still miss you at the school. Bradley asks about you, and he wants to come and visit you."

"Yes, I will bring him in to see you." It would do him no harm to see that the world was made up of the quick and the dead, and many that were neither quick nor dead.

"Let's see how your arms and legs are today."

I would move the arms and the legs to see if they were stiffening up. Sadly, I was sometimes too busy and hurried to do this, and both I and the physical therapist became a little slack in our duties.

"It's time for me to go, Mrs. Pompa. Time and tide wait for no man." I was just making noise, but I was a believer that a few comforting words in a friendly tone did make a difference.

I had other patients there, many of whom could speak and move. Mrs. Gonzalez had had a huge seizure that had left her a paraplegic. Alberto was large and had frequent spells of apnea and other bad breathing problems and needed constant suctioning.

Very few if any would ever leave for a better life. Sometimes I would think sadly that the motto there should be 'Abandon hope all ye who enter here.' But I couldn't say that, and I kept up a brave front.

One weekend I did decide to let Bradley come into this other world. It was a quiet Saturday afternoon, and I had been called in to "pronounce." As always, when a life began or ended it was not official until someone had signed a piece of paper. I thought I could leave him to talk to Mrs. Pompa while I "pronounced." I explained the situation carefully.

"Brad, I'm going to see Mrs. Pompa."

"Oh Dad, can I come too?"

"I don't know. The last time you were in a hospital you were a wild Indian."

"I'll behave, Dad. Please, let me come and see Mrs. Pompa. I'll be good, I promise."

"If you make trouble, Brad, this will be the very last time I take you. There will be no more visits to the ER."

"Dad, I was good then, wasn't I?"

Maybe it was all the blood, I thought. He had been in the car when I got the call to the ER, and I didn't have time to go home first. A stab wound to the left arm, bleeding heavily. When I got there the head ER nurse had it under control with a pressure dressing.

"Stay here, Brad. Don't move."

"Dad," he strained his head up. ""I can't see."

On his a previous visit to the ER the charge nurse had given him a stool to stand on. I nodded to Marcella, and again she got him a stool.

When I lifted the dressing to look a jet of blood shot out. Obvious an artery had been nicked. Brad was fascinated. He watched with intense concentration as Marcella helped with the tourniquet, and the wound tray to repair the artery and the deep laceration. There was a slippery puddle of blood on the floor, and one of the nurses mopped it up. All in my family had seen only small amounts of blood at the weekend clinic, and Brad seemed to think that this was a special performance just for him. He had been good.

"Yes, Brad, you did behave. But this is different. Mrs. Pompa is lying in bed, she can't move or speak. I think she can hear, and all you can do is talk. That won't be fun."

"Please, Dad. I want to see her. I'll be good."

As I drove, I told Brad I would have to leave him alone for just a bit. I had to look at someone that had just died.

"Dad, can I ..."

"Brad, there may be family there, and it is sad and serious for them. Even if you were quiet, they wouldn't like it. Just stay with Mrs. Pompa. Okay? Promise?"

"Oh alright, Dad."

I should have recognized that he gave in too easily.

At the nursing home, he was subdued. The smell wasn't too bad that day, but it was a solemn, mournful place. In the quiet room with Mrs. Pompa, there was no TV blaring. I took her hand.

"Mrs. Pompa, this is Brad. He is in First Grade, remember? He's a bit of a problem sometimes, but today he promised to behave. Right, Brad?"

He just nodded. Mrs Pompa breathed quietly.

"You can talk to her. She is sort of sleeping, she can hear you, but she can't speak. She likes it when you talk to her. Tell her how you can stand up on the surf board now."

Part of Brad's charm was that he was truly sympathetic and liked people. He seemed to realize that she was helpless, and he opened up. And he was proud of standing up on the board in the waves. As he talked happily to the sleeping woman I slipped out, and quickly walked down the corridor to the room of the 67 year old male that had quietly died that day. There was no one in the room, but when I arrived the nursing aide gently pulled the curtain around the bed.

I stood there for a moment. I always mentally said goodbye to a recently departed soul, even if my theology and beliefs about life after death were rather hazy. I pulled the sheet back from the face. I was watching for any signs of life, but there were none. The mouth was closed, and his chest didn't move. When I drew a strand of cotton across the cornea, there was no reflex blink. He was cool, but not yet cold. I lifted the arm and let it drop. It was not stiff. Rigor mortis had not set in yet. I pressed my stethoscope on his chest for more than sixty seconds, but there was absolute silence. The carotid and all the other pulses were absent, and there were no reflexes anywhere.

I stood back, and covered his face with the sheet. I stood there silently. It was always a solemn moment, but then I was startled.

"Dad, is he dead?"

Brad's face was between the curtains, but his hands held them together under his chin. He looked like such an angelic cherub. One of his many faces.

"Yes, Brad. He is dead."

"Mrs. Pompa is not dead?"

Not an easy question to answer. I did not want to lie, that she was only sleeping, but I didn't want to talk about being comatose, brain dead, that her body was still working while her brain was not. I was on shaky ground theologically, so I didn't want to go there. I also didn't want to lose my reputation as someone with all the answers. But there was no easy answer.

"She may wake up, she may not wake up, it is something we can never be sure about. We will do our best, and see what happens."

The months went by, and I cut my visits to Mrs. Pompa down to one a week. She had not changed, and I didn't want to bill Medicare for doing nothing. I had other patients that were more demanding. Like Dan and Bessie, both about ninety years old. I had had to put them in the nursing home after Bessie had nearly burned the house down a few times. She would forget that she had something on the stove until the neighbors called the fire department about the smoke. Their one son lived alone, and could not take care of them.

They were both confined to wheelchairs, but that did not slow them down. Plus Bessie had an obsession that someone was stealing her toilet paper, and she would turn into an empty room, steal the toilet rolls and hide them under her leg blanket. Until the nursing aide helped her into bed, and the whole collection spilled onto the floor.

Dan was also mobile, and logged many a mile every day. He had been in the cavalry in the First World War and galloped in his wheelchair from room to room, making friends. Until Bessie became suspicious that he had a girlfriend, and became very jealous. As a souvenir and a touch of home she had been allowed to keep her frying pan. With no form of heat in their room it was considered harmless, until the day that she was certain that he had been dallying too long with one of his lady friends. She hurled the pan at him, caught him on the head, and I had to sew him up.

I visited them all once a week. I was just leaving Mrs. Pompa's bedside when suddenly she opened her eyes. I stood stock still. Her eyes moved, looking around the room and she saw me.

"Doctor Rogans! So nice to see you again. How is Bradley today? And your daughter? What is her name? No, don't tell me."

She wrinkled her face in thought. "She is called ... I didn't see her as much as Bradley ...."

She frowned as she concentrated.

"She is called ... Julia, she is called Julia. How is she?"

Mrs. Pompa had been in a coma for a whole year. Everyone had given up on her, yet here she was, talking as if she had just seen me yesterday. Suddenly her mind was clear and sharp, and her memory was perfect. She remembered everything, except for parts of the time when she had been unconscious. She was a little hungry, and I removed all of her tubes. She was back in the land of the living.

There was one major problem. The range of motion exercises had slacked off a bit. Her arms and legs had become frozen with contractures. They were bent at the elbows and knees, and the physical therapist could not straighten them and get her mobile. She had some use of her arms, but she couldn't walk. Tendon release surgery would help, but that was major surgery. She has just come back and I didn't want to lose her on the operating table or to complications. She adapted to a wheelchair, and soon gave Dan a run for his money.

The question remained, where had she been? We were beginning to understand that the brain could sometimes heal itself. Neurons could grow and reconnect or find alternate pathways, but where had her soul been all those months? We were learning a lot about the structure of the brain, but the electrical paths of thoughts and feelings were a big mystery that we were solving so very slowly. I brought Brad in to see her whizzing around, and when my back was turned he borrowed a wheelchair and gave her a race. It was many days later before he asked the question I had been dreading.

"Dad, where was Mrs. Pompa when she was asleep?"

Chapter Fourteen

Brad's sea monster

At one time I owned a duplex not far from the beach on South Padre Island, a favorite vacation resort. I knocked a hole in a wall, put in a door and it became our family home for a couple of years. When the ambulance crew discovered that I was there and available they started bringing patients, 'Just for a quick look' before they drove all the way into town and back. Most problems were minor, and soon I became the first doctor to practice, unwillingly perhaps, on South Padre Island. I was not available during the week, as I had to commute twenty-five miles to my office in town, but I did enjoy helping out on weekends.

    A routine developed. I would be on the beach, supervising the children, with my beeper handy. If a patient showed up at the duplex Jean would give me a beep, and I would gather the gang of two kids and a collie dog and walk the half a block back home. The patient was often dressed in a bathing suit with sand on their feet, and so was I. Jean was quite happy with her fancy sewing machine, but she would come and chaperone me if the patient was female. Then back to the beach, until Jean beeped us for lunch. The kids loved it. The surf board that Bradley dragged down to the ocean was a lot longer than he was tall, but he was as happy as a clam., spending all of his free time in the water. I was not quite as happy. I was starting to see some of the water hazards that lurked in the inviting water so popular with swimmers.

I knocked another hole in a wall and set up small rooms as waiting room, exam. room and office, and I became an expert at treating people in pain inflicted by the sea monsters. I never saw a shark bite, but I did my best to educate the children in the dangers lurking in the shallows. I showed them how to stamp hard when they walked in the water, to warn any lingering stingray fish lying flat on the sand that they were coming, and to keep a sharp lookout for any jelly fish or their tentacles. Both species could inflict extreme pain.

The Portuguese Man of War, the jelly fish was quite common. After high tide there were several of them, looking like balloons blown up, almost clear with an attractive iridescent blue sheen. Inviting to the touch, but covered with a poisonous jelly designed to deter ocean predators. It burned like hell.

The patient seeking fun in the sun would be in great pain.

"I saw this pretty looking football and I couldn't resist giving it a kick. Now my whole foot is on fire."

"Okay," I would say. "The first thing is to wash off the very sticky jelly with rubbing alcohol. The poison is in little bags in the jelly which explode and shoot the poison into the victim."

After I had done that, I explained.

"The poison has started to eat into your skin, and we need to neutralize it. Now we use some high tech neutralizing enzymes."

Their eyebrows would go up when I picked up a container of meat tenderizer, usually Adolf's.

"Sprinkle this where it hurts. You can also apply it to any steak you have on hand. After about 20 minutes wash it off. By then your steak should be ready to grill, and the poison of the Portuguese Man of War should be neutralized."

The pain relief from these simple remedies was dramatic. This was before the days of Google, and the early search engines did not overwhelm you with so many conflicting opinions. The world is now plugged in, and words of wisdom from Australia and all over can be contradictory.

Even more painful was an attack from a stingray, acting purely in self defense. The flat fish is lying peacefully on the sand under the sea when an offending foot stomps near it. Up comes the short tail at the rear and the sharp end is stabbed into the presumed attacker. It is covered with a poison that produces one of the worst pains known to man.

It often started with a phone call.

"Doc, I was stabbed in the foot by something and it hurts worse than my kidney stone did."

"Where are you?"

"At the XYZ hotel. I'm coming right over."

"Put your foot in hot water first. For about fifteen minutes. That will neutralize the poison quickly. The pain is as severe as a bad heart attack and hot water will really take a lot of the pain away. Then come and see me."

After I had been doing this for a couple of years I got the hotels and the ambulance crews trained. They thought it was hogwash at first, but one or two cases convinced them.

At my little clinic I would ask about allergies, and if it still hurt I would stab in some local anesthetic. I might have to dig into the wound to make sure that I had got all of the poison and bits of the stinger out while I heard the rest of their medical history.

"This is worse than my heart attack' would probably make me reach for the morphine, plus a tetanus shot if needed and antibiotics and pain pills and a call to the ambulance for a ride to the hospital. Most healthy young patients working on a suntan would be given detailed instructions for follow up and I seldom saw them again.

In spite of my in house medical expertise, another sea monster gave Bradley a wound that needed long-term hospital care.

At one end of our street was the ocean, at the other end was the bay between the mainland and South Padre Island. Jim's Pier ran tourist fishing boats to favorite spots in the bay for half day cruises and a mess of trout. Fishermen from the deep sea boats also docked, and cleaned their fish. The insides and trimmings were rich pickings for the scavenger fish, which in turn attracted small boys with fishing lines. One day Bradley hooked a small catfish, a monster all of eight inches long, and soon it was flapping on the dock. He couldn't get his hook out easily. Always impatient, he lifted his foot to stomp on it and then get the hook out. He had ignored the sharp pointed one inch dorsal spine, which went through his plastic flip flop and into his foot. All the way to the bone, where it became stuck. Finally, pulling hard he jerked it free, threw it back into the water in disgust, and limped home. The spine had been covered with a poisonous slime, and hot water would have helped, had he known.

From the story I knew that the poisonous spine had gone through the layers of tendons, nerves, arteries and veins, and from the location I knew that it had lodged in the distal end of the first metatarsal bone, the big one leading to the big toe.. The bone would have to be exposed and scraped clean. Opening up either the hand or the foot is a delicate operation. The comparable area on the hand is known as "No man's land," an area entered only by a hand surgeon. I phoned one of my specialist friends, arranged to meet him at the hospital and we all left the sunny beach to spend our Saturday waiting on Bradley.

When the surgery was over, I picked up crutches and a bunch of potent antibiotics, and we headed back to the beach. At first Brad enjoyed the novelty of hopping around on crutches, but they didn't work at all well on sand. So, the beach and swimming and surfing were out. Brad was a bit hyperactive at the best of times, and looking after a wounded young lion would have been a comparative walk in the park.

"Dad, it doesn't hurt much when I walk on it. Watch me."

Soon after the stitches were out, the surgeon got a bone scan. This showed a small patch of infection in the bone. In those days the only way to get enough antibiotic into an area of osteomyelitis was with high dose intravenous antibiotics, which meant a stay in hospital.

I was sorely tempted to leave town.

"Brad, this is an IV line to get medicine into your foot. It must not be moved or pulled out or they will have to stick another one into you."

"Brad, when we let you loose in a wheelchair yesterday you knocked over a nurses medicine cart, and you were doing wheelies in the corridors. Some of the patients and visitors are old, and they can't move fast to get out of the way."

"Brad, the patients in the rooms in the wing across the way are complaining about the bright lights flashing in through their windows. Give me the mirror, and don't sweet talk a nurse into getting you another one."

I truly was sorely tempted to leave town.

That was part of the problem. Bradley's charm was irresistible, and he had the gift of the gab. He had an equal appeal to the young and pretty nurses and to the older motherly ones, and they seemed to take turns aiding and abetting his pranks. My office phone was always ringing.

"Doctor, it's the hospital. About Brad."

Sometimes his mother took the torture, but when she could she willingly handed the baton to me when I was free.

I never did tell him about my only stay in a hospital. As a young boy I had made an unwise turn on my bike, and a car had dragged me underneath it along the road, scraping my knee down to the bone on the macadam. The skin grafts and stitches kept me bedridden, and I persuaded the pretty night nurse in the rural hospital that my mother had always given me a goodnight kiss to help me sleep. I was fourteen, and hormones were running wild. Normally I was very shy with girls, and this worked to my advantage with these angels of mercy, who were truly interested in the patients welfare. I did look like a shy, innocent young boy as I slowly turned the goodnight kiss into an embrace of passion every night. When I was allowed to get out of bed, and stood taller than the nurse she realized that to this innocent young boy looked on her as more than a mother figure. She turned a bright red, and kept me at arms length ever after. No, I never did tell that story to Bradley.

The agony finally came to an end. Brad had turned the hospital completely upside down and inside out. He was continually making new friends with other patients within wheelchair distance, running errands for them, legal and otherwise. He was on a first name basis with all the hospital technicians that came to take portable Xrays or give physical therapy, and he did his best to help every one of them, whether they wanted him to or not. "The Doctor's Son" became a living legend in his own time, and unfortunately the name was the same as mine. His mischief was always defused by his charm, and he had a great time. The first thing he asked as we took him out of the hospital was

"Dad, when can we go fishing?"

* * *

More on Brad and Jewel will appear in Book 2. Both got married, and produced a wonderful variety of grandchildren from James to Jolie, Ashley to Brandon. All unique in their talents for mischief, and later accomplishments, all so fascinating to watch as different genes expressed themselves.

Jerry

One medical family gave me more worries and more problems than any other. And became good friends as well. Every member of the family had a different problem in a different body system, and to see them in the office was both a delight and a challenge. I poked and prodded every part of their anatomies, dosed them with medications or repaired them. Sometimes I had to share them with specialists, who remembered them well many years later. The cardiologist Doctor Cockins always greeted me with,
"Hello John. How is Ben these days? Remember when we made you go to Stage 5 with a stress cardiogram.?"
Ben, the father had just had a stress test, and he and Doctor Cockins told me that Ben had reached Stage 5 before I went for my own stress EKG. Stage 5 was the highest level, with a horribly steep incline on the treadmill. The track was racing along at an Olympic speed. I barely survived to

complete Stage 5, puffing and with legs hurting when Doctor Cockins grinned

"Ben only really got up to Stage 3. I was kidding. We knew you would want to try to beat him."

This was not quite grounds for justifiable homicide, but it was a close call.

The one with the most eye-catching routine was the mother, Jerry, She would burst through the doors of my emergency clinic and yell

"Get the EKG and Dr. Rogans."

She already had her blouse off and as she raced through the waiting room she stripped to the waist, yelling all the time for a cardiogram. and for me. In the waiting room patients went into shock from this wild striptease as the crazy woman took off her clothes, yelling all the time.

She was screaming in pain. She had a condition that gave her severe chest pain which was exactly like a heart attack. Sometimes I had put her in ICU because of the severe chest pain, even though the cardiogram was normal. Before I knew the diagnosis it was dangerous to ignore the pressure like pains so typical of a heart attack. Jerry knew that I wanted a cardiogram. before I treated her, and she wanted it as soon as possible. The pain had started slowly, not very bad but had increased to a crescendo in the car on the way to the office and became unbearable.

A sub-specialist out of town finally made the diagnosis of spasm of her swallowing tube, her esophagus. He had to lower a special tube down her throat to measure the pressures in her esophagus to prove the diagnosis. Life became much simpler. When she felt a spasm starting she simply swallowed an anti-spasm pill and drove sedately to the office. The days of the drama and the strip show were over, and the waiting room was never the same.

She still stripped quietly in the exam. room, when I had to examine her breasts. They were largish, nicely shaped and would have held their own in Playboy. For a doctor, they were a nightmare. Searching for a pea sized lump that could be a cancer was nigh on impossible. They were really deadly booby traps.

Her sixteen-year-old daughter developed the same syndrome, and before I could get the diagnosis pinned down she went through the same routine. Exactly like a heart attack, rare - but not impossible at her age.

Another problem with Jerry was that she had a severe allergy to shrimp. Iodine, the active ingredient could send her into shock. Once she badly needed a diagnostic Xray study that involved an intravenous injection of iodine. For this I sent her up to a special diagnostic center in Houston, where there could be every type of specialist on call. There would be the radiologist and an allergist and an anesthesiologist all immediately available with all sorts of life saving drugs on hand.

She was loaded up with meds to prevent an allergy reaction, the specialists hovered, and the iodine was injected. Nothing happened, and she smiled happily. I had urged them to keep her for several days, in case there was a delayed reaction, and this they did. She flew back three days later, normal and happy and relaxed. Shortly after she returned, she started getting symptoms of an allergy reaction, and phoned me. She was starting to have a very tight chest and problems breathing. The preventative meds they had given her had worked too well and lasted too long but there was still iodine in her system. I called an ambulance then jumped into my car with a bag full of medications and sped round to her house. My foot was hard on the gas as I gave the engine a Stage 5 stress test.

I got there before the ambulance and gave her adrenalin and other good stuff and she was recovering on the way to the ER. My engine never did recover, and I couldn't claim a new transmission on her medical insurance. They had been very good with some of our other experiences, but I thought that a mechanics bill would be too much. Things evened out, and I enjoyed many a happy meal with the family which more than compensated for the loss of a transmission.

Her husband Ben had been a football player, and college football gave him many problems in later life. But it wasn't his knees, or his back or any other part of him that had been abused by football that springs to mind. Instead I remember a flying piece of a screwdriver and a collision with a dishwasher, He was hammering away in his workshop when an unfortunate blow of his hammer hit a screwdriver with sufficient force to fracture the steel. A piece of the screwdriver went flying and with unlucky accuracy hit his lower lip. It penetrated the skin and the obicularis muscle and was protruding like a modern metal ornament, long before they were popular.

"It does improve your manly appearance, Ben," I commented. "Maybe we should leave it there. You would get plenty of sympathy."

His comments were mildly obscene, and I removed the piece of steel, irrigated the wound and finished with a suture and a tetanus shot.

Our next little adventure started early one Sunday morning when he slipped in the kitchen of their home. I am not sure of the details, but I think the floor was wet and in the dark he slipped and fell. A sharp edge of the dishwasher collided with the bridge of his nose. For various reasons he did not want to go to the ER.

"John, could I come over to your place? It really is a small thing, and perhaps you could fix it there."

"Sure, come on over. I have a bag full of things and a suture set. Maybe trade for a cup of coffee, if you could pick up one on the way."

Jerry drove him over, and she became the ER nurse. He lay down on the dining table. With the instruments at hand

I injected some anesthetic, and the fun began. The face is a very vascular place, well supplied with all sorts of blood vessels. Anyone who has had a scalp or a facial injury will attest that they bled like the proverbial stuck pig. The wound was not too serious, and pressure stopped the bleeding. Sticking in a needle and squirting in local anesthetic started things up again and the blood gushed out. There was very little trimming to do, but as I worked on the wound I felt something warm on my feet. The blood had run down his face, across the table and was making a big pool on the floor. Jerry found the mop and was soon busy keeping the floor clean. Luckily it was varnished wood, and not wall to wall carpet; that would have been harder to manage.

When I finished, Ben insisted on sitting up. The table had not been too comfortable, and he wanted to stretch before I cleaned up. He was not a pretty sight, with blood drying in wide streaks down his face. He looked like a refugee from a chain saw movie, or the victim of an assault with a sharp instrument, which he was. Amazingly he was left with just a small horizontal scar on the bridge of his nose, looking like a laugh line or a wrinkle. This was another encounter that never got to the insurance company. There was no billing code for surgery on the kitchen table.

Chapter Fifteen

Tale of Two Doctors

They were both born in England. One went to med school there, the other emigrated to Canada and studied medicine there. This produced two very different doctors. We will call them Doctor Brit and Doctor C.
    The Canadian system was similar to that in the US. Lots of theory, many big books to memorize, and Dr.C started practice in the 1970's using all the new lab tests, Xrays and the latest miracle diagnostic tool, the CAT Scanner. The Brit became a very different doctor. The British tradition was typified by the fictional Sherlock Holmes. Conan Doyle had trained as a doctor and had studied under a professor in med school who was brilliant at observing details, deducing and making an amazing diagnosis that completely surprised his students. Conan Doyle took these skills, added some eccentric idiosyncracies and created Sherlock Holmes.

Thus Dr. Brit started with great clinical skills, but knew less about pharmacology and lab tests than the Canadian, who thought in terms of proving a diagnosis with lab tests and Xrays. After they had been in practice for a couple of years both picked up the skills of the other, but still maintained their different biases. Dr. Brit had also practiced under the watchful eye of the British National Health Service. Tests cost money, and were sternly discouraged. This enormous difference of attitude may have proved fatal.

The two met in Brownsville, and became great friends, with common backgrounds and a national heritage of which they were proud. In Texas both became Americanized, but still followed cricket scores and soccer wars. They enjoyed racquetball, with the quick reflexes and speed involved, usually followed by a beer or two. They felt ambivalent on July 4th, as they came from the land that had oppressed the Colonists, but they both admitted that one of the things that had driven them from England, their Garden of Eden, was the snobbish class system. Both would have rebelled against Mad King George.

Dr. C learnt a lot from Dr. Brit, who was the better clinical diagnostician, but Dr. C worried sometimes that Dr. Brit's bias against tests could be harmful. Once an attorney returned from a trip to a big city where he had to visit a doctor, and of course had many tests done. One showed a high serum calcium, which he showed to Dr. Brit.

"Don't worry about that," said Dr. Brit. "That's one of the new tests, and the meaning is not yet clear. Better to rely on your actual state of health. You are active, and chase tennis balls around in the blazing sun. That is a better test of your cardiovascular system, and I can't find a thing wrong with you. Come back in a year, or if you have any symptoms."

This was when we were just learning that a high level of calcium might mean that calcium was settling in the coronary arteries. The attorney went for a second opinion, which led to thorough testing and a cardiac bypass. Although he had no symptoms, his arteries were critically blocked. There was no law suit. Dr. Brit was a truly warm and kind man and his patients loved him. He never had a malpractice lawsuit against him.

The Canadian system came at a price. About nine percent of GDP. The British system cost much less, about six percent of GDP. Both were state controlled systems, with health care rationing and many horror stories of harm to patients. Dr. C's aunt, in England, was put on a waiting list after a heart attack for a coronary arteriogram. In the US this was normally done the next day, to see if another massive heart attack is pending. Similar rules in Canada often resulted in patients being shipped across the border to the US. Dr.C's aunt had a second heart attack during her 'waiting period,' and was put on an 'emergency' waiting list of about six weeks. She didn't make it, and a third heart attack killed her. This saved the National Health Service about $30,000 for the test and the bypass. Saving money by rationing care is a hot button issue throughout medicine.

The system in the US is horrendously expensive, costing about sixteen percent of GDP, as all patients demand the very best whatever the cost, and there are precious few controls on doctors ordering repeat CAT scans. Plus a bad outcome usually triggers a huge malpractice suit, even if the medical skills are beyond reproach. With the lawyer collecting his forty percent of the award doctors may feel forced to practice preventive medicine, ordering tests in self defense.

Another patient had blinding headaches, with all the characteristics of migraines. After a thorough exam. Dr. Brit treated her with migraine specific meds, and injections of strong narcotics for the occasional severe blinding headache spasms. Two years later an artery in her brain burst, and she was found dead in bed. His British training had made him reject any expensive tests that might have uncovered the cause of the migraine.

It was at about this time that doctors were becoming aware of the late effects of smoking on arteries. Dr. C had had several patients who had smoked, then quit, and some twenty years later had problems with blocked arteries. Ladies with fainting spells plus a bruit, a whooshing noise that indicated a narrowing, in their carotid arteries he referred to a vascular surgeon. He scrubbed in when the surgeon opened up the neck, and uncovered then opened the carotid artery. They found a tough, brown layer on the inside of the artery. It had narrowed the vessel, reducing the flow of blood to the brain. The surgeon peeled this thick, leathery layer from the inside of the artery and restored normal flow. Without surgery, if the patient was lucky and some blood still got through, only a dizzy spell followed. A severe blockage could lead to a massive stroke.

If this happened in the heart the symptom might be angina. Or not. Dr. C was at a Halloween party and a friend asked him to dance the polka. This was a violent 'one, two, three hop' sort of dance and after six minutes of energetic hopping the lady friend said

"My heart is racing to beat the band. Here, feel it." She took the doctors hand to place it on her chest. Her cleavage was inviting, but he diverted his hand and took her pulse at the wrist. Instead of a normal seventy two it was racing at two hundred beats a minute.

"Any chest pain," he asked.

"No. Just a bit short of breath."

"Let's sit down. You need a cardiogram.."

Woman do not to always have chest pain for a heart problem. Maybe a back pain, or shortness of breath. She flunked the EKG and the stress test, and was sent for cardiac imaging, which showed major blockages in four vessels. She had a quadruple bypass, and lived for many years afterwards.

She enjoyed those years with her children and grandchildren. She took them fishing, and played cards well after their bedtimes. It was a cancer that killed her, not any blocked blood vessels. She had smoked for thirty years, and had quit twenty years before dancing the almost deadly polka. She had never had a chest pain in her life.

The evidence that late blockages years after quitting smoking caused problems was slowly mounting. Dr. Brit had smoked heavily during med student days, but had quit, thirty long years before a period of intense stress occurred. It concerned one of his adult children. Calls in the middle of the night to get her out of jail, calls to a judge friend to avert prosecution, these were all starting to build up. He still played violent racquetball, for hours, three times a week. He was made of solid muscle, and bumping into him on the court was like hitting a brick wall. This game was a more severe test of his heart than any stress test, and he consistently beat all but the pros, including Dr. C. To counter the additional stress he upped this from three times a week to six. The mild heartburn he occasionally felt he diagnosed as 'stress gastritis.' His clinical suspicion of a more severe problem was low, and he never went against his long apprenticeship under the National Health System to do a cardiogram. on himself.

Dr. C was aware of the stress, and later felt extremely guilty that he had never pressed Dr. Brit harder for details of the 'heartburn.' Dr. Brit mentioned it one time only, and then insisted that "it was nothing." Doctors make lousy patients, and Dr. Brit was no exception. He always pushed away any enquiries into his health, which he said he knew better than anyone. Not long afterwards, Dr. Brit was found, dressed for racquetball down to his white tennis shoes, laces neatly knotted. He was lying on his bed, smiling, and dead. If he had trained under the Canadian system, he might possibly still be alive. Who knows? The pathways of life are strange indeed. Dr. C smoked part of one cigarette at age eleven, didn't like

it, and quit at age eleven. Yet all around smoking was the norm. It was an easy habit to acquire, and a hard one to quit.
There was standing room only at Dr. Brit's funeral. He was a lovely man, adored by his children, and well loved by both patients and colleagues. One of natures truly good persons. Dr. C lived on for more than fifteen years. Such a pity that the truth about nicotine took fifty years of publicity and education to become widely known.

My Fair Lady

Inside Brownsville's Camille Theater the house lights were dim, it was dark and mysterious, but an empty theater has a special atmosphere, from all the crowds that had laughed and cried there, from the amateur thespians who had donned costumes and make-up to perform on stage. The three hundred red plush seats were empty, except for three figures way down in the second row. A piano was playing, and an actor on stage was singing his heart out.
    This was an audition for 'My Fair Lady', and the actor was singing 'With a Little Bit of Luck'. My feelings exactly, and I slipped into a seat in the back. I knew one of the three. Dr. Larry Siegle, the director, well known and well liked, with a presence that came from many years on stage in New York. I didn't know the others but the pianist was familiar. It was my wife. She had been slipping out of the house all week to come and play for the auditions. She played well, but then she had been to an excellent school of music in her native New England. Tonight was the last night, and my curiosity had been too great.

"Thank you very much", said Larry to the actor. "That was great, well done! We will let you know." Before calling "Next" he got up and stretched, and looked round. He saw me, even in the dim light.

"John," he exclaimed. "What are you doing back there? Come down and join us." Soon we were chatting away.

"This is the last night of auditions, and we only have to choose Professor Higgins and the dustman, Alfie Doolittle. Stick around. You'll find it fun, with all these actors trying to speak proper English."

I didn't want to tell him how poorly they were doing, but after we had chatted some more he looked at me.

"John, why don't you try out? You speak such beautiful English."

"Larry, I'm not an actor, plus they have to sing and dance. I can't act, I can't sing, and I can't dance."

"That's no problem. We will teach you."

I objected strongly about my immense lack of talent, but once Larry had made up his mind he became confident and persuasive. I felt his presence beginning to envelope me, and eventually I said "Okay, I'll try."

"Here, just take these two pages."

A few words of dialogue, and the words to the song. I climbed onto the stage, and went to give the pianist a hug. She frowned in surprise, then smiled, and nodded to center stage for me to get on with it.

It was fun. 'A little bit of luck.' It was my philosophy of life, and I gave them a genuine Cockney accent. By the end I was even doing a little dance, a small chain step, very simple.

Larry was still clapping when I came down.

"That was perfect", he gushed. "That part is just you. You've got the part. Congratulations."

I was still shaking my head when he had an inspiration. "You know, John, you would be perfect for Henry

Higgins. Why don't you read for the part? It's the best one in the play. You'd be the star."

"Larry, be real. You've seen I can't sing, and I could never remember all those lines. I've seen the movie. At least Doolittle only has two songs, and a couple of short scenes. Higgins is on every page of the script, and he has, what, eight songs?"

So I ended up with the plum, small 'starring' role of Alfie Doolittle, a common dustman. Sliding down the social scale again, but it was getting easier every time. A few of the actors that had been regulars on this amateur stage many times were initially peeved that this juicy little part had gone to an outsider, and we were soon part of a team..

Next came a full script read through for the 'stars.' Eliza was there, Higgins, Colonel Pickering, Freddy and me. We sat in a circle in the Green Room, clutching our scripts. Except Higgins. He was being played by a very mature high school senior, Joe, and Joe had no script.

"I don't need it", he said when Larry asked. Joe was good looking, the youngest one there, but he seemed very confident.

And he didn't need the script. We read through the whole play, muffing our lines, coming in too late after a cue, all except for Joe. He was word perfect, and knew everyone's lines backwards.

As we moved towards the dress rehearsal he grew into the part, and became more mature every time. Then it was costume, make up, a small 'orchestra' in the pit, and we were on. The first performance was for the First Nighters, who had paid extra to see the pre-performance show, always a bit rough, with lost lines, stage craft still a bit jagged, and a few off key notes from the 'orchestra.'

I was having a ball. Half singing, half talking my songs as I belted them out, dance steps and all, with vigor. I always forgot my lines and improvised, and they came out different every time, except that somehow I almost always ended up with the correct cue line for the next performer. At the end of my second song, 'Get me to the church on time,' I was carried out, horizontally, on a six hands held high. Rather like a bunch of pall-bearers with hands that were just a bit shaky and slippery. I was certain that one time I would drop crashing to the floor, but, that's show business. And I never did, and they always remembered to hand me a rose to hold as an ensign for my triumphal exit.

We played to packed houses, with standing room only as the word of mouth got around. I had a lot of free time, sitting in the green room with my books. Larry paid me the compliment of asking me to play Henry Higgins in Pygmalion later in the season, but I knew that that was way too much for my limited talents.

It was fun all the way through, and the only minor let down came about a week later when I was working, as an Emergency Room doctor. One evening the nurse gave me a chart, and told me about the ten year old girl with bad asthma in exam. room two.

"Her mother's with her. Give me a shout if you need the nebulizing tent."

When I walked into the room the girl sat up, with horror on her face.

"Mummy, that's the dustman. I want a real doctor", and she wouldn't have anything to do with me. At least, I thought, my performance had been realistic for someone.

Chapter Sixteen

The End of The Affair.

Divorce is too painful to talk about. I was to blame for many things, I was far from perfect. It was bitter, very expensive and Jean left town with our little girl to go back to Vancouver. Bradley was left with me. To regain my sanity I took us both down to Cancun, to the Club Med. We had a great time, and came back refreshed. I carried on, as Dad to Brad and hired a Mexican housekeeper to help and life went on.

A year later Jean phoned.

"I had a vision", she said. "I have to come back to you." I didn't know Baptists had visions, but there was no stopping her. She took an apartment nearby, and was soon visiting often, even taking over the cooking. That was too much for the maid, and she quit. In a flash, Jean had moved into the housekeeper's room. I had objections, but they didn't count.

"It is best for the children," she said. And it was true, they were much happier to have Mum and Dad back together. This was the dream. of most kids when their parents split apart. Even if I was keeping my distance from Jean. I could not forget the vicious testimony in the court room.

Life went on, and the only one not quite happy was me. Impossible though it may seem, Jean could be as bossy as me. I tried to keep my dejection to myself. It was Jean that brought things to a head, about eight months later.

"We can't go on like this", she said. "We should make things legal. That way the children won't have to explain things to their friends." True, the kids were happy, and for me time had healed some of the bitterness, but I was absolutely in no hurry to do the marriage gig again. Jean kept up the pressure, and she issued an ultimatum.

"Either we get married, or I go back to Canada. This time I will take both of the children, and you can't stop me." That ultimatum was too painful to think of and It sowed the seed of a conflict to come. I caved in. A small consolation was that I chose the date. For our first wedding I had chosen February 14th, partly because it was romantic, partly because I would always get reminders of our anniversary. This time I chose November 11th, Armistice Day, the very day that war ceased in 1918. The truce was cool. Celibacy and sadness.

We had been remarried nearly two years when I was asked to do a three month locum job in Saudi Arabia. One of the ER docs there had a family emergency. I had been looking into getting away from Texas.

Over there I spent most of my free time reading the Bible. I was still a bit of a Baptist, and I was looking in the good Book for reasons for divorce. There was one, one only - adultery. That was no good, but being apart had clarified my determination to end the affair. I phoned her from Dharan.

"I am very sorry, Jean, but I can't go on like this. When I come back, I want a divorce." There was a brief silence, then a long string of angry words. No way did she want to change.

"If you think the last divorce was rough, just wait and see what happens this time." She immediately moved out of the house, Bradley was in boarding school, and our collie dog went to the kennel. Lassie type dogs are emotionally sensitive, and with no friends visiting for months, she died. Friends came in later to check on the house.

"The house is a mess, and the food left in the refrigerator is covered with green mold."

I came back in January, just in time for Brad's lonely birthday in boarding school, then stopped in Houston to hire an expert divorce lawyer.

Divorce war stories are always a bore. I ended up with custody of both children. After many years of reflection I know now that that my taking custody was a mistake. Mothers, even foolish ones, are better at raising children, but at the time I couldn't stand the thought of not seeing both of them. It was fitting that my next theatrical adventure in Brownsville was as Jason, the hero in the Greek tragedy of Medea. When she finds that her Jason wants out, her anger is so murderous that she kills as many of the cast as she can, including her own two children.

Alice in Saudi Land.

I had been bitten by the acting bug. I was always willing to make a fool of myself. I knew that I had no talent, but fooling around on stage like a complete idiot had become addictive.

The next episode of my acting career would take place in Saudi Arabia.

"Doctor Rogans, this is Medcom Recruiting in Los Angeles. Are you still interested in working in Saudi Arabia?" I had put out some enquiries. Arabia had seemed exotic, lucrative, with a hint of danger. And this was long before the Gulf Wars.

"Yes, I'm still interested."

"One of our ER docs in Dharan has a family emergency. Could you fill in for three months? Fare, food and rent paid, of course." I only had one question.

"When?"

"Yesterday, as soon as possible. And would you do us a favor - they are running very low on an injectable anesthetic. Could you take a box of vials with you?"

The plane stopped for customs clearance at Jeddah, the entry port for pilgrims going to Mecca. We were not pilgrims. The villainous customs guards with ferocious black mustaches and AK 47s knew we were a bunch of barbaric infidels and treated us accordingly. The short, portly woman in front of me was not a Saudi. Probably coming in to do domestic work, which was beneath the Saudis. She carried all of her belongings in a circular straw mat folded up with handles at the sides.

The customs officer waved his AK threateningly and made her dump all the contents on a table. Mainly intimate clothing and a few personal belongings. He shouted at her, enjoying her embarrassment so much that he passed me through with a single contemptuous gesture. The one hundred vials of injectable narcotic could have landed me in jail, or on the next plane out. That happened to one businessman who forgot the one airline size miniature bottle of whiskey that he had in his pocket, enough to have him thrown out of the country.

I had been traveling East, but they put my jetlagged body to work right away.

"We get some nasty road accidents. Young men with money and fast cars drag race outside the city. They can't drink or date girls, so that's how they get their thrills."

The broken limbs and ugly lacerations were similar to the ones in any emergency room, but if I suspected that alcohol was involved, I soon learnt to sniff loudly, look suspicious, then leave the room. When I came back five minutes later the patient had gone, taken to a private doctor who wouldn't have to report him.

The hardest job was evaluating a sore throat. A young woman was always brought in by her husband, plus there was an interpreter who relayed my questions. To the husband, who asked the woman, then if her replies were acceptable passed them to the interpreter. A lump in a breast, a pain in the pelvis were no problem. If I asked, she took off all her clothes. Anything above the neck was a problem. One had a sore throat.

"I want to look in her mouth."

Not possible. Even if the husband told her to, there was no way she would lift her veil in front of strange men.

The hospital was in Dharan, and the Western staff lived in an apartment building in Al Khobar. This was long before the Gulf Wars, and the religious police, the matawa, enjoyed doing a thorough job of watching the infidels. One was stationed on every floor outside the elevator. Single men to the right, married couples and single women to the left, no exceptions. Two police cars were always parked outside. The nurses going to the store wore long sleeves, ankle length dresses and traveled in convoys of two or more. Walk two blocks, turn right, and wait outside a shop window for the man. Then pretend to be married if questioned.

One nurse wanted to visit the 'gold souk', full of shops selling nothing but gold, in a town about twenty miles up the coast. She knew she would get less harassment with a male companion, so we met discreetly and walked to the bus station. The rear of the bus was partitioned off, with a separate entrance for the women, and we made it safely to the souk.

Inside a shop was an Aladdin's treasure cave, walls and counters covered with gleaming, lustrous, shiny solid gold baubles, gold on every wall, nothing baser than 22 carat. Elegant necklaces, brooches and ornaments in exotic Arabian designs, set with priceless precious stones. Probably worth millions, yet the iron bars guarding the windows were less of a deterrent than the punishment given a thief. To have his right hand cut off meant that he would forever have to eat and wipe his backside with his unclean left hand. While my companion was drooling over the shiny metal I asked the owner,

"Is it alright if I take a picture?"

"Only inside, and no heads."

Images of heads were censored from Western magazines, and even pedestrian crossing signs had headless figures walking across the road. My mistake was slipping out to take a photo of the shop front. I checked to be sure there were no humans anywhere near, but just as I clicked I saw in the view finder a Saudi male walking by. He heard the click then gestured and cussed vigorously and strode off. My sigh of relief was premature. He was back in a flash with two soldiers, armed with AK 47s.

I had heard tales of Westerners caught breaking the law being carted to the station, stripped and interrogated before being thrown in jail or out of the country. My friendly smiles may have helped, or my Guardian Angel spoke Arabic. The film was stripped from the camera, and to my surprise I was let free, and even allowed to keep the camera.

Many customs were different. Before operating on a Saudi Prince or General a Western surgeon would have in his pocket an airline ticket and an exit visa out of the country. Any complication after a surgery could be very dangerous for the surgeon. Getting an exit visa would become impossible. They hoped for the best, and prepared for the worst. After a successful operation it was a different story. A big box would arrive at the ward, full of Rolex watches. Gold, inlaid with diamonds for the surgeon and down to stainless steel for the nursing assistants.

Being invited to a Prince's home was a high honor, and my friend the scrub nurse took me along as a chaperone. A male servant let us in, and we just saw the wives scurrying away to the back of the house. Then the Prince asked,

"What would you like to drink? I have all the usual poisons, gin, Scotch, rum, you name it."

The nurse and I exchanged glances. Was this a test, a trap? Would we be hauled away if we indulged? The Prince smiled.

"Please. I am. your friend. Do have a drink with me."

The Princes and Generals were a breed apart, above the law.

One case was hopeless. A little girl was born with thick, scaly skin which had dried and cracked and resembled the scales of a fish. Before oil and foreigners had come to Arabia she would have been buried in the sand and left. The condition is called icthyosis, from the fish like appearance, and severe cases are hopeless. The mouth was large and round and open. She had no external nose, but two holes where the nose should have been. There were no ears, just holes. The hands and feet appeared to be swollen, were cramped up and felt quite hard. She lived about forty-eight hours.

As Muslims the men were allowed four wives, but when I asked a young fighter pilot who had trained in the US he snorted.

"After a woman has been spoilt in America, one wife is too many."

I treated one of his brother officers who had made a simple mistake on the runway just before takeoff in his jet fighter. He pressed the 'eject' button, and flew about twenty feet into the air. Luckily he was still strapped in his seat wearing his helmet, and suffered nothing worse than a battered ego on landing.

The muezzin's call for prayer came five times a day, over loudspeakers high on mosque towers, and things could be tricky. Once I was in a supermarket pushing a cart of groceries. Cash registers closed and carts were abandoned as the faithful hurried away to pray. Another time I was in a barber's chair, and he had cropped all the hair from the left of my head when the call for prayer came. It looked most peculiar, and I asked "What now?"

He put his finger to his lips, pulled down the window blinds, and finished shearing on the right. He knew there would be no tip if I had left half sheared.

Entertainment for the ex-pats was mainly home made, which is how I came to spend a month rehearsing and performing in Alice in Wonderland in Muslim Saudi Arabia. In their compound the British Airways crowd had a small theater, and were staging a musical version of 'Alice' for the pantomime just before Christmas, an old English custom. Somehow I heard that the cast was one member short, and that is how I came to be singing and dancing as the Third Gardener, having a lot of fun.

Chapter Seventeen

More matrimony

It was not a lot of fun going back to the States. The travel was pleasurable, via Bahrain, Bangkok and Tokyo, completing my trip around the world. I had a pocket full of money, and it was a delight to visit Bradley in his boarding school. But then to Houston, to hire an expert lawyer. My pockets emptied as the money flowed to his bank account. Then to Brownsville and the empty house. My beloved Collie, Min, left in a kennel, was dead. Jean had rented a house, and I was only allowed to see my daughter Julia occasionally while we went through with the divorce. In the end I was given custody of both children by the jury, and Jean was given custody of all of the assets by the judge. Jean wanted to sell our house, and I had to move out. I should have learned my lesson.

I was a fairly good looking doctor, rather broke, but

with prospects. And with two young children to raise. She was a tall, willowy blonde OB nurse, also with two children to raise. It seemed logical, and it lasted nine months. Hindsight told me that I should have looked for a psych profile. On both parties. I was far from perfect, but I didn't realize this in the early days.

Medea

As Wikipedia explains, Medea is a woman in Greek mythology. She was the daughter of King Aeëtes of Colchis, niece of Circe, granddaughter of the sun god Helios, and later wife to the hero Jason, with whom she had two children, Mermeros and Pheres. In Euripides's play Medea, Jason leaves Medea when Creon, king of Corinth, offers him his daughter, Glauce. The play tells of how Medea gets her revenge on her husband for this betrayal, even killing her two children to spite Jason.

  Not exactly a gripping modern thriller, but there was something intriguing about doing a Greek Tragedy. I had never even seen one, but afterwards, for what it's worth I could put on my resumé 'Star of Stage, Screen and Radio'. The director was Will Everett, a talented producer with a Golden Voice, as distinctive as the modulated tones of James Stewart. I had listened to his show 'Theme and Variations' which had played for years on National Public Radio. It had a limited distribution, and he planned on putting on two Greek Tragedies to boost his profile. It worked. After they aired, his show went national over National Public Radio.

  The cast were locals, from Port Isabel. It was a small South Texas town, mainly inhabited by shrimp boat captains and their crews yet Will dug up a motley crew of actors with radio credits. I was the lowest on the totem pole, with zero radio experience, but I still had a slight English accent, which sounded different. He put us through rehearsal after rehearsal, smoothing out the rough edges and injecting drama into our wooden readings. One of the final rehearsals was in the conference room of a local bank, and Medea's murderous screams penetrated the glass walls, alarming the customers. We were ready. Will made the final recording, and we all gathered at his house, clutching beers and assorted beverages to listen to the first airing.

To sound authentic on radio may seem easier than strutting the stage in makeup and costume, but it needs just as much acting ability to make it sound realistic and convincing. Most of the cast were nodding happily at the performances, but I was cringing. I sounded like the rank amateur that I was. It was well received, and I was surprised when colleagues came over to me in the hospital and said "Was that you on the radio on Sunday? I couldn't believe my ears."

I was modest and humble, and in this case I had a lot to be humble about.

Ram.

For the moment I will skip a few years. The next memory comes from a time when my children were grown, and had moved to Austin. I was living with Brad, in a separate Grandfather apartment.

Brad has a male sheep, a ram., and with inspired originality he has called him Ram.. He is a special South African breed, about 200 pounds, with a big coat of grey wool on either side, and a head covered with solid concrete six inches thick. He is very aggressive and will charge at anything that moves. He makes big dents in cars, and if he catches you, boy does it hurt.

I certainly don't mind the cat. 'Lucky' is a Siamese, he is always talking, or yowling but he loves everybody. I never notice the tropical fish. The rabbits have their own agenda and they never bother me. The Rottweiler does look horribly ferocious with jaws twelve inches wide full of teeth, but she is an amiable nitwit, loving and not very bright. The Doberman has pointed ears, sharp looking teeth, suspicious and menacing eyes but Misha is a wimp scared of her own shadow, with a sweet personality. She is not a problem. It's the sheep.

My son saw this breed, a Dorper I believe, on the Internet. Three times as big as normal, three times the wool, three times the meat, a good business opportunity. Also useful for eating grass and weeds and he had been loaned to a neighbor for this just this purpose. I came back late on a dark Saturday night and I didn't know he had been tied twenty feet from the gate on a thirty foot rope. My mind was miles away as I was opening the gate when suddenly, out of the black of the night a two hundred pound monster came charging, hooves pounding and he slammed into my leg. His concrete like head crashed into my hip, and boy, it hurt. As I got up, hurting and cursing, he backed off and was ready to charge again, but I hurried inside. I had a new appreciation of a battering ram. smashing into a castle gate. I knew how the gate felt,

The next day, Ram. needed to be moved inside. Outside the fence he was a public menace. My son was away and his wife wouldn't go anywhere near Ram.

"He's mean. He got me once, and I'm not going to give him another chance." I found a long stick to use as a shepherds crook, untied his rope from the fence and led him to a succulent corner of long grass and weeds. He should have been grateful, but I turned my back to him for a split second as I tied his rope to another fence post. He repaid my kindness by charging again, ramming his thick head into exactly the same spot as before. This time it hurt even more. It seems he is programmed to charge anything that does not look like a female sheep, but I was not in the mood to be sympathetic. I was angry, even murderous. I told him very forcibly how I felt about the situation.

     I thought I was done but a cable crossed the patch of ground. He might munch on it or get it tangled in his legs. Just as I was clearing the cable I heard the pounding of hooves. Ram. was galloping again, straight at me. I hadn't realized how wide he was, a great mass of solid muscle with all four hooves digging into the ground as his thick, wooly coat flapped up and down. His eyes were fixed on me and he lowered his thick gray head for the butt. I jumped out of my shoes and yelled mightily and swung the crook in his direction. Luckily he stopped.

     It's not his fault he is such an aggressive idiot. He is genetically programmed to charge at anything that moves. He is full to overflowing with the male hormones which can make males of any species act foolishly, but I do wish my son could choose softer and kinder animals. Why such a mean looking Rottweiler, albeit rather sweet and dumb, an intimidating Doberman, even if she was in fact a wimp and above all why have an aggressive idiot like Ram, with such a thick and painful skull? Why can't my son collect butterflies, or at maybe birds? When I suggested canaries, he grunted derisively. Once Brad has his mind made up, especially about a business proposition, he seldom makes any changes.

Chapter Eighteen

None of the doctors sent bills

In the last few years the public image of the physician has changed, with the kind old family doctor being replaced by a heartless scrooge, his bony hand forever dipping into the patient's pocket. The physicians here in Brownsville, Texas, a city of 120,000 residents that sits on the Texas-Mexico border, are an average lot, no better or worse than most. In the last 6 months of 1988 we were faced with three crises: a collapsed store, a major hurricane, and a flood of refugees from Central America. The story of the doctor's response to one of these disasters was typical.

    Dr. Mike Berg looked like Papa Hemingway, with a bristly white beard and a generous corporation. Quiet, humorous and fond of action, he had been in the first wave of medical help sent in when the US embassy in Beirut was bombed several years before. Now he was washing brick dust out of the eyes of a young volunteer, one of the links in a human chain snaking up the pile of rubble that used to be La Tienda Amiga, a department store in downtown Brownsville. On Thursday, July 7, 1988 a thunderstorm dumped a record amount of rain onto an aging store roof, and it had collapsed.

Berg had been in the emergency room at the hospital kibitzing with the ER doctor when an ambulance raced in to drop off a patient. Then they were en route to downtown. A call had just come in that a building had collapsed during the thunderstorm, and many people were trapped. Berg rushed to the site in the ambulance. The store was a three-storey building whose flat roof had survived many other storms, but this time it had collapsed from back to front, blowing a huge cloud of dust out the front door.

"The lights went out", said a survivor, "then the whole building came down. I just dived under a table."

La Tienda Amiga was now a pile of rubble 2 to 5 meters high, and screams from survivors could be heard. Within minutes teams of ambulance, fire and police workers began hauling out survivors, as well as those that had not been so lucky. Although many more doctors soon arrived, there was not a lot they could do. An empty store across the street was turned into a first aid station, and gradually routines developed amid the confusion. Human chains stretched up over the pile, passing pieces of debris from hand to hand down to the street, where it was loaded onto trucks. With other groups lifting the larger beams and messengers scurrying to and fro it looked like an anthill that had been rudely disturbed.

Keeping these 'ants' healthy became a priority for the medical crew.

"My proudest contribution," said Berg, "was organizing the Gatorade."

With the temperature 35°C and humidity at 66%, conditions were ripe for heat-related syndromes.

"They just wouldn't stop," added Berg. "They were working like fools on that pile without a break because everyone felt there were people underneath."

That pace continued through the night with emergency spotlights. The medical teams catnapped on cots, then returned to treating minor injuries as workers arrived from the human chains. In the early hours of the morning someone thought he'd heard a cry beneath the rubble.

"Hush" was called, and the area became as quiet as a sound stage. Nothing. Work resumed, only to be 'hushed' again. This time there was a sound, and a hole was started.

Slowly, carefully, a little girl was pulled out alive, apparently unharmed. She was rushed to hospital. More survivors were found, but it was agonizingly slow work.

"They've tunneled through the rubble," said a police spokesman. "Basically, it's digging them out without killing them."

By 8:30 am they had checked all of the possible leads and had pulled out six in total. There was a mother, her 8-year-old son and 13-year-old niece. The mother was fine, but the boy's kidneys had been crushed - rhabdomyolysis developed and he needed dialysis. The girl's right leg was amputated below the knee.

By noon, nearly 24 hours after the collapse, the top layer of tangled rubble had been removed. The temperature rose again and it was like laboring in a sauna bath. Falling bricks crushed fingers and toes, rusty, twisted steel tore through clothing and drew blood, and thick dust got into eyes and lungs. Doctors and nurses came to the aid station in informal shifts. It was now run by a nurse, Tammy Cowen, who had commandeered enough equipment from her employer to set up a small field hospital.

As the second evening came there were occasional

calls for silence but no more sounds were heard. By now a crane was lifting the larger pieces of concrete and as these were pulled loose heavy fragments crashed onto the pile. Onlookers shuddered, wondering what was below.

Help came from all over. Sniffer dogs scrambled over the wreckage but made no finds. A mine emergency expert arrived from Pittsburgh. From California came a sophisticated minicamera mounted on a flexible tube, the kind used in mining disasters. It snaked about in the depths of the rubble, seeking out bodies. By Sunday, hope was gone for any more survivors.

"We have checked and double checked and quadruple checked", said Walter Plitt, whose company supplied the crane. "There are no more survivors."

He gave the word for the bulldozers. They started to scoop up the beams and bricks and each time their blades tore at the pile the question was, "Could Walter be wrong?" He wasn't. The site was cleared down to the slab.

In all, 14 people had died and 47 were injured. Aside from the official response more than 300 volunteers were involved, including 28 physicians. They gave anywhere from 5 to 50 hours of their time. It had been a disaster, but out of the dust of the collapsed store rose a feeling of camaraderie and pride. Both local hospitals treated volunteers for free. None of the doctors sent bills.

Two's a crowd in the ER

The same rule holds in the ER as does in OB. It is 95% routine, 5% panic.

The ER nurse often said "Sniffles."

This would announce a welfare family with simple coughs and sniffles but no money to see a private doctor. They had no funds for a collection agency to dig into. Then there might be absolute quiet, followed by an old lady with a fecal impaction. This was not an emergency, but elderly women who had not moved their bowels for ten days would often show up frustrated as well as constipated in the ER.

Usually the ER nurses were quick to demonstrate their skills, but this did not include inserting a gloved finger to dig out a hard accumulation. Somehow it was not in their contract, and they always found other more pressing duties, leaving the ER doc to do the work. All those years of training to put a gloved finger into an old woman and dig. And dig out piece by piece, until there was a big brown mound. Undignified for the patient, but they were happy when they left.

Then the first part of the evening rush began, with one patient to be sutured in Room 3 when the ER charge nurse said

"There's a gunshot wound to the head coming in by ambulance."

The head is not a good place to have a gunshot would. A bullet blasting through skull and brain would usually have only one ending. One smashing through the fragile bones of the face could bleed like stink and do permanent damage to the eyes or the facial features but they might live. We didn't have long to wait. She had probably been a grandmother, with her cap of grey hair, but she was nobody's grandmother now. There was a small round hole on one side of the skull, and a large area of skull and brain missing from the exit wound on the other side. She was a DOA, 'Dead on arrival,' and should not have been brought to the ER. There was nothing we could do, but the EMT's had been doing CPR on her, so I didn't say anything to them except

"Put her in Room Two."

While she was being cleaned up and the paper work done the family began filling the waiting area. Most patients were Catholic with big families. Dating young Hispanic ladies could be dangerous for a young man's health if he jilted her. The girl often had the sultry beauty of South America, and under the gorgeous exterior that was as glamorous as Ava Gardner there might be the passion and fire of Carmen Miranda. Her displeasure might bring several large brothers out of the woodwork, and the result might be a family feud.

Shooting grandma might have been part of a shot that had gone wild, a family feud or just a random drive by shooting, and I was anxious to have the funeral home come with their gurney and blanket. Especially when I heard "A gunshot wound to the chest coming in, ETA two minutes."

That just gave us time to get the equipment for a chest tube set up in the larger Room One before the ambulance arrived. This was a young man, with a wound to his lower right chest, but stable.

A portable XRay showed a collection of blood at the bottom of the lung, and the chest tube went in and was hooked to suction.

"Get me the surgeon on call," I ordered. We were not a Trauma Center with surgeons in house. I had to handle anything that came through the door for the first part of 'The Golden Hour,' until expert help arrived. Luckily the patient was in no distress, as it might take half an hour to get a surgeon in.

The Charge Nurse pulled me to one side.

"We have a problem. This man was one of the gang that had killed Grandma, and the relatives of both victims are coming into the waiting room." This was dynamite waiting to explode.

I could call Security and the Police to come and be peace keepers but I could see them in the middle with both sides shooting. That idea lasted for about a millisecond. I picked up the phone and dialed the other hospital in town.

"Give me the ER doctor, Doctor Rogans here.'

We were a two hospital town, and we knew each other and cooperated.

"Hi Jim, John Rogans at BMC in the ER. I need your help, or we might have World War Three on our hands. I have a thirty two year old male, gunshot to the right chest, chest tube in place and stable. Surgery is on the way. Can I send him over to you?"

I explained the possibility of the two families feuding, and he gave the go ahead. It took just a moment to bandage the patients unhurt head as a disguise, and he was on his way. When he was safely in the ambulance I announced the transfer, and half of the waiting room crowd also left. Women, children, and many tough looking males with black moustaches. It was almost time to let the Police know that we had just had another routine day in the life of a border hospital Emergency Room.

Chapter Nineteen

The Tontine

The original Tontine was devised in France by an Italian, and modified all over the world. In its various forms, members contributed to a bank account which increased as members died. The last survivor took the whole pot. If he was fit enough to carry it.

I was back in Vancouver taking a break and I thought this might be a good excuse for members of 3276 to meet occasionally, but not for mere money. We sent John Mitchell hunting for the most expensive bottle of brandy he could find, and we devised a formula for 'x.' 'X' was the number of ounces that could be taken out of the bottle on the initial gathering for each member, and how much would be taken out at every meeting thereafter, on the demise of a member, with a double dose for the lonely last man standing.

There were four of us, all retired. Mitchell, Payn, Rogans and Stagg. We had lost touch with Roy Ferris. We first met at Peter Stagg's place on October 7th 1999. We were basically of English stock but our origins were widespread. Mitchell The Brewer had been born in Singapore, Payn the All Round Engineer in Natal, South Africa, Rogans the Engineer and Medic in London, and Stagg the Architect in Madras India.

'X' turned out to be Two, and we followed the initial two ounces with grub and several beers created by Mitchell at a local pub. We toasted Mitchell for his fine creations, followed by several toasts to each other and the Tontine. It was a happy gathering. We had several other meetings of a non Tontine nature, with grub cooked by Peter or Mitch and several beverages, minus the brandy. At the time of writing, two have departed this vale of tears. Now there are only two of us to go.

Thailand

I retired in '96 and I had the time to travel. I headed first for Thailand. The Far East had long inflamed my imagination. Thailand was exotic, and I went back several times.

Eastern and Oriental girls were especially attractive, alluring, but unfortunately heavily infected with HIV. Not only romantic, exotic, and mysterious but also there were the sites of many former British colonies that had fostered many dreams of a young man. Thailand had never been colonized, but 'The King and I' had been in glorious technicolor. I had made a flying visit to Bangkok on my way home from Saudi. I was taken to lunch in style by an engineer classmate who lived there, John McDermont, who had made a killing in the Hong Kong stock market and retired early. He oscillated between his apartment in Bangkok, another one in Tokyo and his house in London. A delightful host. However, I really missed helping patients, and my next trip let me do that in an exotic locale.

Asthma and the naked lady

It was one hour before midnight in the Amazon. I was relaxing in the Lady doctor's thatched hut when the knock at the door came. I had put down my book, and I was about to blow out the oil lamp. I had already looked around the room. Charley the tarantula was nowhere in sight and the baby boa constrictor was also missing. I was alone, and a bit lonely, although I had learned to live with that. During the day the newness of the Amazon, the mystery of the rain forest, the friendliness of the natives and the staff at the tourist lodge, plus the infinite variety of patients and the helpful good nature of the clinic staff kept me happy.

Juvencio, the male nurse assistant had been trained by Dr. L., and he was now teaching me how to look at microscope slides of malaria. Which one was the relatively harmless plasmodium vivax, and which was the plasmodium falciparum, much more nasty, especially if it got into the brain. The differences on the slide were subtle, but the treatment and effects on patients were very different.

He was also my dental instructor. I had never pulled teeth in Canada or the US. I knew the anatomy of the dental nerve from my text books but in real life the nerve often wanders from its 'normal' pathway. The secret was to inject anesthetic so that it covered as wide a path as possible. I knew from the facial expressions that sometimes I had missed. Then

I would put down the dental forceps and squirt in a little more joy juice.

The female nurse assistant was Edemita, with a sun weathered face that was still attractive when she smiled. The native women were usually short, and shy, and intimidated when they had to bend their necks backward to look up to the tall North Americano. Edemita was the bridge, experienced now to Western males, a warm and loving person that helped them open up and tell their story.

On this late night summons it was Edemita that was sick, said the night watchman.

"Big trouble with breathing," he said.

I knew that she had a history of asthma, and as I walked across the field to the clinic I remembered cases where mild attacks had rapidly progressed to life threatening crises. Death was rare but it did happen, and I was always wary. This night there were no water buffaloes. Maybe they had gone back to their jungle to wait until I came out.

Edemita was alone in an exam. room sucking into an oxygen mask. She hadn't brought a chaperone, but I could see from the tightness of her chest that there was no time to spare to wait for a woman from the village. I sent for one, but help was needed now. My stethoscope revealed the high pitched wheezing of bronchial tubes squeezed tight by spasm. I quickly drew up the first round of medicines and injected them into her deltoid.

She had stripped to the waist. Her breasts were well formed, but they were not involved in the problem. I asked if she had used her inhalers, and gave her another dose of each of them. Over the next fifteen minutes she improved slowly. I could see and hear that her lungs were getting less tight, and she was not as frightened. She looked at me and smiled. A happy smile, that could also be taken as an invitation. I quickly gave her another round of injections and grabbed her blouse.

"Here, Edemita, you can put this back on."

"Oh, that's alright doctor. I am. feeling much better."

I knew that most women were proud of their breasts, and I also knew from disgruntled patients that they knew when a doctor was stepping out of line, gently squeezing their breasts or stroking the nipples to watch them stand up. I had sent the night watchman for a chaperone, and I did not want to be found in a room with a half undressed woman. The grapevine would have that all over the Amazon by morning.

"Here, Edemita, put your arms in here."

She looked at me and smiled again, and maybe it was my imagination but I felt that she had picked up on my nervousness. She slowly put on her blouse, just as I could hear footsteps on the wooden stairs.

I stayed with her and the chaperone until the patient, and the doctor, were out of danger.

Chapter Twenty

The Music Doctor

There was another lady doctor, a Ph.D. in music, who had left the concert scene in Washington DC behind her. I never did get her story, and I asked, but she came to the Amazon, and stayed. For something to do she started a library for the native children. It was a great success. Friends donated many children's books in Spanish. Spanish is an easy language to read, and I enjoyed helping, especially when I saw their rapt attention and the shy smiles afterwards.

Nancy missed her music. A couple of times a year she went back home and gave a concert, but that wasn't enough. There were plenty of ancient pianos in Iquitos, and she splurged a hundred dollars on the best one. She had it wrapped in a blue tarpaulin and lashed across the bow of a small cargo boat. It was very conspicuous, and they were stopped by the Peruvian Navy.

"No Señor. It is not drugs, just a piano." She had to raise the tarp to prove it, and they waved her on. Her house was near the narrow Yanamono tributary of the Amazon. The Amazon was about two miles wide, but the Yanamono was only fifty feet across.

"In here. That path leads to my house." Turning the boat so that its nose was over the path was tricky. The boat was nearly fifty feet long.

Nancy had several men from the village waiting. They appreciated her library for the children, and her slim figure, but her living room was fifteen feet in the air. Like most huts it was on stilts to rise above the annual flood of the Amazon when the snows melted high in the Andes. They somehow managed to get the heavy thing up the many stairs. Nancy took some time to get it in just the right position, but finally she sat down to play.

The men were all Yagua natives with wrinkled sunburnt faces, but they lit up in rapture. I have never heard a classical piano recital that moved me as much as that one. The notes went out, along the river, into the thick green jungle of the Amazon rain forest and even the parrots stopped to listen.

Lizbet

It was at the library that I met Lizbet. Twelve years old, a sweet round face, and big brown eyes. At first, she stayed as far away from me as possible. I occasionally read books aloud to the children, and they would line up along the bench waiting their turn to be read to by the strange gringo. Reading a children's book in Spanish was not a great linguistic feat, and like all children they enjoyed being read to. All except

Lizbet, who never came and sat on the bench to wait her turn.

"Oh," said Nancy. "She is a bit shy, and she doesn't like strangers to look at her leg."

I had noticed the crutches, and I asked Nancy what had happened.

"She had walked a little way from her village to relieve herself when she felt a sting at the back of her ankle. She looked, but there was nothing moving on the path or in the brush. By the time she got back to her hut, her leg was hurting. Her mother looked, and saw the two puncture marks from a snake bite. That was a problem for the mother. It was getting late, and it was a long paddle up to the clinic of the Lady Doctor. The Amazon River was flowing at about four miles an hour. It was a long way and hard work, even though the small dugout canoe was not very heavy. Plus, her husband was away and she had two other small children to look after."

"Well," said Nancy, "there was a simple solution. She took Lizbet to the curandera that lived in the village."

When the native healer saw the small wounds she said,

"That's no problem. I have treated many snake bites. I will use the black bone treatment.""

"That's a new one to me," I said.

Nancy explained.

"The curandera produced a couple of old bones from a long dead dog, and grilled them over her small fire until they became charcoal. When they cooled down she crumbled them into powder, added some river water, and spread the mixture on the leg. "This will draw the poison out." She bandaged it with a once clean rag and told the mother to come back the next day, when all would be well."

I was very skeptical. I had heard tales of healing,

and even magic being performed. Miraculous cures had been described, visions seen, but there had always been cause for doubt. The healers could be very persuasive, and almost hypnotized the patient, magnifying the placebo effect. In some cases the use of mind altering drugs to had explained strange visions.

"What happened?"

"She was worse the next day, in a lot of pain, and her leg was swollen to double its normal size. The healer convinced the mother that this sometimes happened, and had the girl brought back for many 'treatments.'"

"I'm surprised she survived," I said. "Snake venom can be very toxic."

"It seemed to be destroying the muscle, and causing a deep ulcer."

Different venoms had different effects. Some were hemotoxic, which mainly effects the clotting and cardiovascular systems. Others attacked the brain and the nervous system. This one was probably a type that caused digestion and destruction of local tissue.

"The mother finally decided to take her to the clinic of the Lady Doctor," continued Nancy. "The healer said that that would not help. There was nothing the gringa doctor could do."

"And she was right. The deep ulcer was not the only problem. The increased pressure in the swollen leg had cut off circulation. The leg had to be amputated," said Nancy.

Lizbet was kept in hospital until the stump had healed, but she was never fazed.

By the time she got home she was an expert with her crutches, and easily managed the slippery mud paths through the jungle. She was cheerful and happily climbed into and out of the tippy dugout canoes that always gave me palpitations when I got in them. When I met her she was twelve years old and as lively as any of the other children, except for a shyness with Westerners.

I kept on reading to the children occasionally, and one day I was surprised to see her at the end of the bench, waiting her turn to be read to. By me. When she got to my side she looked up at me with a smile so sweet that my heart melted. She was a lovely, loving girl.

Sometime later, when I was back in the U.S., I heard that her charm had worked on the craftsman that carved wooden prostheses, and she was now fully mobile. I only hoped that Lady Luck would smile on her, and help her through the trials of poverty and many pregnancies that probably awaited her. Without a smile from Lady Luck it might not be a comfortable life, but Lizbet was a survivor, with energy and lots of charm and personality. If anyone could prevail, she could.

Up the creek, to Santa Clotilda

Somewhere in the middle of Iquitos I finally found the Mission, which I was told supplied outposts in the surrounding jungle.

"No, señor, the Padre is not here."

The middle aged woman in black explained that the priest would be back soon, and I could come in and wait.

The church was on one side of an inner courtyard, and she pointed to the various buildings, saying I could look.

They were dark and dusty, and in one was a pile of boxes thickly covered with dust. I had just decided not to 'look' inside a box when man in black came in..

"Can I help you, Señor?"

The priest was almost as dusty as the box. Perhaps he had come on the same yellow and rust colored bus as I had, with windows and doors open to let the heat out and the dust in. I said I was a doctor and willing to help, and his eyes lit up.

"Ah yes, Santa Clotilda. I am Father Ramiro. Come with me." On a wall in his cluttered office was a large map showing big areas of the Amazon rain forest, many rivers large and small, several villages and a few red spots indicating outlying missions. His finger traced from Iquitos down the Amazon.

"Here is Mazon. A taxi will take you over the neck of land to the Napo river, and the Rapido goes at about ten o'clock every day." His finger traced the winding river upstream deep into the jungle.

"It has a very big engine, only takes six or seven hours to Santa Clotilda. Father Marcelle will be alone for two weeks while Father Grant is away." Both of the Fathers were also medical doctors, ministering to the bodies and souls of Santa Clotilda. He pointed to a red dot deep in the rain forest, which was a special outpost with two doctors, several nuns and a Mother Superior. Between them they ran a clinic and a school. This was Santa Clotilda.

There were very few formalities, and the next morning I was in a small battered white boat chugging down the Amazon to Mazon. The three wheeled taxi was even more battered, but whisked me across the narrow isthmus and I found the Rapido loading. She was about twenty five feet long and on her stern was a huge outboard motor, a black Yamaha, 250 hp. We were sixteen passengers, and we put our baggage in front of the engine and found a bare wooden seat. Next to me was a young Yagua woman, Irma, cheerful, poor, and friendly who was going to work as a cleaner in the hospital. I was about to question her about the hospital when the engine roared into life. The boat edged into the middle of the Napo River, then the captain opened the throttle and let her rip.

    We were speeding along, swerving to dodge the logs and other floating debris. The breeze on our face must have been about 40 miles an hour, and refreshing. About every three miles we passed a small native village, many deserted but otherwise it was solid green where the forest came down to meet the river. After a couple of hours one of the crew passed out 'lunch,' a small box of juice, which was palatable, and a couple of greasy tamales wrapped in paper, which were not. I gave mine to Irma, and munched on my fruit.

    An hour later, as I was trying to doze off, there was a grinding sound, the engine raced and screamed, then was silent. Then we were drifting in the middle of the river, with the current pushing us backwards at four knots. The two crewmen were examining the engine and came to the conclusion that we had hit a submerged log at high speed. The propeller was missing. The Capitan got out the emergency equipment, one paddle, and told the crew to paddle.

    As we drifted by a village a couple of canoes came out, paddled by bare chested natives. I hoped they were friendly, and looked for their blowpipes which could send poisoned darts flying at us, but they simply paddled around us, and laughed.

    We drifted on, and the canoes from the next village were more helpful. They pushed us to the side of the river, and we landed at the next village down river. The passengers climbed out, and the Captain and crew tied up the boat so that her stern was accessible. The drive shaft was indeed naked, missing the propeller. Out came wrenches, hammers, and a spare propeller.

    "No problem," said the Captain. "We fix, pronto."

    I wandered up to the village. Of the twelve thatched huts on stilts, only three looked inhabited. An old lady, bent and weathered came onto the porch. Behind her were two young girls, about eleven and thirteen.

"Nobody here. All hunting in the forest."

She pointed, and didn't seem too friendly.

In the middle of a field was a big round hut, empty. Then a clapboard hut with a red cross. It had been the center for rural health care, once upon a time.

"That was the clinic," said Irma. "Many people leave."

Back at the boat, the Captain was muttering words I didn't know, but they didn't sound good.

"Propeller no good. I go to radio."

He marched up through the village. This had been an important village, with clinic and radio to talk to the outside world. The battery was still working.

"Curillo to Mazan. Curillo to Mazan. Speak to me."

Soon there was a reply, but the news was not good. There was no other Rapido that could come and take us anywhere. We were stuck. It was getting dark and we were hungry. I went to the hut, and the old woman was still alone with the girls. Maybe the hunters were staying in the forest, if they existed. Finally she loosened up and agreed to broil a couple of chickens over a fire, and one of the passengers had a big basket of eggs. We dined on burnt chicken and boiled eggs.

"You can sleep anywhere," said the old crone. "All people gone. The big hut is empty. That's the best place. It used to be the church."

It had been empty for a long time. The dust on the floor was about an inch thick, and trying to sweep it up raised a big black cloud. The only furniture was a few narrow benches. Irma had brought all of her worldly possessions, including a sleeping mat and a mosquito net. One of her candles flickered next to her, and soon she was comfortable. I spread my rain poncho on the floor, with my rucksack for my head and laid down. The dust smelt just like dirt from the jungle, which it was.

At least we were up on stilts, and the pigs running wild obviously looked on the space under the hut as theirs, snuffling and arguing. However to judge by the communal human night music we all eventually got to sleep.

At dawn I was down at the river, cleaning up. Interestingly, so was Irma. She had stripped to her underpants and was carefully taking a bath. Then we heard a motor, and then the Captain shouting. He was guiding a Rapido towards the bank.

"Hey, you peasants, time to go."

He had borrowed a dugout canoe in the night and had paddled down to Mazan. Soon we were on our way after breakfast of boiled eggs and water from the river, and we reached Santa Clotilda before noon.

I knew from the map that we were now more than two hundred miles deep into the jungle, and I had been expected to find Marlon Brando in 'Apocalypse Now.' I was surprised to find a bustling community, with cement pathways, a big aluminum sheathed church, and a twenty five bed hospital. It had been started by a group of courageous nuns. When they made a success of their mission the church sent in a couple of doctor-priests and built the small hospital. The nuns now ran a large school, which was also a great success. The Mother Superior ran it with a firm hand. They were expecting a thousand students and sixty teachers. There were several 'stores' along the main pathway, with yucas and bananas and even rum for $3 a bottle. There was even a discotech which could be heard all over the village when the generator ran between 6 and 11 pm. All told there were three thousand people in this busy remote outpost, deep in the middle of the jungle.

Father Grant had left on his trip up river, and Father Marcelle welcomed me. Sort of. I got the impression that he didn't really want to share his flock with an English doctor.

He was from French Canada. His manner was abrupt. Very French Canadian.. He showed me the Rectory.

"We will have lunch when the clinic is finished."

The menu was the same every day. Soup and stew and rice and beans. The priests, of course were bachelors. They expected little and did not complain when they got less from the lady that did the cooking and flipped an occasional broom over the floor. The priests made their own beds and washed their own clothes. The food was cooked some time in the morning and put in a screened cupboard and the rule was help yourself at anytime.

"You will sleep here." He pointed to one of the six empty rooms. "I still have clinic patients to see. You can come if you like. Put on some green scrubs," he pointed to a pile in a cupboard.

"Just follow that path, past the church." And he was off.

I put on the uniform I was to wear for two weeks, green O.R. shirt and bottoms, and down the path I found the small hospital. Again, buildings around a courtyard. In front was an office, a dental room and an emergency room. One side was the inpatient wing, mainly an open ward with a few private rooms for the really sick or contagious. One side was open, and one side had several exam. rooms where outpatients were seen from about nine until two or three in the afternoon. I found out that there was no break for coffee, and lunch was sometime long after 2 pm when the last patient had been seen. The rule was buy your own luxuries like jam. for the bread and butter, and I bought a few bottles of beer to add to the evening leftovers.

The day started at 5.45 am with the thudding of heavy boots clumping to the bathroom and then the kitchen.

Father Marcelle was tall and imposing, with dark eyebrows permanently arched, as if questioning everything. He was a brilliant doctor and had a photographic memory. He could remember every patient he had ever seen, and knew the names and relatives of every one that had ever come to be seen going back three generations. I had met a few doctors before with photographic memories, and they always made me feel jealous and inferior. His gifted brain however had no use for pleasantries. Lunch was a lecture, and a recap of the clinic.

"The woman you saw with a rash is from a village four miles downstream. She must be hurting to paddle all the way up here. Her mother had twelve children, and six of them lived. I have tried to teach them to come here if they have problems, but it is like pulling teeth."

Then he named all of the children, their ailments, and then all of the grandchildren, and when they were born

Then he added sternly "Make your notes so people can read them. Their next visit will probably be with another doctor."

It was hard enough to write my notes in Spanish. My small vocabulary made it tough going. Now I had to make it legible. That was asking a lot, but I tried..

"They have a different dialect from the Yagua you hear down on the Amazon. If you want, I can let you borrow a book with the important words in it, but you must not take it with you. People are so careless, I have lost so many important books that way."

One morning it was pouring with the daily dose of warm Amazon rain. Even with my umbrella I would get my legs soaking wet walking to the hospital. So I wore shorts, and when I got to my exam. room I dried my knees and was about to change clothes when Father Marcelle came storming in.

"You should know by now you do not wear shorts when you see patients. They are used to giving their respect, and doctors do not dress in shorts."

I was a bit annoyed, but I didn't say a word. I reached into my shoulder bag and brought out a pair of long green scrub pants. I held them up, and just gave him a look. An intense look.

"Don't examine patients unless you are dressed properly," he growled as he stormed out.

He was also very possessive of 'his' patients.

A pretty young girl, thirteen, was brought in by her mother with stomach pains. When I had her lying on the exam. table, I thought I could feel something. I went out to get the small portable ultra sound machine, and sure enough, there was a small skull inside her pelvis. She was about twelve weeks pregnant.

There was no discussion, as every one was Catholic and abortion was not an option. However, she was very young and would need prenatal visits, if she would come. I went and described her to Father Marcelle.

"I will see her now."

He came striding to my room, and hastily dragged her down to his exam. room. He had a nurse, and I could see from his preparations he was going to do a complete exam., including a pelvic exam.. The young girl was scared, and I left. I didn't want any part of this.

Over lunch he explained aspects of the case I hadn't been aware of.

"The father of the child is her grandfather, and that raises complications. He is a good man and works at the hospital. I am. going to have to send one of them away. I will do some thinking."

Sometimes his duties as a doctor-priest overlapped. A woman in hospital was dying from liver failure. A gallbladder removal several years earlier had been botched, and she had been turning yellow for years. We saw her every morning, stoically accepting her fate. One morning as we made our daily rounds of hospital patients, he finished checking her, then asked for his priestly things.

"She will die soon."

He prayed, absolved her of her sins, anointed her head and hands with oil and solemnly gave her the last rites there in the room. He normally looked after their souls at church at five in the afternoon, with a long white priest's robe over his scrubs. He and Father Grant gave a complete service package, ministering to both body and souls. He was right. She died later in the day. There was a wake at the municipal building that night, with the body on a wooden table adorned with palm leaves and red flowers and candles everywhere. The benches around the big room were full, and many people would probably stay all night. Children were asleep on the cement floor on blankets.

There were many replacement patients for the dead woman, with lots of babies waiting in the arms of their mothers, often at the breast to keep them happy. The native genes were dominant, but there were the occasional blue eyes and brown hair from some wandering Western influence. The gene for narrow hips must be dominant, but that didn't stop them having lots of babies.

Spanish medical abbreviations were different. A URI is an IRA, a CVA is a PRU, AIDS is SIDA etc. Making rounds on hospital patients was a trial. The doctor who had admitted the patient gave the history in rapid fire Spanish, then the nurse added her report in a different dialect. If I admitted a patient that meant writing the history, and orders for drugs and IVs in Spanish. It was a challenge.

One evening I had 'the duty,' which meant staying on a cot in the emergency room all night. About eight o'clock a woman came in with a small child in her arms. About three years old, and unconscious. As the child was laid on the exam. table I started to get the history. She had been sick for five days, starting with a fever, then vomiting and headache, then a rash on her abdomen. The mother had not been too concerned, as there was a local healer in the village who took over the case. When the child did not get better, the mother got worried, and got someone to paddle her to Santa Clotilda.

The healer, the curandera, had given herbal brews and had cupped the abdomen. This was said to suck the poisons out, using a small amount of burning wood to heat a metal cup which was then placed on the patient. A suction was created as it cooled and it left a characteristic round bruise.

As soon as I saw the purple rash I knew that it was a serious problem. I hardly needed to examine her for a stiff neck. She had meningococcal meningitis, which had a high mortality at her age, even if she had received antibiotics at the beginning. She had been sick for days, now she was in a coma, and as I watched she started a type of deep breathing which meant that the end was near.

"I am. afraid that she is very, very sick. She may even die." The mother looked at me blankly. "I will give her some medicine, but I think it is too late."

Just then Father Marcelle burst into the room. Obviously the grapevine had told him. I mentioned my diagnosis.

"You are probably right, John, but I think we should do everything we can."

He started giving orders for oxygen, for an IV, for IV antibiotics, and was getting her set up to do a spinal tap.

"Marcelle, she is dying. She has just started Cheyne Stokes breathing. It won't be long. Do you want to use up our valuable medications?"

All supplies came by boat from Iquitos, taking over a week to get up river. Injectable antibiotics and oxygen tanks were in short supply. I understood that he wanted to do something to make the mother feel better, but ...

"Marcelle, she will be dead very soon. She has been sick for five days already. Maybe you might want to go slowly with all this."

"No John, absolutely not. Now is the time to pull out all the stops as fast as we can."

Just then the child gave a deep breath, and stopped moving. After a long pause there was another deep breath. Then nothing. She was dead.

All that remained was to comfort the mother and give her and her family antibiotics to hopefully prevent them getting the disease. I took them too and my urine turned red, like blood. We had a discussion about medication for the curandera, but in the end we sent some up for her. Maybe she had learnt a lesson.

Chapter Twenty One

The Wild Men of Borneo

Traveling was fun, but I did miss seeing patients. I tried to combine travel with doing locums, standing in for local docs going on vacation.

One such place was Kuching, the capital of Sarawak, on the Northern, Malaysian part of the island of Borneo.

Google helped me find a hospital in Kuching, and then I faxed and e-mailed the Malayan Medical Association to get all of my licences. I sent these on to Kuching. Soon I was ready, with a pile of papers two inches thick, to head for Kuching for a three month stay. I was also ready to drop in on a few Toastmasters International clubs. I had been active in Toastmasters, learning how to handle Public Speaking, in

Brownsville, Harlingen, Austin and Bangkok. Toastmasters was a good way to meet and interact with the local people.

When I was a child we heard scary stories about the Wild Men of Borneo. They were cannibals, they ate people, and being headhunters they cut off people's heads. There were still tribes that had never seen a white man. That was several years ago, but still I thought "This should be an interesting place to visit." Cutting off heads was made illegal in 1959, or so I was told, and they had stopped eating missionaries, so there was nothing to worry about. Probably. With primitive communications, I hoped that this was known by all concerned, especially all the tribes concerned.

Chopping off heads had a lot to do with impressing the women. A young warrior was not a good marriage prospect until he had come back carrying a head still dripping with blood. If he found an enemy to fight, that was good, but anyone he met by chance from another tribe was good enough. Man, woman or child would do, so a walk in the woods might be bad for your health. The First White Rajah worked very hard to stamp out this time honored custom, but old habits died hard. The head would be hung high over the fire until the meat all came off and the skull was bare and blackened.

Where is Borneo? North of Australia, South of the Philippines, China, Vietnam and Thailand, and around the corner from India. It is the third largest island in the world. The South part used to be run by the Dutch and in the North Sarawak and Sabah by the British. They are now part of the Federation of Malaysia. Brunei is very tiny and is now very rich from oil and gas. It is run by His Majesty the Sultan.

I ended up exploring all over. I found many mosquitoes, I fed quite a few leeches and visited many tribes. The Kelabits were tall, intelligent, kind and had never cut off heads, they said. The Bidayuh, the Kenyiah, and the Ibans were different. I stayed in one Iban village, and hanging from the roof was a bag of blackened human skulls. One night I saw them chopping meat off a large leg. I wondered if a missionary or an insurance salesman was going into the pot.

"No Meester, This is wild boar we hunt in jungle."

They all treated me with great friendship and hospitality but the most friendly tribe of all was the tribe of T.I., Toastmaster's International..

In Kuala Lumpur, on the Malay Peninsular I had been met by the District Governor of District 51 of Toastmasters International. We had been talking by email.

"Yes John, if you want to work as a volunteer doctor in Sarawak I am sure we can help you."

I stayed a few nights in his luxury apartment, and of course went to a Toastmaster meeting. I even have a certificate to prove it. A word of warning. If you visit a Toastmaster club and you are a foreigner they will pick on you to see how it is done in the your hometown. I did Table Topics, Word of the Day, General Evaluator and gave a speech, the whole Toastmaster experience. The founding club had been started in 1924 in Santa Ana California by Ralph Smedley, a director of the local WMCA. He organized it like a social club, with a formal program that let members practice different aspects of public speaking. There are clubs all over the world. I have given small speeches in Thailand, Malaysia, Canada, but mainly in the United States.

Next I went to Kuching, in Sarawak and a Past District Governor, Dr. John Lau took over.

"We are going to take very good care of you, my friend", and he did. Almost every evening there was a Toastmaster at my hotel for a meeting, or a dinner at a private home. One night a very pretty young woman. Law Lee Poh said "You're coming to our C.O.T." They are very fond of acronyms. SAA and VPE were easy, Sergeant at Arms and Vice President of Education, but I had to stop for TOE. Okay, that was Toastmaster of the Evening. COT was Club Officer Training. Lee Poh was the Division Governor and the training session was very good. Another time John Lau said "Today it's the DOT. You will be the VIP guest." He gave a great power point presentation for the District Officers Training and his delivery was indeed powerful. He had the charisma of a strong leader, and he later became an International Governor of TI at the Conference in Toronto. He is now the International President of TI, which has almost 300,000 members world-wide.

It was several days before I could get out to the hospital where I was going to work for three months, but I finally made it. The Administrator made me feel very welcome, he had all of my credentials, and we chatted about patient care in general before he dropped his bombshell.

"By the way, Doctor Rogans, you do have your work permit?"

I knew without looking that there was no work permit in the thick bundle of papers. I shook my head "No."

"That's no problem", he said. "We can get one from here." I started breathing again.

"Of course, it will take time, wherever you apply from."

"How long?" I stammered.

"It all depends. Months, of course. Sometimes a year."

I found out that this was a common occurrence. Sometimes doctors wandered around the hospital for a year, not allowed to lay a hand on a patient, until the work permit came through. After the end of World War II the third and last Rajah, Sir Charles Vyner Brooke ceded Sarawak to the British Crown in 1946. The education system was great, but British bureaucracy was now in complete control. It had been one of the reasons I had run away from Britain, but however far you run, you can't hide.

However, there were plenty of Toastmasters. In most clubs the Chinese outnumbered the native Malays. They worked much too hard for anyone else to keep up, and they were determined to perfect their English skills. Usually I was the only Westerner but at one club there were two other Brits. Val was the British Consul, and Dr. Simon was a professor of English at the university. Everywhere the level of energy and enthusiasm was amazing. One night John Chuang was TOE and he apologized.

"We only have five speakers tonight. Most nights we have six or seven."

It was the same in Sibu, Miri, Sandakan and Kota Kinabalu. They were all fired up. That may have something to do with another thing I noticed. They kept to the basic TI format but there was a great emphasis on having fun and fellowship. After most meetings they usually gathered for a snack and shooting the breeze. One club held most meetings on a boat, and they talked while they fished.

At the Kota Kinabalu installation banquet they put on a skit based on the songs from *The Sound of Music*, including the nun's songs, although some of the nuns had suspiciously hairy legs. Executive committee meetings were often held at private homes, and throw in the dinners and picnics and you get an idea of the fellowship that bonded the members together. The message seemed to be that the club that plays together, stays together.

The natives of the interior of New Guinea and Borneo were amongst the last people to be discovered by the civilized world. Now, some seventy years later their jungle has been cut down for precious hardwood and their minds improved by missionary education and some of them are asking, "Why do all the pale faced people have so much more 'stuff' than we do?" It is said that civilization started heading down this way about 12,000 years ago from Northern China, and the Chinese have been a driving part of the landscape ever since. When the British took over Malaya they decided that the Malays were best suited for farming and fishing and imported Chinese and Indians for everything else.

In the corner of every longhouse was a large, ceramic vase, usually green. Highly valued, storing everything. They were obtained on the coast by barter, imported, and they were "Made in China." There is nothing new under the sun.

By the 1930's there were 1.6 million Malays, and 1.7 million Chinese, with the Malays controlling less than three percent of the economy. After racial riots at the end of the sixties the government set a target for Malays to own 30 percent of the wealth within thirty years. By 1990 the percentage of wealth owned by Malays had risen to 19 percent.

Sarawak in particular is a racial stewpot that bubbles gently with a lot of interracial tolerance. I was at a meeting in Sibu where all the races were represented. The Chinese led the way and the others, the Malays, the Indians from India, and the indigenous people with their different temperaments functioned at different levels, at different speeds. At an abandoned gold mine at Bau, outside Kuching my young guide said "The Chinese took all the gold. They had the equipment and the know how. They hired us, the Bidayuh, to do the manual labor. We are still

That's how it's been for 12,000 years. A fascinating book 'Guns Germs and Steel' by J. Diamond that claims that civilization spread across the world from two regions. South and East from North China, West and North from the Fertile Crescent, mainly the area that became Persia and Iraq. It claims to explain why the Chinese and the Westerners now own all the 'stuff' the world values and why on large lumps of land like Borneo and New Guinea and Australia the natives remained hunter gatherers until recent times.

It's been told often, but the story of the White Rajah is still fascinating. He was a military man in the British East

India company, wounded in Burma, who inherited a nice fortune, probably worth about four million dollars US today. He bought a well armed fighting ship, and seeking adventure he sailed to Singapore, where he learnt about fighting pirates. He heard that the Sultan of Brunei was having problems with pirates and rebellious natives and offered his services. He easily out gunned them and started winning battles.

The Sultan had nothing to give him but land. He fought more battles, and was given more land until he was the Rajah of all of Sarawak. He became the first 'White Rajah' in 1841. His inheritance, plus guts and luck brought him about a thousand miles of waterfront, plus timber and later oil, worth billions. The third White Rajah didn't want the job, and sold it all to England for a million pounds. He retired, spent all the monsey, and died in the arms of one of his seventeen year old companions, so the story goes.

Now in Sarawak they have officially divorced themselves from Britain. Tour guides in Kuching don't even know where cricket used to be played, but they have kept the legal system, the education system, the infrastructure, and the overwhelming bureaucracy. They still drive on the left but all other things British are out.

I met a British prof, who had been here for five years. He had met a lovely Malay woman in school in the UK and married her, which meant that he had to convert to Islam.. He likes the laid back life style here, but grumbled about the slow service and lack of respect. "Sometimes I have to get out of my car and tell them I am Professor Matthews, Head of the English Department and then they move. I don't like to do it, " he says, with a smile. Foreigners don't get tenure, just two year contracts, and a French prof was 'non renewed' recently.

"That gave me a scare, but as long as you don't say anything political you're safe. The bureaucracy is crippling. Everyday I get long forms to complete, in legal type Malay and it's a struggle. I can't find a teacher. Mandarin teachers are easy to find, but not Malay."

I found a young woman, Carol, a Bidayuh, who helped my with Malay pronunciation and also acted as a tour guide. One day she picked me up to drive deep into the country with two long haired males. I had a momentary qualm, but what the heck so I let myself be taken for a ride.

They were really quite pleasant. The driver spoke a bit of English, and drove with a young man's impatience, and young people type music on a CD screaming out of the speakers. The current trend seemed to be to repeat three words a hundred times. Suggestive is good, offensive is better. There was 'All night long,' and 'Crazy, sexy bitch' repeated ad nauseum. The other male was Carol's husband, a quiet type, who watched more than he talked. Carol chatted more with the driver, and the husband seemed to be making mental notes. He was Muslim, and Carol had had to convert when they married.

We got to the 'Fairy Caves' and climbed two hundred steps straight up, while they told me legends and ghost stories. The driver was Catholic, and all sorts of missionaries have been busy. St. Thomas' Anglican Cathedral in Kuching was overflowing on a Sunday, but they also try to keep their animist Gods happy, just in case. So many Chinese have been converted that the prime time for Sunday service, 10.30 am is for a service in Mandarin. Chinese college entrance exams are critical for their future, Chinese mothers raised a big stink about taxis and school buses with bad numbers that might bring rotten luck, like the number four, which sounds like 'death' in Mandarin.

The next day I was stocking up with survival rations for the two four hour boat trips up to Kapit, changing boats at Sibu. The menu on the Express Boats was unlikely to be appetizing or sanitary. I had a pleasant dinner before I left with a Chinese family. I knew the hostess from Toastmasters and the meal was cooked by her mother-in-law. Her husband's parents lived with them, for life. They also had an Indonesian maid, and a cute three year old daughter. Two nice cars, a big house and plenty of 'stuff.'

The Express Boat to Sibu had many buckets on the floor for the bumpy first long leg across the South China Sea. On that particular day there was a gentle swell, just enough to make the running Chinese children crawl on all fours, but not enough to disturb many stomachs.

The Romance of the South China Sea! Home to pirates, Western navigators and adventurers looking for spices and gold. I bet they didn't have padded seats, air conditioning and a James Bond DVD playing with Chinese subtitles. I couldn't hear the dialogue over the roar of the diesels, but the action as usual was fast, furious and utterly ridiculous. I only hoped I would get to Sibu in time for the last boat to Kapit, or else I would have to hunt for a hotel in Sibu.

Longhouse Living.

I caught the last boat to Kapit, complete with a Chinese martial arts movie with the slaughter of a cast of thousands. I talked with an Iban coming home from Guyana. Short, stocky, big smile, chain smoking. He had learned hardwood logging in Sarawak and his skill was in great demand wherever they were chopping down precious hardwood. He comes home every six months, and makes a baby every twelve months. He grew up in a longhouse, but with his earnings he had bought a house in Kapit. After the close-knit, condo type of living in a longhouse did his wife like living alone?

"No problem. With three children and many shops she is busy."

I had booked into a 'budget' hotel. If the Lonely Planet guide book says 'budget' it means a bare cell suitable for monastic meditation. I moved to a luxury hotel the next day, for 40 USD a night. There were no travel agents in town. A 'Travel Adventure Service' listed on the wharf didn't answer its phone so I went into an internet café to check out its web site. It was empty. The power had just failed, and the screens were blank.

I walked across town to the hospital. The ER doc was a pretty young Malay woman from Sibu. She did her two years matric, then five years med school in KL and was now into her first houseman job. She earned about 800 USD a month, which was good. The hospital had 300 beds and serves three districts, about a hundred thousand people. If they are sick up river it's a long boat ride, unless it's a matter of life or death and the flying doctor is called in.

Doctor Normy is learning Iban, the main local language, and writes her notes in Malay. I would have had a problem there, even if I had waited a year for my work permit and learned the language. It would take me that long to learn Iban, even with the aid of a sleeping dictionary. Dr. Normy is young and smart, very tiny, very shy. She will have to do up to four years community service to pay back the government education costs before being able to practice privately.

As I was walking with her amongst the patients a skinny tall young woman jumped up and grabbed my arm, speaking good English, but wild, agitated, and not making much sense. She had recently been discharged from the psych hospital in Sibu and had not been taking her meds for schizophrenia. An injection of haloperidal soon calmed her down.

I finally managed to arrange a stay in a longhouse, and I hoped they had given up their old customs of chopping off heads and eating 'long pig.'

On Father's Day I went to a feast. An Iban feast, which in the old days might have included a pale faced father like me on the menu. For once I welcomed progress. There was no more 'roast leg of insurance salesman' or visiting missionary. Now there is running water and corrugated tin roofing. Oh, for the good old days.

The books all tell of the romance of the longhouse, the fascinating, different lifestyle of the Borneo tribal communal living. You don't get your Boy Scout Explorer badge if you don't stay at a longhouse. So I did the Longhouse, and I'm glad I did because now there won't be any unfulfilled desire to do that in the future, ever.

It was an Iban community, Sea Dyaks, 22 families living side by side in a long, primitive wooden bungalow, with a common veranda in front, all of it some two hundred yards long. Seemingly laid back, living with tolerance, almost harmony, for generations. A family has a backroom, about 40 feet by 20 feet for cooking and dining, usually on the floor. A front room, same size, for entertaining and sleeping, also on the floor. A ten foot space in between for storage and even an indoor privy with running water. All were spacious, and furnished according to their means with status symbols prominently displayed.

In the wealthy houses were antique shields, spears, wire corsets for the ladies after childbirth, and ancient Chinese ceramic jars, some several hundred years old. Outside the door was a bunch of round things hanging. Looking closely I could see that they were heads, human skulls, blackened over the fire, with lower jaws tied in place with a permanent grin. Terrible teeth. I was in number seven. The fancy houses started at number eight, and the Chief lived at the North end in splendor.

My guide had promised a special ceremony to mark the end of Harvest Festival, Gawain. There was another tourist, a Dutch professional tourist that you find all over. He was older, 43, dedicated to traveling and having a good time. Lived on odd jobs as ski instructor in the Urals, dive trainer in the Philippines, salmon canning in Alaska. Still able to pick up an occasional girl friend who might hang on for two or three years before giving up hope. Spoke enough languages to monopolize conversations and top stories in English, German, French, Spanish etc. He couldn't speak Iban, and neither could I.

Before the feast I was waved into the back room of one family and saw a meat cleaver whistle down into something that looked like a leg. There was hardly any light, and I wondered if they had caught a wandering missionary and this was to be the feast. Then I saw the short black hair on the skin. It was a wild boar brought down by a shotgun, headed for the barbecue.

At eight there was a gathering outside the Chief's rooms. Ah ha, the feast? The Chief talked nonstop for twenty minutes, followed by other men, and the guide, until my backside was sore. They don't call it hardwood for nothing. The whole building was hard wood. Lasts forever, but recent repairs made in soft wood only last a few years. It was a community meeting to announce higher fees for guides to bring in tourists. I was glad to see a new group form up a few rooms down, table with white cloth - at last, the feast?

Then they started singing from black books, full of Methodist hymns. The group had voted to convert a few months ago, which explained the crosses on a few doors. This didn't interfere with their animist beliefs. Like the Chinese and the Thais they also bet on many horses, spreading their risk.

Finally at ten thirty the feast began. A household brought out greasy fried cakes, fried fritters dripping with oil. Gourmet cuisine has not caught on in Sarawak. In many homes and restaurants, plain or fancy the food ranged from mediocre to inedible. Then glasses of rice wine, home brewed by each household helped wash down the food. A dish full of rice and uncooked eggs was waved over a couple of heads to appease the Gods.

The party moved along the veranda and we sat on the floor in front of the next house, and they brought out their bottles of rice wine etc. I slowed my consumption of food and wine. Then we moved our bottoms to the next patch of ironwood floor, and then the next, and the next. I was wilting at two am at the last house and I headed for my mat on the floor in number seven, but many hard core drinkers, including the Dutchman settled down to some serious drinking. I was drifting off but my host reached sleep first, a very sound and very noisy sleep. His grown son also started up with his own night music and their duet penetrated my ear plugs. I had finally got to sleep when, bang, every one got up, stamping and calling out loud. It was five am, and most of the adults were going in to the town miles away to work.

In the morning there was pain. The outhouse had the Asian style squat toilet. My knees had been battered by twenty years of downhill skiing, and they were full of sharp spikes of calcium, arthritis changes. When I sat down to squat there was intense pain, sheer agony in both knees, and it almost made me forget what I was supposed to be doing.

During the day there was only me and the old people. My host, an old man, skinny and bent led me into the forest to find the 'real jungle.' After an hour and a half of hard trekking we still hadn't found it. Not even a leech to spice things up. The woods of BC in Canada are more beautiful and fragrant, and by this time the old man had walked me into the ground. I gave up, he grinned, and we turned back. I had brought my compass, but didn't need it. We were basically following a small river, with short cuts to add variety, and even an idiot like me can find his way down a river to get home for lunch.

Lunch was handfuls of congealed boiled rice cooked the day before, plus left over fried fish, and pieces of barbecued wild boar. I had seen them butchering it, and they had cleverly cut it so that every piece was fifty percent gristle and fat. Chicken was chopped into small lumps, bones and all and boiled. Just be very careful chewing. They chewed with gusto but I would have willingly swapped for a less glamorous but edible burrito from Taco Bell.

One of the Ibans had given me a different rationale for the palang. The dictionary says this is a small round crosspiece. Not to be confused with a parang, a machete. I could never understand why a man would have a hole drilled through the end of his penis and have a crosspiece inserted. About an inch and a half long, of bone, wood or metal, the books said it was to give enhanced pleasure to the woman. There were several specimens in the Sarawak museum in Kuching, giggled over by the locals and the tourists. The Iban told me a different story. It made the woman scream., and it was this that made the man feel good. He didn't have one, and anyway the fashion had changed. Now a small glass bead is inserted under the skin, and now this allegedly gives a woman pleasure. When you don't have good books, music, culture or TV to improve the mind you have to enjoy the pleasures you do have.

The afternoons were bad. It got hotter and hotter, it felt like a hundred and twenty, no air moved and we slowly cooked. I'm sure a meat thermometer stuck in me would have shown medium rare. I was horizontal, desperate to snooze, but I could only ooze. My sweat glands were working overtime, and I could see blobs of perspiration pop out, join up and run in small rivers down my bare arms and chest. The heat was so heavy it was an effort to breathe. Nothing moved except for the chickens, not the brightest things in the world. Of course the English had never complained.

"Mad dogs and Englishmen go out in the mid-day sun."

Noel Coward must have been over there. This is the opening line of one of his songs.

'The toughest Malay bandit, can never understand it.' A few feet from my melting body the tough old Malay was equally comatose. From his vivid tattoos I'm sure he was a bandit when young. He wasn't moving at all.

"At twelve noon the natives swoon, and no further work is done, but mad dogs and Englishmen go out in the midday sun." And the chickens.

When I get to the Highlands, and the weather is not so cruel, I might try a Kelabit longhouse, but no more Ibans, Sea Dyaks for me. Jumping into a boiling pot might come to be as appealing as a cool bath.

After a couple of days I couldn't stand the excitement any more. The road back to Kapit was a winding bulldozer trail blacktopped over, with gaping holes and angry rocks waiting to bust into the van but at least there is civilization, of sorts, at the end. It will be a cold water bath but there is a half decent Chinese restaurant behind the hotel with Tiger beer. Tomorrow I could run away on a boat down river to Sibu. There they have a four star hotel, forty dollars U.S. a night, with a rooftop swimming pool.

Chapter Twenty Two

Sibu

After Kapit I went back down to Sibu. A Chinese doctor showed me around the Specialist Hospital. Most docs had been to med school in Australia and then had done post grad work in the UK to get the prestigious 'FRCS (Edin.) after their names. They really were 'Fellows of the Royal College of Surgeons.' And had earned that widely respected degree in Edinburgh, Scotland.

One was spending some time with a problem patient. She had come in with a bad belly and a huge moon face from the steroids that a local 'healer' had been sticking in to her. This had affected her so badly that many of her vital functions were failing. She probably had a ruptured appendix, but she had gone into cardiac arrest and septic shock. She may die without surgery, but surgery might kill her. The Chinese doctor had to explain this many times over to the huge extended family that came in relays.

On the boat back to Kuching from Sibu I found my perspective had changed. Coming up I had been saddened by the empty longhouse, and the signs of exploitation of the forest, and the river yellow with sawdust.

After a week in Sibu I was looking through Chinese eyes. They had been refugees from oppression and poverty, establishing a colony in a strange and distant land, overcoming crippling hardships. In the 1800s there were just a few Chinese on the river. They couldn't speak the local language, and often had their heads cut off after a disagreement with a headhunting native. In Mainland China there was even greater poverty and oppression. There, for the majority there was no chance of owning land, and a good chance of being robbed and raped by warlords. A few enterprising Chinese Methodists sailed to Singapore, then to Kuching, then up the Rejang River. They found empty land, and a White Rajah who wanted to stop more native Ibans from occupying the land. He gave them land grants and subsistence rations for six months.

The Chinese Methodists went back and brought over eight hundred more, mainly from Foochow in Fujian province. They had very few tools, but hacked away at the land with wooden tools and in six months they harvested their first crop. They endured tropical heat and humidity, and nearly half of them died from malaria. The fittest survived, and in 1905 they planted their first cash crop of rubber trees. The price was high. Henry Ford's model T's needed four tires each.

Typical of the third generation Methodist Chinese is Steven Wong. Both parents came from large families, ten sibs each, to make up for malaria losses. Marriages were arranged, often within the extended family so that the wealth would not be lost to outsiders. They were extremely smart and hard working, with a knack for business. Strong traditions governed communal life, and they had a civilized gene pool going back twelve thousand years. They valued education so highly that they would mortgage everything to ensure the education and prosperity of future generations.

Steven was a Toastmaster who bought a durian for me, even though he knew his car would smell like dirty socks for weeks. The odor of this tasty but stinky fruit is as notorious as the extremely moldy smell of truffles. Durians are banned from many hotels and airplanes.

Steven's many cousins have almost all gone to University, with every profession represented by graduates from Australian and UK universities. I was entertained by so many Chinese that my skill with chopsticks improved, even if I often feel hungry later and yearned for a good burnt steak.

Bario

I caught a puddle jumper to Bario, up in the highlands of North Sarawak. It landed in a field near a small village not far from the border with Kalimantan, which used to be Dutch Borneo. In Bario there are a few lodges that cater to intrepid tourists who want to hunt, fish and trek through the jungle. I didn't know yet how intrepid I would be.

The plane was a twin engined Otter, carrying fifteen. I'd flown around the Canadian bush in Otters. I hoped that this one was as reliable. The pilot flew at about two thousand feet, which meant that with an engine failure the glide path would be a short one. Not that it would matter. There was solid jungle for miles in every direction, no empty field to land in. A few rough logging roads and a small lazy river twisting through the green. Occasionally a flooded rice paddy field. Dropping in on any of those would mean a quick end to the story.

If we did survive at least there would be jungle experts with me. I was the only Caucasian on the flight, and none of the others had much use for cold showers judging by the strong, pungent yellow mist of body odor. Reminded me of treating Carnival workers in Texas. They seldom had access to running water and when they came in for medical treatment I tried to keep the door open. If they had to undress it was a real olfactory challenge.

Planes that go down are immediately swallowed by the jungle, hardly leaving a trace. The year before a chopper flying from Bario called an emergency ten minutes out. There was a government official on board, and the army was called out for a massive manhunt. They knew where to look, but it still took them two weeks to find the wreckage.

The missionaries have been here. Doug the lodge owner who met me was a keen Evangelical, and took off for Saturday church. On Sunday with more church he was too busy to show me a longhouse.

"Just walk that way, you'll find a longhouse, just go in." I did find a longhouse an hour down the trail, empty. All at church. When Doug finally got back he had arranged a guide for the next day.

The life blood of Sarawak is brown. It was a treat to walk amongst the tall trees, brown and tough. Ironwood so hard that I had used it for piling in a Vancouver harbor terminal. There had been a marine contractor that tried the cheap way, with Douglas fir. The waters of BC are full of marine worms, teredos. When tiny, these hungry little babies find a crack in a piece of wood and burrow in. Feeding, they track up and down. The first time a freighter gave the wharf a bump the piles crumbled and the wharf collapsed. The big piles were honeycombed with teredo tunnels, some over an inch thick. They never did get their little teeth into my south east Asian hardwood piles.

I didn't try to explain this to my Kelabit guide. I had no breath. We were on a hillside going up at 45 degrees. He had hunted these woods, and he glided effortlessly up the slope. Every part of my anatomy screamed that I was stupid to try and keep up. Oh, the vanity of man. Lungs bursting, pulse dangerously fast and knees crunching painfully. He looked back.

"Do you want to rest?"

While I panted he showed me how to get good water from a thick bamboo. With a simple flick of his machete he opened windows into the compartments. Some had muddy, cloudy water. Others had clear clean water that tasted so good.

For jungle survival lesson number two he suspended a pole horizontally, tied to trees with flexible vines. Next he cut six foot long sago leaves and propped them to make a waterproof lean to. One never knows when these tricks will come in handy.

After the jungle we headed for a longhouse. Dickson, my modern Kalabit hunter doesn't measure time in terms of days marched. He had an imitation Seiko and a fifty cc Suzuki motor bike. His cousin at the longhouse was older, a grandmother, baby-sitting a grand-daughter. She had pierced ear lobes that had been pulled down to her shoulders with heavy ear rings. Without the weight little ropes of light brown flesh that flapped wildly when she moved her head, until she put in her big brass ear rings. She suddenly disappeared and came back with all her finery. A hat, and a sort of velvet like bodice all richly embroidered with beads of every color. Her daughter, a cook in a school, doesn't bother. She has normal earlobes and blue jeans.

"Not pretty any more," grumbled grandmother.

Dickson had warned me about the ferns. They are as pretty as roses but they had very sharp thorns which left bright red railroad tracks when they dragged across my legs. That wasn't all. When he dropped me back at the lodge my dark brown socks had somehow grown black lumps all over. When I took off the socks the lumps fell to the floor and started wriggling. About an inch long, tear drop shaped with a suckers at each end. The narrow end of the leech squeezed out into a three inch tube that started waving around, looking for fresh blood.

One has to admit that leeches are considerate and they do get so attached to you. They use a local anesthetic and an anticoagulant and blood was oozing painlessly from many places. It didn't stop oozing for forty minutes. Fascinating little fellows, but my new blood brothers ended up in a watery grave.

The lodge was simple but pleasant and I had it all to myself for a few days. At night the generator powered a small color TV set on which the owner and his family watched game shows in Malay while I read. I was hoping for their stories of the Kelabit, but the language barrier and the TV got in the way. It was a pleasant change when another guest arrived. A good looking young woman, alone, but I soon found out that she was married to a French engineer at an oil company meeting in Paris. She was from Madrid, with light brown hair and blue eyes. A geologist, but Brunei wasn't keen on ladies working. She found her lonely life in Brunei so boring that she would rather trek the jungle.

She was somewhat negative about most races on Earth. Except the Japanese.

"So polite, never raise their voices, never push in front of you like the Germans."

I was glad of the company and cheerfully let her deplete my beer supply while she sounded off about everyone. It wouldn't help to argue so I let it all run off. By now I was down to re-reading my favorite novels, and her provocative opinions made a change.

Miri

Back to Miri. To appreciate a comfortable hotel bed one should sleep on the floor in Bario, separated from the bugs by two inches of foam rubber. The ants weren't too bad, they just crawled into intimate places, but disturb a Kelabit cockroach and he doesn't run. He flies. With a mad flapping of wings he takes off, circles wildly, then comes right at you in a Kamikaze attack.

A hot bath is best appreciated after shivering under cold showers. And what a joy to have a bathroom near at hand. In Bario two or three beers with supper always meant a dark midnight trek down rough wooden stairs, across creaking floorboards and out to the facilities lit by the light of the moon, or a flashlight. But, the night sky was dazzling. So many stars, like brilliant, dazzling white light shining through a million pin holes in the black curtain of the sky. No wonder the ancients were awed.

Maria the Spanish lady had taken off on 'The Loop.' Five days of hiking through the jungle from longhouse to longhouse. It rains hard every day. so she will arrive soaking wet. She will change into dry clothing but has to put on the wet stuff back on the next day. Leech socks and all. Still, she will see some of the 'real' Borneo. I chickened out. An eight hour trek would take me twelve hours and I would probably have to pay four guides to carry me back. Maybe I will save 'intrepid' until my next reincarnation.

Sandakan.

The name sounds as romantic as Samarkand, that ancient city of romance on the Silk Road, but Sandakan on the East coast of Sabah was a sad contrast to Sarawak. Buildings streaked with black, garbage in the streets, and the smell of sewage and rotten fish. Beaten up taxis, that used their horns incessantly. That would be extremely rude in Kuching. "Don't walk the streets at night," said the locals. I intended to stay ten days and explore, but the smell was too strong. I didn't want to take a chance on the local street restaurants. Many more Muslims with a muezzin near enough to enjoy prayer calls five times a day. Little green arrows on the ceiling point to Mecca.

Then a depressing afternoon. The Sandakan War Memorial Park is where 2,400 prisoners were held by the Japanese in WWII. I'll be brief. It wouldn't make happy reading. The atrocities were so cruel, sadistic, and deadly it made the Burma Railway Death March seem like a stroll in the park. 1800 Aussies, the rest Brits. When they moved the camp inland near the end of the war they made the prisoners march. By the time the Japanese had finished starving them, torturing them, and executing them not one prisoner was left alive and marching. The guards destroyed all records to cover their tracks, but six who had escaped from the death march survived to testify at the War Crimes Trials.

But, it was such a long time ago. The rape of Nanking was even further back in time. Best forgotten? War brings out the beast in man, and some were quite beastly. In the years just after the War ex-prisoners were known to have flown into murderous rages at the sight of a Japanese tourist. Then, slowly, time heals and people forget, and start buying Japanese and German cars again.

The twentieth century probably holds the killing record. Russian gulags and Stalin's purges accounted for some thirty million. Germany under Hitler about twenty million. Japan millions more. China's cultural revolution some 30 million. Then add those killed in Cambodia, in Africa etc., etc..

Who can guide us to prevent future massacres? Politicians, the military, the philosophers, the religious leaders? There are no easy answers to these terrible questions.

Brunei

Brunei seems to be a wealthy one man show. There was a whole 'museum' devoted to the Sultan, with his coronation vehicle, and all the presents from world leaders. Soon after his coronation Queen Elizabeth commissioned him a Captain. All of his uniforms are there. I wonder if he ever wore that great big bearskin hat. Nearly thirty years later she made him a General and his uniforms really were fancy, especially the naval one of Admiral of the Fleet, and the light blue one of Marshall of the Air Force. He is on all currency, on billboards, street banners etc. Sort of a 1984 feeling.

With oil and gas discovered in 1929 it became a rich country. It wouldn't have had to give away Sarawak if they'd found oil seventy years earlier. Democracy was tried only briefly but there is free medical care, free education, no income tax, a high minimum wage and pensions for all. Alcohol is banned, drugs carry the death sentence, and the national ideology stresses Malay culture plus Islam. I spent a day there then came back to Sabah.

I was rudely awakened at seven am the next morning. "We are waiting for you downstairs for the Tenum railway trip.' I had made a booboo, and thought the trip to see first growth timber was the next day. I grabbed a few things and was on the minibus ten minutes later. On the train I breakfasted on cheese slices, crackers and beer. There was nothing else. This basic diet was enough to fill me, but after four hours bumping along over a narrow gauge railway watching second growth jungle I decided to develop a disturbed intestine, and my sympathetic guide got on his cell phone and arranged a taxi to pick us up at the next stop, and found a restaurant, with restroom. There was a limit to the amount of excitement for one day. I had to rely on the descriptions of others for a mental picture of magnificent mahogany trees, elegant columns of brown reaching for the sky.

    Next I went back to the ordinary jungle. Hundreds of different sorts of birds failed to excite me, but it was so peaceful cruising along narrow rivers, watching strange monkeys picking fleas off each other. We found a bunch of proboscis monkeys. They gather in two types of band, a bachelor band, or a harem group, with one big dominant male and his many wives. He will last until one of the bachelors gets big enough and frustrated enough to challenge him. In one harem the male was huge, and so was his proud male appendage, prominently protruding in front of him. It was colored a brilliant red. Maybe it pays to advertise. Called 'the Borneo red chile,' by the guide.

    Then long hikes through the forest looking for pigmy elephants. Found only tracks of wild boars and scarlet leopards (The guide said it was a scarlet leopard) and also got attached to several leeches. They climb a low level bush, anchor their base and extend the rest of their worm like body as a waving heat detector that will fasten to any warm object that passes by. Once their sucker is attached it is impossible to shake them off. Sprinkle on salt if available, or apply a flame.

Leeches have had such bad PR since movies like 'The African Queen.' In the old days no doc would be without a jar of them in his black bag. Lately they are coming back into fashion. To drain blood from black eyes, especially those left by the plastic surgeon, and the reconstructive surgeon. They are the most effective way, in fact possibly the only way to remove collections of blood from below the skin that look ugly and impede healing.

I don't think anyone has given a thought to the desperately lonely life of a leech. It may go through an entire lifetime without meeting another of it's kind. They carry both sets of equipment. It lay eggs and fertilizes them and moves on. No friendly chats with other leeches about the flavor of the month, be it wild boar, leopard, and occasional elephant or the rare taste of a passing human. None of the joys of motherhood or fatherhood. Just hang on and suck until you are full, then drop off, climb a bush and fasten your rear end to a leaf, then start waving the long thin end in the air seeking the passing of another warm body. Anything warm will contain blood and their next meal. For my next lifetime I will definitely skip coming back as a leech. I don't know if an ardent feminist would embrace this as a way to make males superfluous. Perhaps the purist liberated female would object to carrying around a set of male type appendages. The only thing sadder is the sex life of the glow worms in New Zealand.

Chapter Twenty Three

New Zealand

Travel does broaden the mind in many ways. After spending several weeks in New Zealand standing upside down my brain must have expanded quite a bit. I also learnt that polyester is ruining the wool business, and I was amazed at the love life of the glow worm.

There should be no problem getting to sleep in New Zealand with so many sheep to count. However, sheep farmers are not happy with synthetic fibers, which they claim are nowhere as good as wool, just cheaper. After a few years of polyester fiber production the sheep population had dropped from 70 million to 35 million, still greatly outnumbering the human population of about three and a half million. Farmers are now turning more to dairy, beef and venison. Large deer farms sell venison to Germany and others for good prices. It was the best meal I had there. The lamb I tried to eat was stringy and tough, probably old mutton, with the best cuts being sent for export.

A sheep gets a really quick haircut, in about thirty seconds. A good shearer can clip over 300 a day, and the sheep don't complain about the rough ridges left behind or the occasional cut from the clipper. They are just happy to lose the six inch wool coat.

Milking also goes fast. By hand, they were up at 4 am, and milking forty cows took all day. Now the cows walk into a carousel, four vibrating suction cups are stuck on and it's over in six minutes. 900 cows, no problem.

Unless they had been eating new grass, which will give them diarrhea. As I was filming, one let loose. My camera was okay, but my khaki pants had a brown and tan camouflage pattern and my hostess didn't really want me back in her car. Luckily all the families we stayed with were kind and understanding, many came from farming backgrounds, and it gave them a chuckle.

The country doesn't seem rich in resources. There was a gold rush or two but the main attraction has been a free passage and cheap land. This was very attractive in the 1800's for farm workers and factory hands in England working almost as slave labor. Children in England in those days started work at six years of age in the factories around unfenced machinery for 12 hours a day and they could be fired if they took Sundays off. New Zealand was a country where people could escape the rigid class system and build a better life even if it meant saying goodbye to family and friends. A free passage was offered to healthy men under forty, and to healthy women under 25. Even in the 1960's it only cost ten pounds, or about forty dollars for an assisted passage halfway around the world.

There are still signs that the country is not rich. Roofs are made of corrugated iron, although it is now stamped and painted to imitate red tiles. When it rains it sounds like a hundred hammers on tin drums. There are still many bridges built with only one lane to save money. Signs tell motorists which direction has the right of way and you wait your turn to cross the bridge.

The Islands were submerged millions of years ago and when they came up again there were no animals. Birds came and the occasional bat, but there were no predators so the birds gave up the work of flying. There are still many flightless birds, including the Kiwi. These got a rude shock when the Europeans arrived with dogs and cats and rats from the ships. The inhabitants, the Maoris were not at all happy to have white men taking their land, and they were big and aggressive and put up such a fight that a treaty was signed giving them equal rights with white men and letting Queen Victoria handle the selling of land. As soon as the ink was dry the treaty was broken and 'differences' still persist.

The scenery is fantastic, as seen in 'The Lord of the Rings.' This was supposed to have happened in ancient England, before industrial pollution. The fields, hills and mountains are spectacular, even better looking than many in England.

I mentioned the strange love life of the glow worm. We went through a pitch dark cave festooned with stalactites covered with glowing worms. Why do they glow? These little worms exude a very sticky glue, and the glow attracts moths and when one lands, zap, lunch for the worm. The worm spins a cocoon and after a baby fly grows inside it emerges for a brief and unusual life of about a day and a half. The boy flies have scent organs on their foreheads, as well as sex organs and they spend their little life flying and hitting their head against the rock of the cave. They leave behind a drop of scent and some sperm. The girl fly, attracted, comes and sits on the rock and that's that. Little girls have sometimes asked "Can I get pregnant from sitting on a toilet seat?"

I always said 'No' but if girl glow worms were asked the answer would have to be different. Travel does broaden the mind. The high points of a male fly's day was when it banged its head into a wall of solid rock, time and time again. It made me question Darwin's theory. Why couldn't Mother Nature let them develop a similar apparatus on their feet, or even their tail?

Roots in Schagen

We are all a bit curious about our ancestors. My father never talked about his family in Holland, and only once did a relative, introduced as Uncle Peter come to visit. About twenty years after my father's death, I became curious. I wrote to Genealogical Institutes in Holland, and to the Postmaster of my father's birthplace, Schagen, in Northern Holland. A long time later the Postmaster replied, and said that my father had had three brothers and three sisters, all deceased, including Uncle Peter. I had known nothing about them. That stimulated me to hunt for cousins, and I found one, still living in Northern Holland. Cousin Simon was a sign painter, and he was kind enough to send me photos of my uncles and aunts. Putting faces to the names made it more real, and then there was another break. A lady with the same surname had found my enquiry at The Hague, and she had published a book with the family tree of the family Rotgans. Her name is Nel Fijnheer-Rotgans.

But my branch of the family did not join up with hers. She had traced three lines of Rotgans back to the early 1600's, in her book 'Genealogie van de familie Rotgans,' which is the story of the 'Rotganzen van Wieringen.' The three lines all came from North Holland, and before that from an island in the North Sea called Terschelling. She came from one line, and my father from another. There was probably a missing link, but she never found it.

Surnames in the 1600's were vague and carelessly recorded. Ours came from a bird that migrated through Holland, and had the annoying habit of pecking away at the layers of grass that held the dams together. Since much of Holland was below sea level, these birds were a hazard. Hunters of the goose began calling themselves after the bird, which had a red ring around its' neck. It was known as the Red Goose, der Rot Gans.

Paper trail

Mention a paper trail and most people think of the IRS. I think of our progress through this vale of tears from birth to death. The papers I think of are some of those signed by that endangered and much abused species, the Family Doctor.

You were all babies once, thought of as beautiful by your mothers, but your entry into this world would not be official without the birth certificate signed by the doctor who helped you arrive. Some of mine stand out in my mind.

She was 49, a chain smoker, a heavy drinker, and she was taking three drugs every day for her epilepsy. So many risk factors. She was five months pregnant when she first came to see me. I sweated blood for months. At 49 she was an elderly primip at high risk for Downs syndrome in the baby, about one in eleven, as well as her other risks. She promised to stop drinking and smoking but she couldn't quit taking her different drugs or she would have a seizure. The baby came a bit early, was a bit small, but otherwise perfect. However, I had failed. She hadn't quit her cigarettes or her heavy drinking. She had promised to have her tubes tied but when she saw how much fun her first baby was she wanted more.

Another birth certificate I signed made me smile. The husband came in with his wife on her first visit. He wanted to be in the delivery room.

"Okay, but you have to realize the nurses and I will be busy, we won't have any time if something happens to you."

"Don't worry, doc. I'm a veteran, I've seen it all. Bodies blown to bits, sometimes nothing left but the boots." He sounded offended, as if I should have known.

He was lean and muscular, crew cut, and if looks could kill I would have been vaporized. The mother was Italian and they strongly believe that the more noise they make the better it is for the baby. When the time came she was yelling and screaming in good voice. I took the scissors and cut a long epiziotomy and the baby came out with blood, mucous and a lot of baby Italian screaming. Then there was a loud thud. The veteran had hit the floor, but I had to sew up mother and check the baby and send them to post partum before I could look at him. By then he was sitting, sheepishly, with a big cut on his forehead.

"Get up on here" I said, and I sewed him up on the same table that had seen the entry of his son into the world. Really a family affair. Togetherness.

When I think of the many Workman's Comp. Forms I have filled out I think of the man in the yellow T-shirt.

"I hoit, Doc, I hoit." I think he was from New York. He had allegedly injured his back at work lifting a fifty pound box and he seemed to be in agony. Touch his toes ? He couldn't even bend. Twist 90 degrees? He could twist 5 degrees without a lot of groaning and facial grimaces. The Xrays were normal, and as he kept coming back I got an opinion from a neurologist, who said there was nothing he could find. He always put on a good show when he limped out of the office, staggering and groaning, hardly able to walk, but one day I was in a side room with a view of the parking lot, and I witnessed a miracle. As he walked to his truck his pain went away. He began walking normally. His brown pick up had a very high step but he climbed up with ease. I recorded my observations on the chart.

On his next visit I told him the good news. He wouldn't have to stay cooped up at home watching TV on full pay. I was releasing him to go back to work, full duties, no limitations. He fired me on the spot and I never saw him again, and I never knew if Workman's Comp cut him off, but I will always remember that yellow T-shirt and "It hoits, Doc, it hoits."

There are death certificates and there are death certificates. At the end it could be easy, with a 90 year old lady dying in her sleep in a nursing home, but it wasn't always like that. Charles was an accountant, 55, with terminal lung cancer. When I saw him for the last time he was leaning back on the pillows, his eyes open, and on his face there was an expression of utter terror. He'd been so scared of dying he hadn't even closed his eyes when the time came.

I was in the ER when a call came from an ambulance.

"Transporting a full code, ETA five minutes. Male, nine months old."

A baby? It really was a full code, and when they pushed through the swing doors one paramedic was squeezing the small chest, the other pumping an ambubag. As I got to work I got the story. The mother had been driving, with her maid sitting next to her holding the baby. Then BANG, they were hit from the side and the baby went flying through the open window, landing head first on the road. After 30 minutes I stopped the code. I'd run all the drugs several times, but nothing helped. For the cause of death I did a post mortem Xray. The skull looked like a broken egg shell. I really felt I had failed when I signed that death certificate.

There was once a very special piece of paper. It was a

few years ago, in Canada, and I was looking after the practice of a husband and wife team of doctors while they were on holiday. I picked up the next chart, Dianne, a 19 year old girl, and went in to the exam. room. She was pretty, and very black, and suddenly she saw me and she was horrified. She was shocked. I know I'm not Robert Redford but I had never scared anyone like that.

"I came to see Dr. Jane."
"She's on vacation. I'm seeing her patients."
"I must see Dr. Jane. When will she be back?"
"In about two weeks."
"That's too late", she wailed. "I must see Dr. Jane."
I had noticed a different accent and I asked
"Where are you from?" She was from Somalia. Dr. Jane had patients from all over the world, and we talked. Dr. Jane had seen this girl, and her mother, and she began to relax and finally told me the story.

Her boyfriend had just dumped her, and her mother was convinced he had had his way with her. In the culture of Somalia virginity is very important. I had once seen a National Geographic feature showing young girls lined up lying in a field waiting to be checked by a tribal elder. That's what Dianne wanted.

About twenty minutes later we were sitting in the office. She was smiling and I was writing on a prescription pad. I wasn't sure exactly what to put. Some things just aren't covered in med school, and you have to wing it.

"I hereby certify that Dianne xxx is virgo intacta, has not had sex, and she is a virgin."

I gave it to her, and she left smiling. Then I realized I had messed up again. I had lived in Vancouver as a young man and I knew there weren't many 19 year old virgins, and I would bet there was only one with a paper to prove it. Such a rare document. And I hadn't kept a copy. Sometimes I really messed up.

Chapter Twenty Four

Welfare Indians

The time is several years ago, the place is Northern Canada where I was looking after a clinic in a small town called Dease Lake, population 900. The lone doctor who was the only medical help for almost three hundred miles was having a vacation with his family. He needed it. His work was all day, all night call, seven days a week, and he handled everything that came in the door. It was far from ancillary services, such as vets.

"Doc, do you do eagles?" said the young woman on the phone. "It was hit by a truck."

She was with the Park Service, and when the eagle swooped into a truck, probably chasing a smaller bird, the driver had passed the problem on to her.

By the time the stunned eagle arrived at the hospital it was recovering. The Park Ranger had tied its feet together, but now it was moving its head, and the huge beak was a lethal weapon. Nearly three inches of tough, sharp beak, with forty pounds of muscular eagle struggling to use it.

"I have a piece of canvas," she said, and soon appeared with a square of tough tent material.

"This is how we do it, " she said. She waved the canvas in front of the eagle and he grabbed it tightly and she pulled. "He won't let go. It's okay now, Doc."

With the trucker pulling on the legs, and the ranger on the canvas, the eagle was immobilized.

I was dubious.

"If I was an eagle I would let go and slash at anything I could reach. That is a deadly weapon."

"Have you ever seen an eagle drop it's prey?" she asked. "That's their way. Until it is ripped to shreds they hold on."

"If it got hold of my hand then, goodbye hand?"

"Not while I pull, and move it a little, as if it was alive."

I was in no hurry to lay a healing hand on the angry eagle, but after watching for a while I decided that the Ranger knew what she was talking about. I started to examine the big bird.

"There is blood on the shoulder, here, on the right, but I can't feel a fracture underneath." Cautiously I felt all over the bird. No bones crunched when I moved them, and when I moved the joints there was no hostile reaction.

"There is a laceration over the injury. I can fix that, but I think I will use sutures that dissolve. Not that I wouldn't like to see you again, but the eagle may remember that I poked and prodded him, and he might carry a grudge. Do you have a large cage?"

"Yes, I do," she said.

"Then you can keep him quiet for about a week, so he doesn't tear the sutures loose. Keep an eye out for infection, and I could come an look at him, in the cage."

"Watch out for swelling, redness, heat or pain, and call me any time."

I saw the Ranger a month or so later. She appeared to be in one piece, with all of her fingers intact. Obviously the eagle had succumbed to her charms.

"Oh, once he got used to me he was an angel," she said.

I had never seen an angel, and I didn't think it would have had dark brown wings and a deadly, sharp beak, but I was not going to argue. In fact, I was a little smug. Another triumph of modern medicine.

It was a lovely Sunday afternoon in August, and they had called me from the lake where I was enjoying the sun, to see a patient.

Sitting on the stretcher was Joseph, Joseph Tikliat, a Tahltan Indian. I saw quite a lot of the Indians. There were 3 villages, each about 20 miles away and I visited them at least twice a week. The government nurse in the village would have patients ready for me to see, and then I would have to go to the houses for the ones that couldn't make it in to see me. I made house calls all the time, and I got to see how they lived. The babies were fat and lazy, the young children and teens were into drugs and alcohol and sex, and so were their parents. I treated many complications arising from all activities. They lived on reservations, they paid no rent and they got an allowance from the government, like a form of welfare, but it wasn't called that. What it meant was that they never had to do any work if they didn't want to. They had nothing to do except watch TV and OD on drugs, sex and alcohol. Some of the houses were well kept, clean and tidy, but they were the exception. I could see the damage that had been done to the morale of the welfare Indians, as some of the whites called them behind their backs.

There were many exceptions. One was a grandmother,

Grandma Peg, who was a patient I saw regularly for ulcers on her legs. She was wrinkled and very old, but she had character. There was a twinkle in her eyes, and she had a spark of life that was missing in the majority of the Tahltan Indians. I had made an effort to learn a few expressions in their language, like "Hello," and "How are you today," and this would always get her smiling. When I had finished with her legs and washed up I usually sat down and talked with her.

She loved to talk of the old days, when she was a girl, and the tribe lived in a camp in the forest, in tents, like wigwams. Animal hides were stretched over spruce boughs, and the women looked after the children and the cooking while the men were out hunting and trapping and fishing in the river. In winter, in Northern Canada, there was a lot of snow, it got very cold, and twenty below zero was a warm day. They were tough in those days. They had a hard life, but they were happy. Grandma Peg smiled a lot and her eyes wrinkled with pleasant memories. When the game became scarce they packed up the whole village and moved. They rolled the tent hides into bundles and moved everything across the snow and through the woods about 30 or 40 miles and set up a new camp.

Grandma Peg certainly wasn't a welfare Indian, and neither was Joseph. He chose to work, as a horse wrangler in the high country. The hunting up there was good and people flew in from all over the US to stay at the lodge down near the road. They were carried up by helicopter to the high country where Joseph looked after a bunch of horses. The hunters were put on horses and guides led them off to the best hunting areas. Early on that Sunday morning Joseph had been alone with the horses. They were not expecting any hunters that day and as he was bending down a horse kicked backwards and caught Joseph on his forehead, knocking him out. When he woke up, his face was sticky with blood. He staggered over to the radio shack and called the lodge. The helicopter came and took him down, and they put him in a pick-up for the long bumpy ride to the clinic.

I checked him over, and he seemed fine. I took an Xray, and his skull was not cracked, so I started cleaning the cut on his forehead. As I cleaned I found that the cut kept on going. The side of his head was covered in a layer of dark, dried blood, and as I cleaned it off I found that the cut still kept on going. I cleaned and I cleaned until I had uncovered a cut running almost all the way around his head. Then I started to lift up the front of the cut, and the more I lifted, the more came loose until I was holding up his complete scalp. All of his scalp held in place by a strip only about two inches long. The horses hoof must have torn the scalp loose, and it fell down and stuck on as the blood dried. It was a wonder that he hadn't bled to death.

The scalp was surprisingly clean, and I only had to trim the edges before I could start repairing it. I had to cut a thin strip from the top and the bottom of the cut to get fresh edges for me to start putting in sutures. It took about an hour, and 80 sutures to sew him back together again. Joseph was lying calmly, quiet, not saying a word, as I did my cutting and sewing.

When I finished I asked
"Do you want to have a look?"

He shrugged, and the nurse brought him a mirror. He looked at the lines of stitches running almost all the way around his head, and he grunted.

"That must have been an Indian horse", he said. "Darn near scalped me."

"I want you to come back tomorrow for an infection check, and then in a weeks time I'll take the stitches out."

He shook his head.

"I've got to work", he said.

He left the clinic, climbed into the truck with the

driver, and I never saw him again. I heard later that he went straight back up to his camp, and when he got the manager of the hunting lodge to take the stitches out there was no problem.

He was another exception, like Grandma Peg. Joseph definitely was not a Welfare Indian.

Appearances

It was Saturday in Dease Lake and the phone rang. It was seven o'clock and I groaned. I was going fishing, and on the days when I didn't have a clinic I didn't like to get up too early.

"Doctor Rogans?"

I recognized the voice of Nurse Ramsey. She was a very good nurse, but she didn't like men, especially men doctors. She was very efficient, but she had a hard face, and she seemed to be one cold hearted woman.

"The ambulance is bringing in a car accident victim, a young male, stable. Another ambulance is bringing in two bodies, and you'll have to pronounce them." She loved to tell me what to do.

"When?"

"In about half an hour. You coming over?" It was more of an order than a question.

"I'm on my way."

I was there when the ambulances pulled in. The live victim was taken into one of the emergency rooms, and I made a quick check inside the other ambulance. Two bodies, no pulse, no breathing, very cold.

Nurse Ramsey had oxygen running on the victim. He

was a young man, a German on holiday. He looked comfortable and the vital signs were stable but there was a horrible dent, a deep depression three inches across just above his left eye. The bone had been smashed in. I gave him a quick exam., nothing else seemed out of line, and there seemed to be no problem on the XRay. The thin bone over the sinus had been stove in, but the skull next to the brain was not fractured. I left the room and got on the phone.

When I had agreed to do this locum they told me "Any serious problems, call the Air Ambulance in Vancouver and it will be here in an hour. It's a Lear jet, room for three or four patients. No problem."

Sure enough, the dispatcher in Vancouver said "Right doc. Depressed skull fracture, we'll have the plane there in an hour."

It was now just after seven, and I breathed a sigh of relief. Young Herman looked stable, but there might be swelling or a slow bleed going on inside his head. He might go sour and have severe brain problems any time. If there was bleeding inside, the treatment was to drill a hole through the skull, a burr hole and bring the pressure down. I knew all about that in theory but it was something I had never done. And I didn't want to.

I went back and gave young Herman a more through exam., and there was nothing out of line. He had been driving in the middle of the night and probably dosed off and skidded off the gravel road. The ambulance crew had told me that his car had flipped a couple of times. His young wife was strapped in, but their little girl had flown out of the open window, and they had found her body some twenty feet away. They had been driving across the North of Canada, and were on their way down South to Vancouver to catch a plane home, back to Germany. He had been deceived by the distance on the map. Canada is a big country. He had planned a 1200 mile drive and he had been running late.

He wasn't a big man, about 24, a bit skinny, and he didn't look strong. I looked again at the Xray. The frontal sinuses, the air spaces, were involved but the bone next to the brain did look as if it was okay. I would have loved a CAT scan or an MRI, but we didn't have one.

I got on the phone to the neurosurgery docs in Vancouver who would be receiving him, and they made some suggestions, but it was up to me until the air ambulance got there.

8 o'clock came, 8.15, and then 8.30. The dispatcher said there might be some small delays, the plane had had to land to check out a warning gauge but it was in the air again and should be there soon. Young Herman was holding up alright, so I asked Nurse Ramsey to come with me.

"I want to look at the bodies. I may need your help." She grunted, in an unfriendly way, but she came willingly to the ambulance outside.

We got in, and there was a stretcher on each side. On the left was a white blanket covering a short body, about five foot five. I lifted the top and looked at the face. It was a young woman, early twenties, and she was pretty. There wasn't a mark on her face and she seemed to be resting, at peace. But her skin was cold, and she was whiter than the blanket.

I lifted the rest of the blanket and started to check her from her legs up. Pressing on her pelvis, her stomach, on her chest. Everything seemed normal, and there was nothing broken. I checked her arms, her shoulders, and ran my hands around her face. All seemed fine. I shifted position and gently pulled on her head. There it was, a grinding sound, the thing that had killed her. Her neck was badly broken.

I covered her face, and sat down. I needed to take a couple of deep breaths. Doctors get used to death. They see it many times in one form or another, but this seemed so cruel, such a waste of a lovely young woman. I happened to glance up at Nurse Ramsey. Her face was blank, no expression, but there was a wetness in her eyes, and her lower lids looked full.

I turned to the other stretcher.

There was a short bundle, covered with another white blanket. I pulled down the top, and it was the little girl, about three years old. Like her mother she seemed to be resting peacefully, not a mark on her face, but she was as cold as death and she had the pale white of death. I lifted the rest of the blanket and did the same, examining her from the bottom to the top. Again, nothing broken, nothing dislocated, nothing out of line. I gently pulled on her neck, but there wasn't a crunching noise.

"Miss Ramsey, I need a post mortem Xray before I can make out the death certificate. Will you bring her into Xray?"

Then I looked at the nurse. Tears were running down both sides of her face. She wasn't making a sound, but she was gulping hard trying to keep things inside her.

"I'll carry her," I said, but she stiffened, and bent down to pick up the little girl's body. I got out of the ambulance first, and turned to take the little girl but Nurse Ramsey shook her head angrily at me, and got out carefully.

It was in the Xray room when she lay the little body on the hard metal table that she started sobbing, and she didn't care who saw her. I was lucky. I was busy calling the shots, telling people what to do. It helped me keep down the squeezing feelings I was having in my chest.

The Xray showed that the back of the little girl's head had been shattered like a broken eggshell. There was no doubt about the cause of death.

I went back to the emergency room and looked at young Herman. He was very still, staring ahead, as if he knew, but did he? Now I had to decide about telling him. Was he strong enough to take the shock? I didn't want to give him any tranquillizers, because that would mask any mental changes he might have if his brain started to have any problems. Would he react violently and shake his head around? I told one of the nurses to put on a neck collar and I went back to the phone.

It was 9.30, and yes, there had been another delay but the plane should be on the way. Ten o'clock came, then eleven. Then I decided to tell him. It was his family, and he had to know.

So I told him, very gently, that his wife, and his little girl were both dead. He made a little shake of his head, as if he didn't believe, or he didn't want to believe, but nothing else. No tears, no crying, no hysteria. He said,

"I want to call my parents in Germany. Can I do that?"

There was one woman in the town that spoke German. The RCMP helped find her, and soon she was in the clinic. She helped him make the call, and he spoke to his mother in German. The translator was telling me that he was just saying what had happened, that it was his fault, and that was when he started to cry. The interpreter took over the phone, and I answered the questions that were coming from Germany. Just then there was the whine of a jet. The air ambulance had arrived. It was one o'clock.

Appearances can be misleading. I was wrong about many things that day. The horrible looking skull fracture that I had been so worried about had caused no problem. The smooth, peaceful faces of the mother and her little girl were hiding the fact that they were both very dead. Above all I was wrong about Nurse Ramsey. She had always seemed to be a hard case, without feelings. She booked off early that day, badly shaken up. The next day she looked at me just as severely as ever, but, appearances can be misleading.

China train, thirty women.

When I travel I like to book tours with a local travel agent, That way I get local prices, and meet local people. I was staying in Suzhou, a pretty little town near Shanghai crisscrossed with canals. These had obstructed modern development and many houses were over three hundred years old. At a local travel agent I booked a tour to Guelin with a Chinese tour group, at a bargain price. $150 for five days and four nights. This was still very expensive for them, with their average wage at twenty dollars a week. I got to see the real countryside by train for thirty hours. There were no seats, just long dormitory cars with six bunks per compartment, and no doors. I chose the bottom bunk, which made for easy access, but I got dive bombed with wrappers from the children above me, who took frequent peeks at this funny looking foreigner.

All of my tour companions were female, mainly mothers with small children, all friends on this big trip. The odd ones out were me and two teenage high school girls, aged about seventeen. The tour leader was a brisk young woman in her mid twenties who spoke good English, and she was very conscientious in organizing everyone to get the most out of the trip, including me. She had an air of authority and she was very pleased to be able to organize my happiness in English. The Chinese are used to being told what to do and I wondered if she was a rising star in her local communist party.

The children and the mothers walked up the corridor quite often to have a look at this strange Western barbarian, the only one on the train. In school they are still taught that the number one enemy of China is the United States of America, or anyone living there, but that didn't stop them from being extremely friendly. The teenage girls were shy. In

China nice girls seen talking or walking with Western males get angry looks from their elders, but gradually their curiosity got the better of them and soon they were coming by every five minutes. I soon figured it out. They would go off and practice an English phrase then come and try it on me. They were young and slim, and quite pretty behind their thick glasses and they bubbled with the happiness of young people on a vacation.

There was no dining car, but the food trolley came by often. I had no idea what I was eating, but it kept me going. I soon found out that the train stopped long enough at the stations for you to get to the food stalls on the platforms. There were bowls of fat for deep frying all sorts of brown things, and cold boiled chicken feet were big sellers, but they also had warm beer. I arrived in Guelin rather ripe and smelly, tired, but happy. I even managed to use the Asian toilet, squatting on my haunches while the train did its rocking and rolling. It was painful, and took balance and skills that were not mentioned in the guide book.

I knew I had to bring my own toilet paper, and the balance bar to hold onto was vital to survival when squatting with trousers around your knees as the train rocked crazily from side to side. There was a hole in the floor through which you could see the railbed racing past, and a feeble flushing system. With the violent movement of the train it wasn't possible to aim well and a thick brown deposit built up around the rim of the hole. By the end of the rail journey visits to the toilet became extremely brief.

About a hundred miles out of Shanghai the urban sprawl gave way to an older China. The standard five story workers apartments were replaced by old low houses with grey tiled roofs. Green rice fields and palm trees, but not a cow in sight. In a restaurant if you order meat, you get pork.

When we got to Gueilin there was a problem. Foreigners were not allowed to travel on the same river boats as Chinese people, and the next day there were no foreign boats going up the river. There would have been big trouble with the tourist police if I tried to get on a Chinese person boat. Nothing could be fixed up, so while they enjoyed the lovely scenic cruise on the Li River, which was the highlight of the tour I was left with Chinese TV in my hotel room.

The group, all women and children, was genuinely upset that their pet foreigner was sad. I personally wrote to Jiang Zemin about it, but he never replied. The mothers ganged up and made such a fuss that the tour guide arranged an unscheduled visit to a smaller river, where there were no tourist police, We piled into a bus after supper, and at 8pm that night we arrived at a tiny town with few street lights. I got to enjoy a real Chinese hotel. No elevator, and the stairwell was lit with ten watt light bulbs. If there were any cockroaches, I couldn't see them. I heard some rustling in many dark corners, but I never did see any little beetles. There was no A.C. but as a token there was a broken fan in my room. Many rooms did not even have a broken fan. All of this for $4.00 a night.

I managed to fix my fan and left all my doors open to get some air. The girls were next door and shyly asked me "Would I come to their bedroom and make their fan work?" We males are always happy to fix things, especially if it is to help a damsel in distress and soon they had air circulating in their bedroom. They were happy and they were then delighted to be invited to my room to play cards.

About twenty minutes later they came bouncing into my room in their grey flannel pajamas and I showed them how to play Blackjack. First I explained my rules of the house. Number One was that the door had to stay open. I didn't want a bunch of Chinese mothers angry at me, and number two they could sit on the bed and play cards but far enough apart to be proper. Sure enough as we played there was a constant parade of Chinese mothers walking past my door. Even though I was their pet foreigner there were limits. The girls learnt quickly and soon picked up the Las Vegas terminology. They were giggling happily on Chinese coca cola. I was happy with warm Chinese beer.

After they left I had a shower. It was a standard Chinese bathroom, a bare cement room with no soap or towels. I had brought my own. There was rusty piping, and a showerhead, and a hole in the floor for everything and that was it. In the middle of the night I made an unpleasant discovery. My hole in the floor was connected to all the other holes in the floor, and someone along the corridor had a bad case of Montezuma's revenge. The diarrhea of amebiasis has an unforgettable penetrating smell. A thick brown evil smell that infused every part of my room. I covered my hole as best I could, opened the windows, and tried not to take a deep breath.

The next day the Zi river was rather small, and shallow, with mild rapids that were no problem for the ancient narrow flat bottomed boats and their rusty two stroke engines. A far cry from the luxury air conditioned tourist boats on the Li, the main river, but ours was more fun, especially now that we were a large happy family. Especially the Western Barbarian who had two pretty girls sitting next to him and a succession of Chinese children climbing on his knees. It was possibly the best hundred and fifty dollars I have ever spent.

Chapter Twenty Five

Chinese girl, Parisian accent.

In Suzhou, at the Foreign Language Book Store, I got a pleasant surprise. I was looking for a book on Buddha, and saw a pretty, young Chinese girl going through the foreign books, obviously reading them. I tried English, but she preferred French. She replied with an utterly charming Parisian accent. Took me back to the days of my youth in that city. She had spent two years with her family in French West Africa, on the Ivory Coast.

She asked, but apparently Buddha wasn't a big seller in atheist Mainland China, and when she asked if I would like her to take me to another place to look, I leered happily. Then she said she would have to phone her parents for an OK. She was only 17.

We climbed into a taxi which took us all over town, for a big $2.75, much more than my usual ride for $1.20 ride to down-town. But it was worth it, just to listen to such a sexy accent.

We ended up in a Buddhist temple, which had lots of books, but all in Chinese. She said she was a devout atheist, because her mother said that only crazy people prayed to Buddha. While we were there, there were plenty of crazy people bowing three times and talking to Buddha.

There, chickens didn't cross the road. The only chickens are in cages at the market, to be fresh for the housewife, and besides they would never make it. Cars sometimes have to slow down for the cyclists, but if a car or a taxi sees a gap he will step on the gas and swerve all over the road to get through the gap. Pedestrians have rights. They can die, or jump for their lives. Cyclists ride like kings of the road. They head right for you, look you straight in the eye as if to say 'Move it or else.' Scooters are the worst. The one you saw coming at 20 mph will see a gap as soon as you take your eye off him, and speed up to 60 and get mad if you are in the way. Pedicabs are sneaky, often going against the traffic. They will appear around a corner coming from behind you, and mutter something rude when they miss you.

There are no wedding rings, but the young single girls have long sexy, silky black hair. Soon after marriage this gets cut short, so it is easy to manage and to heck with hubby.

I have about given up trying to learn Chinese. I can just get by, and last night when I went looking for thread to fix a shirt, I looked it up in my basic dictionary. Then I pronounced the word using all the rules and the four correct tones, but I still got a blank stare. Finally I showed them the word in Chinese characters. they said "Oh you mean . . . " which was what I had been saying with just a slightly different emphasis. I kept on looking in many stores. I found lipsticks, female underwear, and feminine hygiene. They must have thought these foreigners have strange fetishes. There was an exhibition of sex toys, going back 1500 years. On the eve of marriage, mothers would give daughter a ceramic model showing all of the many ways to make love It must have scared them silly. And there was a variety of Buddha with 8 arms. It was fascinating to see what a man with eight arms could do.

Safari with a skull cracker

Angry plus impulsive plus foolish is a dangerous combination. It could have landed me in an African jail. It was the time I took a skull cracker on safari.

The Comanches made a skull cracker from a short, thick stick with a heavy rock tied to the end. In close combat they smash it down hard onto the enemies head. I was going to Africa, full of wild and dangerous animals, so I took a skull cracker. I had never been in a fight, I had never been mugged, but I had an active imagination. To get it through security, I had it dismantled. The heavy, chrome plated padlock was in one corner of my suitcase, and the length of telephone wire was neatly coiled, in another corner, looking like an accessory for my MP3 player. Put together, I had practiced at home, swinging and hitting a steel plate on my bed until I could hit, and make a dent in the steel every time. On a safari we expected to see the Big Five. A lion, an elephant, a water buffalo, a leopard, and a rhino. I wouldn't be looking for danger, but I wanted a weapon. I had also read the U.S. State Department Travel Advisory.

"Attacks on visitors are common. Robbery is generally the reason, but some victims have lost their lives. In 2006 a missionary couple were driving near Nairobi. The woman was hacked to death in front of her husband. Street crime is common in Nairobi. Never wear jewelry, don't wear a camera around your neck." Our safari started in Nairobi.

The taxi from the airport had to slow down when it got into downtown Nairobi. There were multicolored crowds of people, black natives, Arabs in white sheets, plus Chinese and Indians. They were so closely packed it was a wonder they could move. The road was full of bikes, scooters, strange little cars and crowded, battered buses. Every seat was full and they were standing in the aisle. On the outside the grey paint was faded and scratched, and the open windows were framed with dirty brown rust. Every vehicle belched clouds of thick blue smoke as it jockeyed for position.

A safari used to mean a hunting trip, to try to shoot the Big Five, with native porters to carry the tents and guns and food. These days a travel company will call all of their tours 'Safaris.' It was a British company, and my airline connections from America got me into Nairobi almost one day early.

The hotel had an ancient elegance that spoke of colonial days. Shiny brass and polished mahogany, and in the lounge the overstuffed armchairs had supported many British bottoms in the days of the big white hunters. Now they were full of strangely dressed travelers from America and Europe, thumbing through their Lonely Planet guide books.

The front desk, and the manager were polite and helpful, but they discouraged me from exploring outside.

"Some very bad people everywhere. They take all of your things, or worse."

I had the hotel lunch, and dinner, and breakfast the next day, but I was getting stir crazy.

"Can I get a tour of Nairobi?"

The front desk people were very helpful, and gave me several options, but it was lunch time.

"Are there any good restaurants nearby?" I asked.

"Yes bwana. One is about two blocks away. You can

see it from here. But you must take a taxi."

"Oh come on. I can easily walk that far."

"It is not safe, bwana. You must take a taxi."

Then I remembered the call I had made to a friend in Brownsville. He had been a big game hunter, now married to a doctor.

"Arthur, I'll be going through Nairobi. Do you have any contacts there I could look up?"

"Well, uhm, John, yes. My sister. But a gang recently broke into her house, tied her up, beat her, raped her, then stole everything. It's not a good time to visit."

I took a taxi. When we got to the restaurant I gave the driver a good tip. I emphasized that I would need to be picked up.

"Yes bwana. I come back for you. At 1.30. Indio bwana."

It was a good lunch, but there was no taxi. The hotel tried.

"There is no taxi just now, but please wait."

I could see the hotel just two blocks away. At 2.30 I started walking. There were some vacant lots, sandy and sprinkled with garbage. It was hot and dusty. Then I saw a fine looking native walking the other way. Tall, jet black, lean with powerful shiny muscles. He stopped six foot from me. Then he snarled.

"Give me your money. Give me all of your money." He wasn't smiling.

The guide books all say that it is better to lose your wallet than your life, but I have a strange reaction to danger and threats. Instead of getting scared, I get angry. Stupid, perhaps, but it's an automatic reaction.

"Go to Hades, you black faced, black hearted black enameled jumped up never came down son of a ..." When I'm angry, my language is not nice. I pulled my skull cracker out of my right hand trouser pocket, started swinging it in vicious circles, and advanced. The chrome padlock flashed in the sun. He backed away, then passed me by, giving me a wide berth. Maybe he thought I was crazy, more trouble than I was worth. I was standing there, breathing hard, when I felt his hand in my other pocket. He had seen the bulge of my small movie camera. I smacked his hand away, turned, and moved towards him, swinging the skull cracker, yelling obscenities. He ran, and I walked to the hotel.

The safari was perfectly safe. We were a mixed gang, including a solo Canadian nurse, a young Swiss girl with an attractive soft helplessness, a couple of young black women from Los Angeles both with advanced degrees and highly paid jobs in electronics. We saw the Big Five, which included lions, the big black water buffalos, a leopard, several stupid one ton rhinos, and elephants. Plus hippos playing happily in glorious mud. The wild lions came close and sniffed at the tires of our LandRovers, but we were safe inside, shooting pictures. I was intrigued to see them pee backwards on trees to mark their territory. Apparently their male member had a swivel joint at the base. We felt less safe when they roared near our tents at night, but they never came close. As well as the Big Five there were the long necked giraffes, the hideous warthogs, foul smelling hyenas and many skeletons marking the end of successful animal hunts. The baby elephants were still small enough to walk under their mothers. The Masai natives were colorful in their red robes, doing their vertical jump dance. We bounced along rutted tracks that made us fly just as high on our bouncy car springs. It was a fantastic trip, and I'd do it again.

It was only later that the guide told me how lucky I had been.

"You could have ended up in an African jail, and believe me they are not fun. If you had hit him, broken a bone or even his skull, who do you think the local police would have believed? There would have been a dozen witnesses to swear that he was an innocent local, that you made an unprovoked attack on a law abiding native. You were very lucky, bwana." There it was again, a little bit of luck.

I still have the skull cracker, but it has only made one trip to foreign parts. To Africa, which has many wild and dangerous animals. Mostly brown with four legs, and some very black, with only two.

Chapter Twenty Six

The Rake's Progress

For about twenty years, matrimony had seldom been seriously considered. I had experienced what Zorba the Greek had described so bitterly.

"Zorba," the young Englishman asks, "have you ever been married?"

"Married, my friend?" replies Zorba. "Am I not a man? Is not a man stupid? I am a man. Wife, kids, house, the full catastrophe! Yes, I married!"

There had been romantic interludes after my divorce with ladies from England, Canada and America, but few had been really serious. As the pain of separation from children had increased, so my inclination to become deeply involved became smaller. Living alone can be sad and sorrowful, but being raped in divorce was more painful than the loneliness. A few relationships did reach the 'thinking about it' stage, but with Margaret the barrier crumbled, and conjugal bliss seemed attainable and desirable.

She was exceptional. Not too tall, very attractive plus smart and confident as well. She owned and ran a business with branches in several cities. She was opening a new branch, and I was there for the Chamber of Commerce committee that welcomed new enterprises. On the platform she was poised and pretty, and as I gazed at her a familiar moment of madness signaled that she was something special. I had had this before. A coup de foudre. Literally being hit by a bolt of lightning, the highly irrational state of love at first sight. I struggled, and maintained my composure over the small talk. I was at ease. I was a youngish, fairly attractive bachelor doctor. I had been one of a bunch of males auctioned in a charity event, and a date with me had attracted a goodly number of bids. The price went so high that it was shared by two young ladies anxious to get up close and personal with me. But that's another story.

I was calm and friendly as I handed her my card.

"Here is my basic information. I was impressed by your composure, and the way you handled this gathering. You did very well. Perhaps we can meet for lunch." She was almost shy as she gave me her card. Certainly not the hard business woman I had expected.

We talked easily at lunch, and only one thing gave me pause.

"You are different from most men here, and I had you checked out," she said.

She had checked me out!

"Did I get a good rating?"

"Absolutely. We have both been through the torture of broken love. Maybe we have both become wiser."I almost said "And poorer," but while that might have been true for me but it would not have been tactful, or accurate. She may have made out like a bandit. The rest of that meeting and the many more that followed was delightful. She was certainly liberated, and could hold her own with men in her business world but she was not aggressive at the personal level. She was highly intelligent, well informed and articulate but so easy to be with it was like a dream. All this and sexy too.

Soon my car was parked overnight in her driveway, and we became an item. Her grown children seemed to approve, which was gratifying. They had inherited her brains and good looks, and we seemed to be forming a new family.

The closest I got to a sea test was when I took her on a cruise for Christmas. Things looked warm and inviting in the Caribbean but the forecast for Orlando was frigid. I had checked the forecast, and I had brought my Arctic parka. She brought a fur coat.

There was a cold wind coming off the ocean but we laughed at the weather. It did get a bit bumpy and she had a sensitive stomach, but I had brought the right stuff for that. It made me feel good to be needed.

We seemed to complement each other, and I bought a large house, five bedrooms and three baths, right on the water. It was big and fancy, with a mortgage to match, but so were my dreams. I could feed the catfish from my dock, and the prospects seemed rosy. There was no formal proposal of marriage, but as we talked about the details of the coming merger we seemed almost telepathic. It looked like we were reading each others minds.

Then something started as a small uncomfortable feeling. I couldn't put my finger on it. I had known all along that she was tough and successful, but she seemed kind and gentle away from her work. And she was, but there was a feeling of something and I couldn't say what.
Finally I said

"Margaret, we have both had failed marriages. I know that I am not perfect, and whatever my faults are, I don't want them to ruin what we have."

"What are you saying?"

"Do you think that a professional opinion on what we are like might help? A professional assessment of our emotional assets and liabilities." That should appeal to her business sense.

"We know that already. We are not children, we have both of us been out in the world and have learned to judge what other people are like. Especially you. What is that has you bothered?"

"That's it. I don't know. I do know that I have flunked matrimony, and I don't know why. Would it do any harm to get an opinion?"

We eventually agreed, it wouldn't hurt. We would both get a psych assessment from a respected psychologist.

I went first.

"John, what are you doing here?"

We knew each other, and had shared patients over the years.

"I am getting married, and we thought we might benefit from your assessment of our strengths and weaknesses."

We did the fifty minute hour, and repeated it a few days later. There were no surprises, we had known each other personally and professionally for years.

Then Margaret went in. I waited at her house, reading. I didn't have to wait long. She was back in less than half an hour.

"He wasn't there?" I asked.

"He was. I just walked out." She had left after twenty minutes.

"I am not going back to see that man," she said.

She wouldn't tell me why. Neither would he, when I phoned him the next day.

"John, you know I can't tell you. Patient information is absolutely confidential."

"Oh come on. Give me a hint. I am going to marry her. Just give me a tone of voice, or something."

"It's confidential, John. You know that."

She did go back a week later. And she didn't stay as long.

"I walked out, and I am not going back," she said angrily. And she would not give me a hint about the reason.

Our telepathy wasn't working. I had absolutely no idea what had happened, and why she was so angry. Was it something to do with me, or the shrink? I had never had any complaints from patients. It was a barrier between us, and I began to back off. We finally broke up, and I had a big house to lose myself in. About six months later I met the psychologist for coffee.

"We have broken up. I am not getting married, and I still don't know why."

"Not getting married?" he echoed. I had never seen him agitated before. "Thank God," he sighed.

"What do you mean, Thank God? This is something big, and you would have let me get hitched? Was it me, or her?"

"I told you, John, it's confidential." And that was the end of the story. I never knew why, or what "Thank God." meant. I was obviously doomed to a life of solitude, never to share things with someone, never to grow old with a feminine best friend. Somehow I had failed again.

Burma and Paying it forward.

For some strange mind - body connection, happy people seem to have better health than sad ones. So when I bought a tricycle rickshaw in Mandalay it may have been good for my health.

Burma is a country as big as Texas, between Thailand and India and the people are poor. Fifty dollars a month is a good salary, especially for men that pedal bicycle rickshaws around all day. Now why would I want to buy a tricycle rickshaw?

On top of most big hills all over Burma there are white, pointy pagodas, some several stories high. A few are even gilded. Most are solid, ringed by a small ornamental wall, usually with no access roads. They are seldom visited, and may be lonely for centuries. They are perhaps remembered in local legend, or recorded on some dusty page, or they may be forgotten by man. It doesn't matter. Buddha remembers. The Buddhist merit system seems even more popular here than in Thailand, which is 97% Buddhist.

The Buddhist believe in reincarnation, coming back to do better next time, and in karma. Bad karma is all the rotten things you do, even those ugly thoughts you believed were secret are all recorded somehow and accumulate as bad karma. If you die with a big debt of bad karma your next life will be full of tests and learning situations to work off the bad karma. Things can be really miserable and every Buddhist knows this. They are always looking for ways to build up good karma to cancel out the bad stuff.

So, a wealthy man or a rich war lord who probably did many a dirty deed to accumulate his wealth will spend a bunch of money building a holy pagoda on a hill. Perhaps his motives are selfish, but giving is good for the soul as he acquires some good karma. When I thought of giving Tutu his own trishaw I felt good. I would improve his life. You can picture a rickshaw, with a skinny Chinese man pulling something like a wheelbarrow with a seat. A trishaw is a bicycle with a sidecar bolted on for the passengers.

He had spent the last ten years peddling a rented

tricycle around Mandalay twelve hours a day. He is raising three boys, and his wife spends most of his money. So far he had saved $26, and it would take another thirty years to get the $100 to pay for his own trishaw.

Very few foreigners travel by trishaw. Taxis are cheap and quick, but you rush by, everything is a blur and you don't see the details of the sights and smells. The washing on the third floor balcony, the street vendor frying her snacks, the kids playing kickball. The roads could be a lot better. The bumpy ride on a rickshaw with no springs is just as therapeutic as a Swedish massage. Every bone is well and truly separated from every other bone and all the joints are well loosened. So, I got to know Tutu quite well on our leisurely journeys around Mandalay and he seemed to be a good man so I told him I would buy him a bike.

Maybe my motives were mixed. When you visit the country you have to bring in cash, because they don't take credit cards or travelers checks anywhere. I found out that I should have declared all my cash, and that leaving with undeclared money could land a foreigner in jail. The country is run by ruthless military dictators, and they like dollars but do not like Americans.

Tutu got all excited. Perhaps he had told this tale of woe many times and had finally got lucky, but I don't think so. I didn't see any other foreigners on trishaws. One fancy hotel didn't even want him coming through the main gate. When I came out he was parked on the street round the corner. It's not a classy way to travel.

He started calling me Father, asked me to come and meet his family, and the next day he said he hadn't slept all night. He kissed my hand with lips and teeth scarlet from chewing betel nut. Over a cup of tea the deal was done. The seller produced the all important licence, and a Promise Agreement and they both signed it. I gave Tutu the money and we rode away on his new possession. He stood on the pedals and the trishaw flew. And I felt better. Doing good is definitely good for your mental health. I may try it again sometime.

Chapter Twenty Seven

Butch Cassidy in Patagonia

Patagonia is the Southern half of Argentina, and goes right down to the tip of South America. Butch Cassidy and the Sundance Kid, the real outlaws, arrived there with satchels full of money. Somewhere between twelve and thirty thousand dollars US. Which was a lot of money in 1902. They were not worried about being robbed. That was their specialty. They robbed banks and held up trains. In the US they were number one on America's Most Wanted list. The reward had risen from two to four to ten thousand dollars as their haul from train and bank robberies had grown. Many freelance bounty hunters and Pinkerton's Detective Agency were getting close. It was time for a change of scenery. A boat was leaving New York for Buenos Aires.

In 1902 Buenos Aires was a wild, swinging city, full of fun and entrepreneurs, and one of these was an American dentist George Newberry who was trying to set up a Shangri La in Cholila, a small peaceful community in the foothills of the Andes. It had fertile land, forests full of game, and rivers packed with big, shiny Rainbow trout. There were Hereford cattle. These had been introduced a hundred years before and abandoned and were running wild. It was an ideal place to start a new life. It was cool. I was there in November and it was springtime in the Southern Hemisphere but there was thick frost on the grass. Butch had grown up in Utah, and he didn't mind the climate.

He had always been a good kid, polite, popular, and very hard working, but his childhood heroes were the gunslingers of the Wild West roaming wild and free. They didn't pitch hay, or get their hands cold and wet panning for gold. When they wanted gold, they took big bars of it from trains and banks and galloped into the sunset. Butch always wore a gun, as part of the costume, but seldom used it. It is said that the only time he killed a man was on the day he died.

He grew to be a warm and charming man. Children loved him, and once in a peaceful year between robberies he was hired to protect payrolls and he never betrayed these to his 'Wild Bunch' gang, that lived in 'The Hole in the Wall.' He even got a great reference, which would not have helped him later as he was always changing his name. In Argentina, in Chile, and Bolivia he had a different pseudonyms. So did his sidekick, the Sundance Kid.

Maybe they wanted to settle down, or the hunters were too close, but he and Sundance bought land just outside Cholila. One historian today in Cholila who knows all of his pseudonyms is Myrta, Myrta Cea. Her grandfather had been a compadre of the Boys, and he always spoke to her fondly of Butch. Butch impressed everyone as a really good man, and in Cholila the stories of his life as a bandit were taken as an exaggeration. No one had an unkind word to say about him.

Myrta has a large collection of photos and documents detailing their life in Cholila showing the pair in their three years of domesticity as land owners and ranchers. Somewhere along the line Sundance had acquired a young and pretty traveling companion, Ethel. She was with him from New York to Buenos Aires and on the long trip across country by wagon to Cholila. She and Sundance set up house in the largest of the five cabins they built on the property.

Butch apparently remained a bachelor. Myrta knows of no little Cassidys or any little Ryans, his Argentinian name. There was much talk and many local theories about this. That he didn't like women, or that they both shared the favors of Ethel, or he may have been looking over his shoulder with plans for a quick getaway. Butch's cabin was close to a small river, and a tunnel ran from his cabin to the river bank.

Perhaps Ethel wore the pants too much for his liking. Myrta has a copy of the 1905 taxroll, which shows their four hundred and fifty cattle in the name of Ethel and Butch. Sundance is not mentioned. Or maybe she just had a better head for business.

They became well liked in the community partly because they could afford to throw the best parties in the region. The Provincial Governor of the Territory came to their parties, ate their food, drank their wine, and danced with Ethel. It was during one such party that a bank was robbed many kilometers away. The locals stoutly defended the innocence of their 'gringo rancheros.' The robbery and the party both took place at exactly the same time, and it was said to have been physically impossible for them to have robbed the bank and made it to the party. Myrta even has a picture of the party, clearly showing Butch and Sundance. However, the tales of their previous profession were well known, and eventually warrants were issued. So ended a domestic chapter in the lives of two of the most glamorized bandits ever. They left behind their cabins, and cattle, and they were on the run again.

Somewhere between Cholila and Bolivia Ethel disappeared. In the Hollywood version of their story Butch and Sundance are torn apart by a fusillade of Bolivian bullets. There are many, many versions of who it was that really died. Many graves opened have been empty, and DNA tests on bodies that were exhumed were all inconclusive. No one may ever know the true end of the story, but once upon a time for a few brief happy years there lived in Patagonia a pair of peaceful men. Ranchers, fishermen and law abiding taxpayers. Butch Cassidy and the Sundance Kid.

Peculiar Penguins in Patagonia

Why would an animal that has spent millions of years evolving to crawl out of the sea, that has even soared into flight as a bird, change direction, and evolve back into the ocean?

Penguins are birds that swim in the sea. They have feathers, but their wings have become flippers. They can dive down to five hundred feet, but they still come up to the surface to breath, and out of the water to lay and hatch eggs on land, like a bird. One social peculiarity is that they have become egalitarian, taking turns to sit and hatch their eggs. The husband often spends months alone on the nest hatching eggs, unable to forage for food, starving, while the female is away swimming and feasting on anchovies and sardines.

Together they make massive migrations every year to avoid winter, leaving the cold of Patagonia for the warm beaches of Brazil, then they come back, separately, to exactly the same nest the next Spring. Many experts say that they mate for life. The penguin has this solid reputation for life long fidelity, but if the male is delayed on the way back she will not wait. She will mate with any available male rather than miss out on the chance of being a Mum. There are also homosexual penguins, pairs of males who have bonded so strongly that even lonesome females cannot separate them. You can see them try, and fail. Male bonding obviously cannot produce eggs, but give them an egg and they will make a nest and share hatching duties. Sometimes the nesting instinct is so great that a male pair will take a stone into the nest, and try to hatch it. How these homosexuals pass their genes along is a mystery, but penguins have defied evolution before.

At the Provincial Penguin Festival in Patagonia, at Punto Tumbo about half a million penguins are gathered, getting ready to mate. Young adults, with their first time at bat are crooning love songs and displaying erectile tail feathers. Old married couples are cleaning out last years nest, that is if he didn't dawdle and lose her to a swinging philanderer. Amongst the half a million, there are probably many male pairs bonding, but unless you are an expert it is hard to tell who is doing what with whom.

Swooping seagulls have to be quick to steal an egg, but a sea lion climbing out of the ocean looking to eat a tasty penguin can cause a deadly hysterical panic. There are none here today to disturb the crowd of the waddling waiters. Their white bellies and the black coats are camouflage tricks to fool predators below them or above them in the water. These include sea leopards, sea lions and killer whales. Thus the migration to warm beaches might hit surprises far more deadly than a Florida speed trap, and the penguins may have to swim for their lives. Because they are warm blooded, and need to breathe, the graceful leaps they make that look like play are just regular breaks to take in a little air.

Diving deep to seek food may take them down to 300 feet, or to 1,500 feet for a King Penguin, and this means holding their breath for impossible lengths of time. Again, the penguin has come up with some incredible evolutionary tricks. Their red bloods cells have evolved to hold many more times the amount of oxygen carrying hemoglobin. Their muscles can even feed on their own fat to function without oxygen. In humans this produces a deadly lactic acidosis, but the clever penguin has developed an enzyme, lactic dehydrogenase, to deactivate this deadly acid.

Such amazing birds. They can see well in the dim blue light of the deep ocean, but they have turned off their olfactory organs. They have a very poor sense of smell. To appreciate how smart this is, try standing next half a million penguins all pooping together.

Chapter Twenty Eight

The Last Tango at the World's End

Ushuaia is truly a town at the End of the World, at the bottom tip of Tierra del Fuego. Then there is only the Southern Ocean and Antarctica and the South Pole. In the Club Nautico in Ushuaia an ancient Brit, myself, is dancing the tango with a pretty young instructor, Marlena. She is short, and sweet, with red hair, and she is carefully keeping her distance.
"You must watch your feet, señor. One and two, and three and four."
She is probably worried about her toes inside her soft shoes.
This was very different from the ballrooom dancing lessons the Ancient Brit took at age fourteen in London.
"I am putting this gramophone record between you two. DO NOT let it drop." We were clutched together in shy teenage embarrassment, and it wasn´t fun at all. Not until

years later. Would it be tonight in the Club Nautico that the Ancient Brit and his traveling companion learnt how to dance? Marlena and Sergio are teaching the tango to a couple of Ancient Brits.

"It is very simple. Eight movements and you are dancing. Five and six, seven and eight."

Tango music is exciting and passionate, but the older students were stumbling. Two other students, young and pretty were doing better. Maxie is in her mid thirties, with a well filled tight white sweater and sleek black slacks. Her hair is auburn, not quite red, long and wavy. Her friend Penny has black hair cut very short, her sweater is baggy, and the blue jeans and running shoes were more for comfort than for sex appeal. Both are from New York, they are both in the commodities business, both attractive and smart.

The tango seemed to be a man's dance, until step sixteen. He stands regally, while she twists and turns in a complicated sexy routine. At one point he catches her foot with his foot and drags her foot and her leg and her whole body close up to him. So very sexy. But then she does step sixteen. Suddenly it is scary, and dangerous. She puts her right foot between his feet, then turns. Facing away, she gives a sharp kick, back and up. That's when this Ancient Brit quit. Her heel was flying straight up, aiming right at a very sensitive spot. Luckily just then everyone took a break.

Maxie starts telling the Ancient Brit about her scruffy hotel in Ushuaia. The Ancient Brit asked

"Are you sharing a room?"

There was a sharp, angry reply.

"No, of course not. We are just good traveling friends."

Then strangely, Maxie moved closer, knees touching under the table, head close and she started some high powered flirting. With a grey haired Ancient Brit old enough to be her father. Delightful, flattering, and embarrassing as the Ancient

Brit's partner gave him dirty looks. I'm still not sure what that was all about. Then the music started again and the focus was back to the dance floor.

Ushuaia is the most Southerly town in the world. There are small settlements of people between there and the South Pole, and they may even dance the tango at the Antarctic Research Station at the South Pole. However, the Ancient Brit was so uncomfortable watching the women turn and kick back up in step sixteen that he decided that this was too painful even to watch. This, he resolved, in Ushuaia, at The End of the World would definitely be his last tango.

Revolution in China?

On this visit I went a long way off the main road in China. To country villages of stone huts with mud floors that have changed very little in the last four hundred years. No cars, not even carts. They had electricity, with perhaps one TV in the whole village, but no running water or sewage.

They spoke no English, and I had asked a friend in Taiwan to come and be my guide and interpreter. Her parents had run away from mainland China when the communists took over, and I thought she might be interested in seeing the small villages of her ancestral homeland. However, like most Taiwanese she was anti communist, and felt very uncomfortable being in Mainland China. She was a teacher of English and she spoke it well. More importantly she spoke Mandarin as well as the Taiwan language which survived the invasion of Chiang Kai Chek. When I had met her many years before she was still working, married, with two young children. I knew she was now divorced, the children grown, and I phoned her.

"I am going to Mainland China, and my Mandarin is very limited." I hesitated. I did not want to be rejected as a predatory male.

"I would be very happy if you would come along as my guest, in separate rooms of course. I want to get way off the tourist trail, and find out what life is like for the poor people away from the big cities."

She was a great guide. She helped me get deep into the countryside, and even when we wandered into 'minority' areas where they spoke a different language they still could understand her Mandarin.

She found the small local buses to get to the villages, and talked to the people we met. She was kind and friendly, and they opened up to her, and answered any questions I asked through her. When we got to a village, she started asking and walked to the guesthouses, looking for one that wasn't too primitive. Travel was cheap. The guesthouses only cost a few dollars per night. The food everywhere was authentic Chinese food, but sadly not as tasty as Chinese food in America. I mainly lived on noodles and beer. In six weeks I lost fifteen pounds, on my Chinese version of a balanced diet.

I was looking for any signs of a revolution. I had read about deep unrest in the countryside, where education and healthcare had been drastically cut back. Plus the peasants that had flocked to high paying jobs in the city mostly lost what benefits they had. These were restricted to the rural locations the peasants had come from, and were not transferable. I had heard that there was much unrest. In the last five thousand years China has had many brutal warlords and tyrannical emperors. When their demands for slave labor and more taxes became too much, the peasants revolted. The last rebellion in about 1850 was especially successful.

It started as a religious cult, led by a zealot who claimed to be the younger brother of Jesus Christ. He raised an army of over a hundred thousand, and marched almost to the Imperial City of Beijing. He made the mistake of stopping in the Southern capital of Nanjing, which was empty at the time. He put on imperial robes, ate imperial food, and sampled imperial concubines. This was his downfall. He never got further than Nanjing.

Recently, Tibetans died and Chinese Muslims were killed when they rose up against the rulers from Beijing. These were small, isolated incidents. But I had read that there was great unhappiness amongst the peasants in many parts of the countryside. The medical system was no longer free. The most common cause of bankruptcy was a huge medical bill. Seriously ill patients often refused to go into hospital.

"Let me die at home."

They didn't want to leave their family with a huge debt. Education had always been the pride of China, but funds have been cut and few country people now go on to higher education. Wages in the country are a fraction of those in the modern factories along the coastline. People in the country villages had very little money. I spent six weeks deep in the countryside trying to answer one question. Are the peasants unhappy enough to launch a revolution?

I saw many ancient villages, all very picturesque, all very poor. The one child law of 1979 was making the men in particular unhappy. Many girl babies are 'terminated,' and in some areas 119 boys survive for every 100 girls. By the year 2020 there may be forty million surplus males unable to find a bride.

In one village an old woman said "Come into my house and visit. I will be honored to feed you."

Her life had been harsh and simple. She was 68, and had had her five children before the one child law. There had been no nurse or midwife. Her aunt had told her what to do, but the aunt had to leave for her work in the fields. The woman delivered all of her own children, alone in a stone hut with a mud floor. She cut the cords herself, and was back in the fields working soon after.

We had been drinking beer in the one room store in the village. I was the first foreigner ever to visit them, and people were taking turns to come and look at this peculiar stranger. Many of them were bent forward 90 degrees at the waist, from soft bones and lives spent bending, planting rice in the fields. Plus there were very few cattle, and fewer dairy farms meant no milk. It is not wise to order beef in China, as it may have dried out and hardened with age.

After several beers I needed a potty break. I was shown to an outhouse with two loose bamboo planks, eight inches apart and slippery, and a crude door for privacy. The solid waste was harvested every day by a young woman who shoveled it into two buckets which she carried on each end of a carrying stick. It went to fertilize the rice paddies. The stone outhouse had been in use for 300 years. The odor had ripened over the centuries. Going in the smell hit me like a blast of Mace. I couldn't breathe, and my eyes watered painfully.

Back in the store the old lady became more friendly. "You must come to my house and stay the night."

It was an intriguing offer. I had come to the countryside to get to know these people, and what better way than to spend time living with them? But the thought of falling between the two planks at two in the morning gave me pause for thought. I regretfully declined. Her hospitality was typical. The farther I was from the big cities, the more friendly were the people.

Everywhere the peasants were overtaxed and underpaid. They got rotten medical care, and poor education. They were as unhappy as peasants had ever been in the past. Could it be that they unhappy enough for a revolution?

Then came the earthquake. I was in Guiyang, in the province next to Sichuan where about 70,000 people died. I felt the floor of my hotel room shake. The TV started nonstop coverage, seven days a week. The efficiency of the government's reaction gave me a chill. Within days, 35,000 troops had been rushed in, and they kept coming until 120,000 troops had been sent in. They were there to take care of the earthquake damage. They could equally have taken care of a revolution. These were not the skinny, poorly clad youths in thin green uniforms I had seen several years before. These were smart and fit. China has been spending billions, up to twenty percent of GDP to modernize her military. The Central Government obviously keeps strong grip on all things in China.

There will be no democracy in China, no human rights, no real freedom of speech, and there is nothing that we, or the peasants, can do about it. There will be no revolution in China.

Chapter Twenty Nine

Tontine in 2010

Peter Stagg was a kind man, a good man. When he checked out of this incarnation, on May 21st 2010 in Nanaimo, BC the feeling was unanimous. Just the mention of his name brought a smile to your face. An excellent cook and an avid gardener, whatever he tackled, he did things well.

He was born in Madras, India, now Chennai. His father ran McMillan's Publishing firm there, but the family retreated to the coolness of the hills in the burning heat of summer. By the time Peter was eighteen he was back in England, facing conscription, and he put on the uniform of the RAF. Next he became an architect, and ended up a few years later as the odd man out in a house with three civil engineers. Keith, Roy and I tried to be tolerant of folk whose only aim in life, we thought, was just to make our engineering structures look pretty. With Peter, it was so easy to be tolerant.

We had many good times together, like the camping trip that took us completely around the Olympic Peninsular, in Washington State. We packed into Peter's Morris Minor, and into his green canvas four man tent. Or more accurately two men, two women tent. It didn't matter if it rained, we had a great time.

Peter's try for independence came when he designed and built a camper van body to fit on top of a pick up truck. Two things were against him. Firstly he was ahead of his time. No one had ever seen a neat camping rig that fitted so well onto a truck bed, and one of his employees had sticky fingers and stole all the profits. After that he settled back to the respectable life of a school architect, leaving behind the dreams of being an independent businessman.

My memories of him in later life are more vivid, when Keith, Peter and I had all retired and we would cross from Vancouver to visit him in Lanztville, North of Nanaimo. Like Keith and John, Peter was an expert perfectionist with hand tools, and was always making improvements at a professional level. I was never in their class. If two pieces of wood came within half an inch of each other, that was a triumph for me. I could tackle the gin and beer almost as well as he could, if there was someone to drive the car afterwards.

He spent many a happy year with his one and only wife Molly. They raised Liz and Andrew well, until Molly developed a problem. By then I was a doctor, and it was one of the times that I was up visiting from Texas. Ruby told me about a strange incident.

"We were walking down Georgia Street the other day," she said, "when there was a tremendous accident between two cars on the street right next to us. We were not involved, and soon we walked on. I was in shock, and it was a block or so later that I said to Molly,

"That was a scary accident, wasn't it Molly. I thought

surely someone would have been killed.'"

"Molly looked at me, and said 'What accident?' She had no memory at all of the accident."

Later, when Ruby told me this I realized that something bad was wrong. Molly had a CAT scan, and it showed that somehow her brain had shrunk. Her mental function quickly became worse, and she died not long after she had been confined to a nursing home.

Peter had an Honor Guard at his funeral put on by the Royal Canadian Legion. The uniforms and the bugle were a fitting exit for a really good and kind man. John and I retreated to the bottle of Tontine brandy. We carefully poured our measures into elegant snifters, and gave a final toast to Peter Stagg. I remember thinking back to when we were young, at 3276, and Peter helped train Bloodknok the dog to tangle his lead around the legs of attractive young ladies who happened to be walking along West Eleventh Avenue in Vancouver, back in the good old days. All of us, Peter included had really been carefree bachelors.

Hippocratic challenge

There is a small fishing community only about 70 miles South of the border, but it is in a different era, about 200 years ago. Plus to get there meant going through a war zone.

Crossing any border is always a bit of an adventure, but the US Mexico border can be quite exciting these days. On the Mexican side there is sometimes open warfare, between different drug gangs, and between the gangs and the police and the military. Both sides have automatic weapons, and bullets sometimes fly over the border into cars and buildings in the Brownsville University area. Students have been evacuated, getting an extra day of vacation.

This adds spice to a trip into Mexico but a local church had a need. It had food and medications donated by wealthy churches in North Texas and volunteers were needed to distribute these to a group of small fishing villages on the coast South of Matamoros. Fishing had been poor, and prices had been driven down by competition from giant fish farms in China and elsewhere. The price of gas had risen, which also hurt, and with their small open boats they are no competition for the seventy foot trawlers from southern Mexico and Texas. I was new to the church, and when I enquired one member said

"If you want to help, we can certainly use you. We meet here in Brownsville at six thirty, then cross to our warehouse in Matamoros."

I'll call him Pete, and he had retired after fifty years in the fishing business. He was the chief scrounger, getting the food and medicines from up North. Donald had retired from being a successful electronic engineer who also used to be a wrestling champion. He keeps fit now by wrestling on both sides of the border with heavy sacks of food and critical customs agents. We met up at the Matamoros warehouse and loaded a pickup. Pete drove and talked.

"First we repackage the food into small plastic bags. I will drive around the villages giving out the food, and you can sort out the pills. Have a look around. They have simple wooden shacks, no plumbing, or running water, and sometimes electricity if there is gas for the generator. The outhouses are cold in winter, but still have a strong smell."

"There is a lot of diabetes, and the diet of flour tortillas and tacos doesn't help. There is a local medical facility, but the last doctor quit after two weeks. There is no unemployment insurance, and only a few families qualify for help from a government program.. If they are really sick they can take the long bus ride into town. If they get a prescription from the hospital they are so short of money it is often a choice between food and pills. We have volunteers with good hearts and strong backs to lift the sacks, but there is often a shortage of nurses and doctors to give out the pills."

  We survived the numerous pot holes and arrived at the main village. While Pete drove off to distribute food, I became familiar with the large plastic boxes of medicines.

  They set up the 'clinic' under a mesquite tree. Two card tables held the meds, and there were battered plastic chairs for the patients and for me, and we started when Pete got back. He helped with any language problems, and used the blood sugar machine on about every second patient. They either had diabetes or so many relatives did that they had good cause to worry.

  "We have a special person for your first patient, Doc. Teresa," said Pete. "We have been doing what we can, but she has a major problem."

  He waved, and a middle aged woman shuffled over. She sat in one of the battered plastic chairs and reached down to remove a bandage from her lower leg that once had been white. Patches of yellow showed where some sort of fluid had leaked through. Her foot and the bottom of the bandage were black, coated with dirt and sand.

  "Pete, let's take her over here with a basin and some bottled water." Soon I was washing her foot, which seemed like a good Biblical way to start.

  "No, they haven't helped me," was her first version of her story, but over time a somewhat twisted tale came out. Twice surgeons in Matamoros had cut away dead tissue and tried skin grafts, but these had not taken. The only option remaining was amputation. She was not keen on that and came back to her ramshackle shack in the village.

  When I had finally removed the dirt and the smelly bandage, her ulcer was impressive. Stretching six inches along her lower leg and wrapping almost completely around it, all of the skin and muscle tissue had gone down to the lower layer of fascia. Treatment would be long and complicated, even in the US. Oxygen under pressure in a hyperbaric chamber might help, so would clean dressings and medicated sprays and ointments. Back in Brownsville I got opinions from surgeons and podiatrists skilled at this sort of lesion. They were all gloomy.

"Don't think a graft would take," they said. After several frustrating weeks I asked my Mexican 'sponsor' for an opinion. As a foreigner I had to be 'supervised' by a doctor with a local license. Teresa was admitted to a treatment center specializing in ulcers, but she soon signed herself out.

"They wouldn't let me have my cigarettes." She meant both the nicotine variety and the ones that made her happy. It didn't help that there were several patients who had already had one leg chopped off, heading for a second amputation and a life in a wheelchair.

All the while I had been seeing patients under the tree. I had bought steel fence posts and yellow boundary tape from Walmart to keep the curious crowd back, but as many of my questions were quite personal, the crowd strained their ears to hear the details. To evaluate a belly pain the patient must be lying down to relax the abdominal muscles. The card tables were simply not strong enough. If I couldn't make a diagnosis by poking them as they sat in the battered plastic chair I had to have them lie on the grass. Disorders of the private parts were mainly guess work. It could be a simple bladder infection or an STD. It was impossible to tell if there was a major or a minor problem without an exam. Sometimes I tried a simple treatment on a trial basis. If it didn't work, they would have to get the bus into town. One man described what could have been a hemorrhoid or an anal cancer. I marched him about a hundred yards away behind a shed, and put on gloves while he dropped his pants.

"Why can't we use the new State clinic building?" was a question that I never got a good answer for. There were hints of major problems with bureaucracy but I was never able to get inside the building.

There was no solution. I didn't mind crossing the war zone. Even sitting in the open in 90 degree heat and humidity wasn't too bad. I had lived in deep South Texas long enough to become acclimatized. It sometimes rained, and the branches of the mequite tree gave little shelter. There were many problems, but what was so hard to live with was turning away a patient with a potentially fatal problem that I might diagnose and help if only I could poke and prod them in privacy. This could not be arranged, and I finally stopped going.

Did I feel bad about quitting? Of course I did. The father of modern medicine, Hippocrates had seen and treated patients under a plane tree, a platanus orientalis on the island of Cos, twenty five hundred years ago. Graduating doctors still recite his famous Hippocratic Oath. True, he had no modern medicines or surgery to offer them. Most operations had not been thought of back then. But if he could help out under a tree, why couldn't I?

Cambodia

I had bypassed Cambodia several times on my way to other parts of South East Asia. I had never felt drawn by Angkor Wat or The Killing Fields. Monstrosities from the past and recent times held no attraction. However, I was running out of places that I really wanted to see, and both Cambodia and Laos had been part of steamy, exotic French Indochina and both made for intriguing travel tales.

The French got a couple of things right. But sitting at a sidewalk café in Phnom Penh sipping an Anchor Draft beer was a mixed blessing. Taking a deep breath could be hazardous to your health.

Across the street was the mighty Mekong River. It had wandered down here all the way from China, and there were long-tailed local boats with men and casting nets, plus tourist boats cruising to watch the sunset. There was a promenade with a hundred motor scooters and saffron robed monks, and lovers sitting discreetly on the low river wall. There was also a road used by a million motor bikes, tuk tuks, cars and trucks leaving villainous blue vapor trails. Just don't inhale.

The French left behind the baguette in many parts of Indochina. Some were stodgy, but many were crispy and light. The street vendors make them into sandwiches with a quick longitudinal slice then fill them with good stuff in the blink of an eyelid. Only when you bite in do you realize that the brown paste was 'fermenting' fish paste, and the little red bits are atomic strength red chillis. The rest of the stuff is juicy and tasty, ingredients you can only guess at. The red bits will bite into your stomach lining and stab you with a horrendous heartburn. It's like a knife in the belly, a gut pain that lingers for hours.

Some monks on the embankment may be real, but some are scruffy, dirty, smoking cigarettes. They wouldn't tolerate phony monks next door in Thailand. Ninety percent of the people there are very religious, and every young man from the King on down spends a few months with his head shaved wearing the robes. A man is not considered good marriage material otherwise. Buddhism is very tolerant, and one hundred percent of Thais are also animist, with spirit houses outside the door so that bad spirits and ancestor spirits don't have to come into the house.

In Cambodia communism, especially under the brand left by the Khmer Rouge, had become a religion that tolerated none other. The fanatic murderous rule of the red scarf brigade included daily brainwashing sessions for the kids and the adults. They were taught that Ankar, 'The Organization' was now their Father and Mother and would provide all their spiritual needs. It may be that Buddhism is recovering it's hold, but it will take time.

Chapter Thirty

Ruins of Angkor Wat.

My attitude to ruins has vacillated. The paths at the Temple at Karnak, on the Nile were level, and had been trodden by Soldiers of Ancient Egypt, Greece and Rome. When I walked on the same stones, their ghosts walked with me, young men in armor talking of wine, women and war. Climbing the few steps was no problem. That was before sharp pointed spikes of arthritis formed in my knees. Bending them now, as in an Asian toilet, can bring tears to my eyes.

    Which finally brings me to Angkor Wat. Okay, it may be "The Eighth Wonder of the World" and "The Largest religious Temple on the Planet." But, the builders must have been a pretty crude bunch. Guarding the inner temples are painfully irregular steps, ranging from seven to seventeen inches high. Knees must be bent double, followed by pushing up hard, then jumping jerkily down the other side, both going in and coming out. Pain pills and potent liquid refreshments didn't help much.

They never mastered the arch, so widely used by the Romans a thousand years before. Thus the temple towers are narrow and pointed. Inside, the roughly built ceilings have fallen down in many places. Outside the lines are jagged and irregular. Sandstone blocks have become black with moss, speckled white with bat droppings. Norman Churches, built at about the same time seem more attractive. at least to Western eyes, and have a solid sense of strength and dignity. Even the stairs are civilized.

The temple of Ta Prohm at least partly lives up to the romantic tale of the Frenchman in the 1860s who "discovered" Angkor Wat, leading to it's Indiana Jones name, "The Ancient Temple City, swallowed by the jungle." He became famous, but in fact Portuguese travelers had been writing about the Temple City for five hundred years.

The small temple of Ta Prohm does at least look the part. Huge trees have grown up through the temple walls, with foot thick roots writhing around like big brown pythons. Hollywood used it as a setting for 'The Tomb Raiders."

The tour guide tried to earn his pay by spewing out details of the which Kings did what, and the differences between the Hindu and Buddhist varieties. Perhaps I was restless because after hours of torture my moving parts were creaking and groaning, much in need of pain relief and lubrication.

Thanks to the barmy builders of Angkor Wat I ended up hobbling around Cambodia and Laos, with knees complaining all the way. Give me the Norman Conquest anytime.

A young girl in Dante's Utopia.

She was about fourteen. Large pretty eyes, dark brown, serious. Round bob of black hair. Young breasts budding under a black shirt. Pajama pants black, scarf red checkered. Only the young boys carried AK 47s to pose for the grainy photos. Pictures on a wall, in S21, the notorious 'school' in Phnom Penh. Young fighters for the pure revolution.

Daily lectures from senior cadres. Some had studied in France. Importing revolting French ideas. Cadres preached complete obedience to Ankar. The organization. The anonymous father figure that had abolished religion and the Cambodian family.

Daily lectures taught the 'pure' revolution, of the proletariat. All suspects watched. Intellectuals, doctors, businessmen. Suspicious activity reported, leading to jail, torture, death. Even for her family, her siblings.

The 'pure' peasant cooperative movement started in 'Year One,' of the rule of Khmer Rouge. Cities evacuated, all sent to work in fields, workers camps full of disease, two meals of watery porridge a day.

I shall call her Chantha. There were no names on the wall. So pretty, perhaps she was a favorite of the cadre leader. Ankar did not allow sex, but her youthful enthusiasm became devotion. For Ankar she would torture, and kill. S 21 had been a school in Phnom Penh. Now it was a collection of relics and records. Three stories. Converted into narrow prison cells, chambers for interrogation, torture, confession, and inevitably death at Choeung Ek, one of many Killing Fields.

Sticks, iron bars, machetes saved precious bullets. Babies heads smashed against trees killed future subversives. 129 mass graves, some opened to yield hundreds of skulls now peering sightlessly from the Memorial Tower.

In the end Vietnam invaded. The Khmer Rouge were chased into jungle, starting a civil war. Chantha perhaps killed, wounded, or in refugee camp along Thai border. Probably drifted down to Bangkok, to be a sex trade worker, or legless beggar. If still alive, may have been granted amnesty that ended civil war.

Many brutal Khmer Rouge leaders are still alive and well. A few old men were put on trial, thirty years later. But they were only following orders. Chantha may have been a wife and a mother. How quickly all is forgotten. Or is it? In 1984, five years after the atrocities, AIDS began its deadly epidemic. Divine retribution? Probably not.

The KR blood bath began with a powerful idea. An idea made into religion by one man. Into revolution by another. Into madness by man's inhumanity to man.

Science claims that in the beginning we crawled out of the primordial slime. Atrocities through the ages seem to say that we have not come far. Or even that we are going back.

There has always been killing. With animals we call it the food chain. For humans Stalin probably set the all time record, at about thirty million. Then Auschwitz. In Cambodia, about 2 million. In 2010 the Killing Fields museum is now a tourist attraction.

Did all these people have to die?

Perhaps the clinical trial of humanity has failed. It has lasted for many millennia, and the numbers are overwhelming. They seem to prove that the planet's most highly evolved creature is just an animal. The most brutal and violent beast in creation seems to be evolving back into the slime.

There are several questions that any remaining optimists might ask.

Worldwide, in all countries, in any era have any military, political, religious or educational leaders ever been free of corruption? Have they ever given us leadership, or answers?

Is violence increasing?

Is there any hope for us?

Chapter Thirty One

An ER tale in Laos

There were plenty of problems and people in the back seat of the crew cab, but a critical shortage of language skills. The injured girl and her boyfriend from Korea spoke only Korean. The driver and his daughter only Lao. Me, none of the above.

Bouncing in the back of the pickup were two Korean girls, tourists like me but they spoke some English. They had helped a lot translating at the accident, but I couldn't get the message to the driver that I needed to have one inside. He had been the good Samaritan who had picked us all up, but he was concentrating on his suicidal driving.

"Are you taking us to a hospital?"
No answer.
"Are we going to a clinic?"
"Ah, clinic, clinic." Vigorous encouraging nods.

She had been driving a rented scooter and ran into a bigger scooter coming the other way. He had injured his big toe, but she had a possible head injury and a cut under her eye. She was moaning and twitching, confused and amnesic. The friendly tourist from Korea translated.

I had done the usual sixty second ER assessment. Her body was mainly intact but her brain shaken. Helpful bystanders had been shocked when I ran my hands over her feminine body, checking for fractures. Laos is a conservative place. Brides blush angrily when they are kissed by the groom. but they had seen it done so often in Western movies, so they go along.

On the narrow twisting road the driver was doing a great James Bond imitation, taking all corners on two wheels. Again the language barrier. Maybe he thought that my waving hands were egging him on. If we had met anything coming the other way there could have been a mess of mangled bodies to deal with, if I had survived.

It was obviously a hospital, clad in white shiny tiles, but the parking lot was suspiciously empty. I signaled "Wait here" and checked inside. Yes, an ER of sorts, but no welcoming committee in white coats. Not a soul.

I turned, too late. The enterprising driver had found a wheelchair, pushing it in with gusto.

A nurse type person appeared and looked with scorn at all the foreigners in her ER, but she did get the girl onto an exam table. Next came a diffident "Yes, I doctor" young man. When he heard the babble of foreign languages and saw the injured girl, he turned and left quickly.

The patient was still moaning and twitching, spreading a little panic into the worried young Korean tourists who were trying to get her to take slow deep breaths and relax. The message was obviously lost in translation, and they were all getting more nervous all the time.

A slightly older "Yes, I doctor" appeared, and reluctantly examined the patient. After a cursory exam, he got the nurse to swab the cut on her face with betadine. At least her lungs and vocal cords were working well, judging by the screams.

He retreated to a desk, wrote notes, and entered details into a large ledger. He didn't want the details, of the loss of consciousness, and the loss of memory before and after. He didn't answer when I asked if they had a CT scanner.

I am sure I would have resented a 'know it all' foreign doctor asking pointed questions in my ER. No, he would not do any XRays, or admit her overnight for observation, or suture the cut on her face.

"Twenty minutes she go." Home, which would be her small hotel. With a possible subdural hematoma developing.

I reconnoitered. There were neat rooms labeled 'XRay' 'Cardiology' 'Laboratory', all locked and not a human in sight. It was about four pm, on a Friday. I'd been told that medical personnel were paid so poorly they often went to a second job after their siesta.

A young man, a visitor in a ward nearby full of patients proudly told me that "This the best hospital in the province. He very good doctor. Study in China.. He my uncle. He the best."

The victim's boyfriend, very quiet and nervous, had not taken out travel insurance for medical mishaps, but he did have the phone number for the Korean Embassy in Vientiane on his cellphone.

The scooter rep appeared next. The Laotian victim with scrapes on his big toe claimed that she had been driving on the left, in his lane, and it was all her fault.

I thought of Mexico and their Napoleonic Code that declared that everyone was guilty until proven innocent and therefore all are thrown in jail. It costs significantly to get out of jail, injured or not. I wondered if the French had left their

"Throw them all in jail" code in Laos. No police appeared. I saw very few in Laos, and only one police motor bike.

Two young Laotian ladies came in, representing the Korean Embassy in far away Vientiane. One spoke Korean, so at last linguistically we were in good shape.

Medically, not so. The cut did need sutures, or it would leave a thick scar. The possible head injury could progress to stroke, coma, or death.

Or not. Working in the ER you see a lot of worse case scenarios, so you imagine the worst and prepare for the worst. Especially in the U.S., where trial lawyers get rich when things go bad.

Flying her out to Bangkok or Seoul could be as risky as staying here. A tough call.

After the doctor left I checked her again. An ER without frills. No gloves, masks, or instruments like an opthalmoscope. Seat of the pants medicine. I didn't see gloves used in anywhere in Cambodia or Laos.

Treating a subdural is relatively simple. Take a drill and a half inch bit and go through the skull and drain out the blood to relieve the pressure. In the old days even G.P.s tackled this. Knowing where to drill was the art in the days before CAT scans.

I sat in a corner, brooded, and started writing out a list of things to watch for and what to do, then I explained the options.

One of the girls from the Embassy said she would take the victim to her house. She would call the Embassy. Would call a private doctor for a second opinion and back up. I tried not to scare her too much but I had to tell her what might happen.

"Yes, I will wake her every hour. Then what do I do?"

I gave her my cell number, my hotel number, my e-mail address, and I said

"Call me at any time."

I kept in touch. After I left the doc changed his mind, and she stayed in hospital overnight. Perhaps from Embassy pressure. Or he had seen my little list.

By the next morning she was alert and stable, and they flew home to Seoul in the afternoon.

In my dream that night she died, and I did some morbid mourning. Which was strange, because many patients die on you in the ER, and you must keep your emotional distance. The most disturbing ones were the children. Including a six month old baby with a massive head injury that failed to respond to a full team effort. Yet I hadn't grieved over him, not a lot. I had hardened. Or so I thought, but perhaps my brain had softened with age. In my dream I even cried.

All told, I had worried everyone, including me, for nothing. ER docs are paid well, but they work hard and worry a lot. Many are burnt out after ten years.

All's well that ends well. Maybe. I wonder what I forgot to include in my lists.

I will worry about that tomorrow.

Royal Ballet for the Communists

"Royal Ballet" brings to mind Covent Garden and Sadler's Wells ballet, but the Royal Ballet had come to Luang Prebang, Laos. In the People's Democratic Republic of Laos.

Could it be? Would we see the likes of Margot Fonteyn and Robert Helpman? This slow and sleepy little town in Northern Laos had declined into poverty when the capital was moved down to Vientiane, and the main occupation is said to be watching the rice grow.

It was also a Marxist-Leninist anomaly. That the "Royal Ballet Pralak Pralam" would be held in the theater of "The Royal Palace." This was in the heart of communist Laos. TV, radio, newspaper all state owned, pushing the party line. Strange but true. The communist party of Laos has followed China's lead into almost free enterprise. Plus the ballet was really an ancient folk tale, no threat to dialectic materialism, and it also brought in tourist dollars.

I became addicted to ballet at age fourteen after my first exposure. The significant word being exposure. The red plush curtains of the Royal Opera House at Covent Garden looked opulent, especially with the classical music coming magically from the orchestra in the pit, but the main attraction was the scantily clad dancers.

They had grace and elegance, and lovely long legs beneath very short tutus.

The girls in Luang Prebang were exotic, pretty, but covered completely by gold embroidered silk dresses, except for the naked feet. Males all wore masks depicting their characters, human or animal. The principal dance step was the Frog Stamp. Knees bent, wide apart, feet stamping hard.

Vocals came from a group at side of stage. The voice of Princess Sida came from old crone, sounding very much like a Gregorian monk with a bad sinus problem doing some chanting. Bass drums for volume and rhythm. 'Melody' from six xylophones and pair of two stringed fiddles. Not exactly catchy, definitely an Oriental musical scale. I only wish I liked it.

It will never replace Swan Lake, but in sleepy Luang Prebang, where the ambition is to do nothing but sip a beer and watch the Mekong River go by, and enjoy doing nothing, it was a welcome interlude of unexpected, incomprehensible Laos culture.

Chapter Thirty Two

Asian patterns

One pattern seen in every country throughout the East is the aging Western male and the young Asian woman.
 In the Outback Hotel in Manila the procession was usually led by a large Western male, often American or Australian. Three paces behind, the young Philipino woman is small, shy, submissive, with small breasts and an exotic beauty. Carrying a baby.
 In Thailand, Burma, Sarawak, all over, the man was happy, proud. The girl shy, excitingly attractive. Look into the future, either with a crystal ball or by seeing her mother, the figure has thickened. Features flatter, hardened by rebellion.
 The long term prospects - I don't know. I knew many that started with high hopes. I had a patient, Bill. Retired, he saved part of his Social Security check for a trip every year to Chiang Mai, in Northern Thailand.
 "She is so lovely, Doc," he would tell me after his annual physical.

"She has been true to me, and she is waiting."

Then one year he didn't come back. He always said his money went farther over there. I tried to find him when I got to Chiang Mai. Not a big place, quieter, more friendly than big Bangkok. I stayed a month. I had planned to work in the leprosarium there, but my information was out of date. The patients had all gone. Modern drugs could cure them, allowing them to be treated in their family homes, and the crumbling shacks were empty.

I met many ex pats..

One said "I have to get my papers renewed every year. I hope that this year I will be permanent." He looked a little sad. "I had to buy the house in her name. I can't own property here."

"Pretty soon she moved her mother in. To help take care of the baby. Then her aunt. I've got a regular harem now."

In Laos, I was in an internet café. I was surprised when an attractive local girl sat at the keyboard next to me.

She logged on to Skype, and was soon talking awkwardly. I leaned back to stretch and saw her screen with a video of a red faced Caucasian male talking to her. Looked American, with the shaven head that many middle aged males prefer to advanced male pattern baldness.

"Yes, of course I wait for you." She giggled at one of his jokes.

"Don't look so sad. Soon you be back." She looked up as a young Lao male came in.

"I got to go," and she clicked off, hung up the headphones.

The only experience I have had with long term prospects has been from watching the Philippino nurses hired by our hospital. On two year working visas, then they go back. Unless...

One male nurse in the ER was so happy. Dear Ken. Such a good, kind man, great sense of humor. No luck matrimonially before.

"Doc, I never had it so good. She makes me happy in every way."

And they usually did, until they had been in the US long enough for a green card. Then they were free, and they dropped their American husbands so fast. Ken fell so hard. The Asian weather forecast can be "Sunny, with cloudy periods. Outlook unpredictable."

Dreams of the South Seas

In North America "Go West, young man" sparked many a dream. To get 160 acres of free land, stake out a homestead, build a cabin, and be independent, it was a dream that worked for many. In Europe, especially in England the dream was different, and was inspired by the tantalizing tales of early English explorers to the South Sea Islands in the Pacific.

The first adventurers truly dazzled the natives. They had skin so white that it almost blinded the eye. White was beautiful. The young maidens were equally appealing.

The explorers ships were huge compared to the dug-out outrigger canoes, and the trade goods were wondrous treasures. The natives thought 'These must be Gods.' In particular the young girls were absolutely fascinated by the white men. On the sandy beach they watched the ships, clad only in flimsy grass skirts, long grass stems flattened into flimsy one inch strips. When they swam out and climbed onto the ships, this garment concealed very little. Plus they were so eager to see a white man up close and personal that they literally threw themselves onto the seamen. On the islands, the fruit hung from the trees, the waters were full of fish and there was no reason to work.

Captain Cook discovered several island chains in the Pacific Ocean, all new and fascinating. The penalty for desertion was death. Many took that risk.

The early accounts of Captain Cook became best sellers back in England and soon all young men were dreaming of the South Seas. Not many got there. It was a long voyage, and took up to ten months in a sailing ship. The very few that got there found that the maidens were laid back, even lazy.

They had never had to work. The mean and nasty diseases brought by the first sailors had burnt out after killing many, but silent syphilis lingered on. There was nothing much to talk about, and the girls lost their beauty very quickly. Soon the white man had nothing to do, and many dreamers became drunks and bums, wishing they were back in London but without the money to get there.

I did know that Captain Cook's Islands were mainly romantic dreams, but I had always wanted to see for myself. It was only a couple of plane rides, thirty hours each way from Brownsville. Instead of the better known but smaller islands of Fiji, Tahiti, and Samoa I chose New Caledonia. About two hundred miles long at least it had roads and places to go to, and should be less boring. However, I was not in a hurry to get too close to the natives. They could still be carrying interesting microbes, and were rumored to have a world class body odor.

It was a French Protectorate, and do not believe the guidebook that says most people speak some English. French was the language, rapid, and with an incomprehensible vernacular. My half forgotten French was now as limited as my Spanish. The French speaking Whites had taken all of the good land in the South, pushing the natives into Tribus, tribal villages in the North. The natives were given an education, up to high school, but then there was no work. The villages were full of young people with high school diplomas, but nothing to do. They had no income, and they had lost their native skills.

Before the white man came, they knew all the thousands of plants, animals, and fishes, which ones were good to eat and how to harvest them. That knowledge had been lost. Now there was abject poverty and boredom. In the stores almost everything was imported, and prices were 30 to 50 percent higher than in the U.S.. Many drifted into the few towns, but there was little work to be had.

The white schoolteachers were mainly French, lured by salaries that were almost double what they would get in Paris. They were still ahead financially, but soon they too suffered from the Island syndrome, boredom. I was warmly welcomed as a diversion, and enjoyed their homemade entertainment with them.

The medical system was free to the natives, and ex pats had their own insurance. I stayed briefly with a lady doctor in a village North of Noumea, and we compared notes. The health system was sadly similar to the Canadian socialized medicine system, but with different diseases.

In the Amazon I had dealt with snakes, malaria, and meningococcal meningitis. Here there was no malaria, and she hadn't seen much of the local schistosomiasis or ciguatera poisoning. She was however an expert rugby player. She and her companion kept themselves quite busy teaching school children the secrets of the backward pass.

In the capital Noumea nightlife stops when the sun goes down. Stores often closed earlier at 3 pm, restaurants at 6 pm. The only places that stayed open late were run by Asian people. Luckily I was fond of Chinese cooking.

Young people were attracted to the big city, seeking a better life, but they ended up sleeping on patches of grass in the city during the day, and in a back street at night. At least the gangs of young people on street corners seemed peaceful and friendly. Still, walking in Noumea at night was spooky.

There were miles and miles of streets that were deserted, no cars moving, no people. Then, in a shop doorway a shadow would move, a native would come out and greet you with "Bon Nuit, M'sieur."

I was puzzled by their body odor. It was extremely potent. It burnt the nostrils at ten feet. When I stayed briefly in a native village I found part of the answer.

The bedding, billed as woven native mats turned out to be pieces of thin foam rubber on cement floors. There were two taps on the sink, and two taps in the shower, but only one temperature - very cold. Perhaps the natives didn't like cold showers, which partly explained their strong aroma. The hut had a brown thatched roof, and looked very picturesque, but when the roof leaked they had lost the skills to repair the thatch. Instead, they covered the holes with plastic tarpaulins of blue, yellow, and brown, like Joseph's coat of many colors.

Their cooking technique was simple. Boil everything, in black iron pots, sitting on two steel rails over a line of small wood fires. There were root vegetables, including karo, and yams, tough and hard. These were boiled to the taste and texture of wet cardboard. In the woods there was plenty of deer, and one pot was full of crudely chopped pieces of venison bobbing around in boiling water. Two items in the meal were quite tasty, the instant noodles and custard in plastic packs. These came from Hongkong. The venison was boiled and became as hard as a rock, then was cut into small pieces, with the flavor of burnt meat. The stray cat I was feeding gave up after a few pieces. Even in the 'French' restaurants the only item that reminded me of France was the bread.

On the road, in a rental car, I was a bit afraid of the Napoleonic Code. I had seen it in action in Mexico. After an accident everyone is guilty until proved innocent, and were often thrown in jail until the police and lawyers are satisfied. I asked the car rental company,

"What do I do if there is an accident? Who do I call first, the police?"

"No M'sieur, do not call the police! Never! In the glove compartment is a green form. Your description on the left, the other persons on the right, especially their insurance information." The salesman repeated this forcefully. "The insurance companies will sort things out. Meanwhile, just leave us a small deposit on your credit card, about two thousand dollars. Just in case."

Luckily I didn't hit anything.

As for the beautiful native maidens with bare breasts and grass skirts, I knew that the London Missionary Society had come running when the immoral behavior of the natives was reported by Captain Cook. All that remains of their allure is shown on the colorful 1,000franc note of The Institut d'Emission d' Outre-Mer, the currency used in French Overseas Territories. There is a picture of a very pretty Polynesian girl. It shows her only from the neck up.

They started by making girls and women wear a long, shapeless Mother Hubbard, like a maternity gown that reached to the ankles. This added an air of mystery which was just as well because all the girls lost their figures in their mid twenties. Their distinguishing feminine features were strangely different. In pre-missionary photos the young girls do not have Western type bosoms like Marilyn Munroe, but conical ones. Like ice cream cones, and they point out threateningly. Along with the cone shaped roofs of the thatched huts, and the widening lower bodies of girls over twenty five, and it is a peculiar conical society. Add the potent body odor, and it was not exactly the stuff that dreams were made of. But I knew before I left that this particular dream was over 200 years too late. I'm glad I went, but I won't be going back.

Chapter 33

Epilogue

We have been on many trips together. In China, she was wonderful. Visiting peasants in ancient stone houses she was kind and sympathetic, and brought out the best in the people we talked to. Rather, she talked, then translated for me. All it took was a short conversation and we were invited into homes, to stay for meals. She was genuinely interested in them, and it showed. Also we were sometimes the first tourists to ever walk into their small, ancient villages, with stone huts that had been built hundreds of years before. We were a curiosity, especially the male with the big nose. The country people were too polite to refer to the foreigner as a crude barbarian, but they might make a quiet reference to the size of my nose.

"Y ge da bitze," meant 'One with big nose.' Their noses were less protruding, much more polite than mine. I had never realized just how big English noses were until my first trip to China. To me they had looked quite normal.

She was from Taiwan and the thought of the communists running the mainland country made her most uncomfortable, but the folk in these villages were not in the least bit interested in politics. There had been warlords and emperors for thousands of years. Some were better than others, some worse, and the peasants had learnt to live with the rulers. There were plenty of rice fields, and as long as they were allowed to keep enough to live on, they survived.

I got to pay back the interpreter services later when we went to places like Mexico and Costa Rica. She was learning Spanish but was not confident enough to speak to people, as she had been in China. My Spanish was limited, but I had had plenty of practice and confidence enough for two.

In Cambodia and Laos neither of us could speak the native language, but that didn't slow us down. At temples and museums we got by with sign language and fingers pointing to the entrance fees. At sidewalk cafes the shoe shine boys and urchins selling cigarettes knew a soft touch when they saw one, and we were never lonely. New Caledonia was a French Protectorate and had a lot of native French folk who much preferred to speak French, even if they could speak English. This was a language I had learnt at school, the right age to learn a language, and some of it had stuck. The French don't really mind how bad your French is as long as you pronounce it properly. I had a talent for imitating accents, and fooled a few natives..

All of this traveling brought us closer together. We shared meals and adventures, life histories and stories of our triumphs and disasters.

Neither of us was perfect, but we were tolerant of the other's faults. We wanted to spend more and more time together, but there were problems. Asian women who are financially independent are reluctant to bond with a male. Their males are traditionally very dominant. Old Chinese saying is "Woman has three all powerful masters in her life.

Her father, her husband, and then her son." She had been through all of that, and it had made her wary of attachments. Marriages are fewer, and more couples live together openly. The older generation shake their heads sadly, but the Chinese above all are practical people. Plus she had seen Women's Lib in her own country, and on her many visits to the U.S..

Small town life in Texas is dreary compared to the sophistication of Taipei, and after missing people who spoke her language for too long she becomes linguistically deprived. Life for me in her country would mean a year of hard work to get comfortable in her language. It is the most difficult language in the world to learn, and I have tried many times. It would be a long time before she could share her friends with me.

Chinese people are very thrifty, and she is happiest when she can find the very cheapest way to go. In Mexico the restaurants were not expensive, but she could find cheaper food at the stalls of vendors or in the market. I tried her way, and the extremely cheap chilli relleno at the market was tasty, but soon afterwards my intestines grumbled and misbehaved. After that we would often eat separately.

There seem to be as many things keeping us apart as there were others drawing us together. We are working on a compromise. I'd had success as a doc, but made so many mistakes as a man. Would I ever get it right?

*   *   *

Many names have been changed.
Book Two will include " Bloody Leg in Egypt" " Opera House in Hanoi" "Blood on the Sand in Gallipoli" "Is there a doctor on the plane?" "The Rounding of Cape Horn" "Night voyage on the Grand Canal," and other small stories.

Made in the USA
Charleston, SC
25 June 2013